Forecasting Tourism Demand: Methods and Strategies

Forecasting Tourism Demand: Methods and Strategies

Douglas C. Frechtling

OXFORD AUCKLAND BOSTON JOHANNESBURG MELBOURNE NEW DELHI

Butterworth-Heinemann
Linacre House, Jordan Hill, Oxford OX2 8DP
225 Wildwood Avenue, Woburn, MA 01801-2041
A division of Reed Educational and Professional Publishing Ltd

A member of the Reed Elsevier plc group

This book is an updated and revised version of the publication
formerly entitled 'Practical Tourism Forecasting'

First published 2001

British Library Cataloguing in Publication Data
Frechtling, Douglas C. (Douglas Carleton)
    Forecasting tourism demand: methods and strategies
    1. Tourism – Forecasting   2. Tourism – Forecasting – Methodology
    I. Title
    338.4'791

Library of Congress Cataloging in Publication Data
A catalog record for this book is available from the Library of Congress

ISBN 0 7506 5170 9

Composition by Genesis Typesetting, Laser Quay, Rochester, Kent
Printed and bound in Great Britain by MPG Books Ltd, Bodmin, Cornwall

Contents

Figures

Tables

Foreword

In the five years since Dr. Frechtling published his pioneering survey of tourism forecasting, world travel and tourism demand has risen by more than 20 percent in real terms. This remarkable growth attests to the power of the ubiquitous human desire to visit new places and meet new people. These impulses have been aided by the expansion of the abilities to disseminate and retrieve information on destinations, transportation, hospitality and attractions instantaneously and at little cost.

Over this recent period, Marriott International has grown to more than 2,300 hotels. Our objective is to surpass 2,800 hotels in 70 countries by the end of 2003. This optimism reflects both confidence in our lodging portfolio and the dedication and commitment of our associates as well as trust in the continued growth of travel around the world. This trust is grounded on solid research on the various paths world tourism may follow in the future. History shows that resting on past successes is no guarantee that they will be repeated.

As technologies, tourism markets, political institutions, and social environments are ever in flux, organizations that would thrive in these turbulent times must maintain a factual-based view of their strengths and the challenges they will encounter in the future.

This book's broad survey of methods and strategies for forecasting tourism demand will assist tourism and hospitality managers in identifying these coming challenges and in preparing to take advantage of them.

J.W. Marriott, Jr.
Chairman and Chief Executive Officer
Marriott International
Washington, DC

Preface

This is a book about forecasting for those interested in the ubiquitous phenomenon of tourism.

The purpose is to present strategies for enumerating tourism demand futures, methods using only personal computers and spreadsheet programs, through an understanding of how the methods work and what their strengths and weaknesses are. It is designed to help those interested in forecasting tourism demand to do so without struggling so much with theories, complex equations and Greek letters.

It is the successor to my earlier work, *Practical Tourism Forecasting*. That was my response to Thomas W. Moore's book *Handbook of Business Forecasting*, an amazingly readable guide to the complex world of economic forecasting. This version includes additional tests of the validity of forecasting models used for tourism and over twenty more brief case studies of tourism demand forecasting from around the world.

Once again, I have employed a time series of demand for commercial lodging in the Washington, D.C., area as an instructional tool. These data suggest the monthly demand for the services of a major sector of the tourism industry. They also represent visitor demand in a metropolitan area. Finally, this series portrays the trend, seasonal, supra-annual and irregular patterns we often encounter in tourism demand series. In short, it aptly illustrates the challenges that forecasters will encounter in building forecasting models, or evaluating those of others, regardless of the temporal or geographic context in which they operate.

This book will disappoint trained econometricians. They are understandably concerned with the statistical properties of the stochastic estimators of various relationships. There are a number of textbooks for them, some of which served as references for this one.

Instead, I hope this book will delight those who must produce numerical predictions about one or more of the myriad of measures of tourism demand over the short or long term but who do not have the inclination to master the nuances of statistical theories.

Douglas C. Frechtling
Bethesda, Maryland, USA
November 2000

Acknowledgements

As with *Practical Tourism Forecasting*, I owe a heavy debt of gratitude to Smith Travel Research of Hendersonville, Tennessee, for granting me use of data from its U.S. Lodging Database. Chief Executive Officer, Randy Smith, provided a great deal of encouragement to me in writing the former book and now this one. Dave Swierenga of the Air Transport Association of America furnished me with historical series on U.S. scheduled air carriers. Lynn Franco supplied Consumer Confidence Survey data from the Conference Board. I am grateful for their generosity in contributing their time and data to this book.

Dr Endre Horvath, economist with the Department of International Business of the Budapest University of Economic Sciences, Hungary, was kind enough to generate the initial versions of many of the forecast models described herein. This project would have taken far longer without his faithful collaboration.

I also thank Kathryn Grant at Butterworth-Heinemann and Rik Medlik of the University of Surrey for their patience and support in the prior effort. And once again, I acknowledge Tom Moore of Tampa Electric Company as the source of inspiration for the original book and its current successor.

While these friends and others have contributed to the sound advice herein, any errors of theory or practice remain my own.

My wife, Joy, has had to endure yet another season of my long hours and heavy sighs in birthing this book. I thank her for sticking with us both.

Introduction

Some say that travel and tourism is the 'world's largest industry and generator of quality jobs' (World Travel and Tourism Council, 1995: 1). They estimate that travel and tourism directly and indirectly contributes nearly 11 per cent of the gross world product, the most comprehensive measure of the total value of the goods and services the world's economies produce.

The World Travel and Tourism Council estimated that in 1999, gross world product both directly and indirectly related to travel and tourism would total about $3.3 trillion, supporting 187 million jobs and generating $729 billion in taxes. This activity is buttressed by more than $8 trillion invested in world plant, equipment and infrastructure related to travel and tourism.

While these estimates may be controversial, there is no doubt that tourism activities, encompassing travel away from home for business or pleasure, comprise a substantial part of lifestyles of the world's residents, or that a very large industry has grown up to serve these travellers.

Futurist John Naisbitt (1994), in his best-selling book *Global Paradox*, subscribes to the concept that tourism will be one of the three industries that will drive the world economy into the twenty-first century. He is also author of the idea that small and medium-sized organizations are growing in importance in the expanding global economy. The managers of these organizations have the agility to act quickly and efficiently to take advantage of trend changes, emerging markets and new business opportunities.

In 1998 Microsoft Chairman and Chief Executive Officer, Bill Gates, agreed that tourism would be one of the three leading 'socio-economic service businesses' of the new century. He noted that the Internet would be an increasingly powerful 'vehicle for travel information, marketing and sales' (Maurer, 2000).

These two continuing realities – the continuing expansion of one of the world's most ubiquitous activities and industries, and the advantages of being small and nimble – mean businesses and governments place increasing stress on understanding the shapes of global, national and local tourism futures.

What this book is about

This book is designed to provide the basic and practical understanding of demand forecasting that tourism managers, marketers, planners and researchers will need to thrive in the decade ahead. It can be viewed as an introduction to the range of forecasting methods available to anyone who must forecast future demand for a tourism product. It is also designed to instruct the executive who must evaluate proposals to develop a tourism demand forecasting system, or produce demand forecasts, or assess an operating forecasting system and its forecasts for their usefulness in strategic management.

There is no distinct set of tourism forecasting methods. Rather, quantitative and qualitative techniques developed to forecast variables of interest to business managers and public planners have been used to forecast phenomena for those interested in tourism.

This book is an introduction to a complex issue and no substitute for the myriad books, reports and articles available on tourism forecasting. Many of these appear as suggestions in For Further Information at the end of the chapters and in the Bibliography. This book is intended to provide a foundation for understanding the various *methods* available.

This book is also designed to suggest the most appropriate *strategies* for approaching a given tourism-forecasting task. Each of the various methods has its own strengths and weaknesses. Some are best when you have plenty of data to work with and you well understand the factors affecting tourism demand. Others are superior when little is known about the past, or the future we are interested in is distant. Some forecasting methods take little time and knowledge, while others require a detailed understanding of their intricacies.

Some have been widely employed in tourism, providing a wealth of experience we can build upon, while others have not been used for our subjects.

In short, the book was written to encourage readers to try their hands at forecasting some aspect of tourism demand, and to inform their efforts to help ensure success whatever their objectives.

It is often remarked that demand forecasting has become a very complex process, basically opaque to managers and other users. The following observation is typical, if more eloquent than most:

> Forecasting often becomes an end in itself, rather than an integral part of the strategic management process, because of the complexity of the methodologies used and the consequent need for specialist analysts to be involved. The analysts, however, have become isolated and detached, and forecasting has become a black box as far as most users are concerned ... Effective integration of tourism demand forecasting with management decision making implies the establishment of a meaningful dialogue between technicians and users (Faulkner and Valerio, 1995: 30).

This text is designed to help lift the veil of obscurity from the forecasting process for those who need sound guidance to the shape of the future. We hope it will lead to such a 'meaningful dialogue', as well as better forecasting and better integration of these forecasts in tourism marketing, planning, development, policy-making and research.

The scope of tourism

While there are many definitions of 'tourism' in use today, the World Tourism Organization (WTO), the affiliate of the United Nations (UN) serving as a global forum for tourism policy and issues, is working to standardize tourism terminology and classifications throughout the world. Such standardization will permit comparisons across studies, encourage the accumulation of knowledge about tourism activities and assist those beginning to study tourism in defining their terms. These standards have also been adopted by the United Nations Statistical Commission.

In the spirit of encouraging uniformity in tourism data collection and improving world knowledge about tourism behaviour and consequences, the following WTO definitions are observed in this book. (The sources of these and further details about them can be found in the WTO publications listed at the end of this chapter.)

The **visitor** is the foundational unit in the UN/WTO structure and is defined as any person travelling to a place other than that of his or her usual environment for less than twelve months and whose main purpose of trip is other than the exercise of an activity remunerated from within the place visited.

Tourism comprises the activities of persons travelling to and staying in places outside their usual environment for not more than one consecutive year for leisure, business and other purposes.

Tourists are visitors who stay at least one night in a collective or private accommodation in a place visited.

The **same-day visitor** is a visitor who does not spend the night in a collective or private accommodation in the place visited. This includes cruise passengers who debark in a country but spend their nights on board ship.

Tourism expenditure is the total consumption expenditure made by a visitor on behalf of a visitor for and during his or her trip and stay at a destination.

The **tourism industries** designate the set of enterprises, establishments and other organizations one of whose principal activities is to provide goods and/or services to tourists.

A term central to this book yet not officially defined by the WTO for forecasting purposes is 'tourism demand'. As employed in this book:

Tourism demand is a measure of visitors' use of a good or service.

'Use' in this case means to 'make use of (a thing), esp. for a particular end or purpose; utilize' (Brown, 1993: 3531).

Such use includes the economists' concept of consumption, as well as the presence of a visitor at a destination, port of entry or other tourism facility, and on a transport vehicle, regardless of whether any exchange takes place. Consequently, visitor arrivals in a country or local area constitute tourism demand since visitors avail themselves of the services of a destination in arriving there. Tourism demand can be measured in a variety of units, including a national currency, arrivals, nights, days, distance travelled and passenger-seats occupied.

Archer (1994: 105) aptly describes the objective of tourism demand forecasting as 'to predict the *most probable* level of demand that is likely to occur in the light of known circumstances or, when alternative policies are proposed, to show what different levels of demand may be achieved'.

The importance of tourism demand forecasting

The tourism industries, and those interested in their success in contributing to the social and economic welfare of a citizenry, need to reduce the risk of decisions, that is, reduce the chances that a decision will fail to achieve desired objectives. One important way to reduce this risk is by discerning certain future events or environments more clearly. One of the most important events is the demand for a tourism product, be it a good, a service or a bundle of services such as a vacation or what a destination offers.

All industries are interested in such risk reduction. However, this need may be more acute in the tourism industries than for other industries with other products, for the following reasons:

1 *The tourism product is perishable.* Once an airliner has taken off, or a theme park has closed for the day or morning dawns over a hotel, unsold seats, admissions or sleeping rooms vanish, along with the revenue opportunity associated with them. This puts a premium on shaping demand in the short run and anticipating it in the long run, to avoid both unsold 'inventory' on the one hand and unfulfilled demand on the other.

2 *People are inseparable from the production-consumption process.* To a large extent, the production of the tourism product takes place at the same time as its consumption. And much of this production-consumption process involves people interacting as suppliers and consumers, such as hotel staff, waiters and waitresses, flight attendants and entertainers. This puts a premium on having enough of the right supply personnel available when and where visitors need them.

3 *Customer satisfaction depends on complementary services.* While a hotelier directly controls only what happens to guests in his or her hotel, the visitor's experience depends on satisfaction with a host of goods and services that make up the visit. A hotel's future demand, therefore, depends on the volume of airline flights and other transport access to its area, the quality of airport services, the friendliness of taxi drivers, the quality and cost of entertainment and the availability of recreational opportunities, to name just a few of these elements. Forecasting can help ensure these

complementary services are available when and where future visitors need them, which will rebound to the benefit of the hotel or other individual tourism facility.

4 *Leisure tourism demand is extremely sensitive to natural and human-made disasters.* Much holiday and vacation travel is stimulated by the desire to seek refuge in venues far from the stress of the everyday environment. Moreover, today there are countless alternatives for spending leisure time pleasantly for residents of most developed nations. As a result, crises such as war, terrorist attacks, disease outbreaks, crime and extreme weather conditions can easily dissuade leisure travellers from visiting a destination suffering from one of these, or from travelling at all. The ability to forecast such events and their projected impact on tourism demand can help minimize the adverse effects of catastrophes on the tourism-related sales, income, employment and tax revenue of a place.

5 *Tourism supply requires large, long lead-time investments in plant, equipment and infrastructure.* A new hotel may take three to five years from concept to opening. A new airport or ski resort make take a decade or so for all planning, approvals and construction. A new aeroplane may take five years to produce from an airline's initial order to final delivery. Future demand must be anticipated correctly if suppliers are to avoid the financial costs of excess capacity or the opportunity costs of unfilled demand.

While there are industries that share one or several of these constraints on decision-making, the tourism industries appear to be unique in being shackled by all five.

Alternative views of the future

There are two extreme views of any event in the future that we need to be aware of. One extreme is that the event is absolutely predictable, that its occurrence has a 100 per cent probability. Of course, there is no future event in the universe that has such a high probability, although the positions of the planets in our solar system, the hours of sunrise and sunset, and many other events studied in the physical sciences come close to this, at least in the medium term.

Certain future events in tourism are a 'sure thing' as well. These include that at least one person in Europe will begin a trip away from home tomorrow, that at least one hotel will be partially occupied and that at least one government will accrue some revenue as a result of tourism this year.

These nearly certain events have at least two characteristics in common: forecasting them accurately is quite easy, and these forecasts are useless to tourism managers. They are useless because they are trivial. Furthermore, no action we can take will change these occurrences.

Indeed, the discovery by German physicist Werner Heisenberg in the 1920s renders this approach futile. His 'uncertainty principle' states that it is impossible to determine both momentum and position of a subatomic particle at the same time, only the probabilities of each (Paulos, 1991: 119–20). One consequence is that there is no deterministic theory that we can rely on to precisely forecast tourism futures of interest to us.

At the other end of the spectrum, as indicated in Figure 1.1, are those future events that are essentially random, that is, each possible occurrence of an event has the same probability. Flipping a coin or choosing a card from a well-shuffled deck are examples. The numbers selected in a lottery are designed to be random as well. In tourism, whether the next person to enter a restaurant is a male or female is a random event under most circumstances.

---

1. The future is totally predictable (i.e., unalterable) implying sound forecasts are useless.

2. The future is totally unpredictable (i.e., random) implying sound forecasts are impossible.

3. The future is somewhat predictable and somewhat alterable implying sound forecasts are useful and feasible.

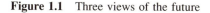

Figure 1.1 Three views of the future

These quite uncertain events are, by definition, impossible to forecast with any acceptable degree of accuracy. Consequently, forecasting them is not a worthwhile endeavour.

Fortunately, there is an alternative to these pessimistic views of the future that gives hope to forecasters. That is, future events important to tourism operations are somewhat predictable and somewhat changeable. We can predict events with probabilities significantly greater than zero and markedly less than 100 per cent. And these events can be affected by other events, including our own actions. This is the view adopted in this book.

This is also the hope of marketers and managers: that we can infer enough about the future to choose certain actions to shape it toward our preferences. Some call this 'inventing the future'. We obtain these inferences from reviewing the past. A forecasting method is simply a systematic way of organizing information from the past to infer the occurrence of an event in the future.

The two extreme views suggest a warning. We make a mistake if we invest heavily in trying to achieve a near perfect forecasting method. If we can achieve such, the results will be useless. Rather we must expect that our forecasts are not going to hit the mark each time, and this is good news for those trying to invent the future. The other caveat is that we can find a forecasting method that will tell us something useful about future tourism in most cases. That is, it will increase our probability of making an accurate forecast.

Bernstein (1996: 7) points out that these two extremes are independent of whether we try to quantify past patterns or use subjective means of indicating possible futures. Even if we could build a mathematical model that accurately reflects past behaviour, we would have no reason to believe that a true knowledge of the future is in our hands. Bernstein (ibid.) quotes Nobel laureate Kenneth Arrow (1992): 'our knowledge of the way things work, in society or in nature, comes trailing clouds of vagueness. Vast ills have followed a belief in certainty'. Tourism forecasters beware!

Forecasting definitions

Forecasting is fundamentally the process of organizing information about a phenomenon's past in order to predict a future.

A *phenomenon* is simply 'A fact or event that appears or is perceived by one of the senses or by the mind' as *The New Shorter Oxford English Dictionary* (Brown, 1993), defines the word. We can organize information about a phenomenon's past in many ways. One way is to manipulate objective, quantitative data by mathematical rules. Another is to analyse the opinions of experts about the phenomenon, past and future. Both of these classes of forecasting methods are treated in this book.[1]

Many who study the future believe as Herman Kahn did, that there are 'alternative futures, that the future is not a single inevitable state, but change can evolve in strikingly different ways' (Coates and Jarratt, 1989: xi). In effect we can 'invent' a future by making changes in the present. Forecasting, then, allows us to predict a single future or a set of futures, each associated with a different set of postulated changes.

In summary, at its most basic, forecasting 'takes historical fact and scientific knowledge . . . to create images of what may happen in the future' (Cornish, 1977: 51). This book describes much of the realm of scientific knowledge that has been applied to tourism demand in the last quarter of a century.

This book focuses on ways of forecasting the behaviour of tourism markets, that is, demand for some tourism product. This product may be a hotel room, a restaurant meal, a visit to a destination, a day at Walt Disney World, or even a trip away from home. In most cases, we want to know how many consumers there will be, how many units will be sold, how much will be spent on the purchases, or any combination of these.

> This book will use the term, **tourism demand forecasting**, to indicate a process designed to reduce the risks of tourism marketing and other management decisions through the use of forecasting. This is assumed to be synonymous with **tourism market forecasting**.

Other definitions

There are other terms that are not specifically related to tourism but are basic to understanding and discussing forecasting techniques:

> **Data point:** an individual value in a **time series**.

> **Data series:** same as a **time series**.

> **Forecast time series:** a **time series** of future values produced by some method.

> **Historical time series:** refers to the **time series** of past values.

> **Observation:** same as a **data point**, reminding us that each data point must be observed and measured, introducing the possibility of error.

> **Time series:** an ordered sequence of values of a variable observed at equally spaced time intervals.

> **Variable:** any phenomena that can be measured; usually refers to all of the **data points** associated with it.

It is important to understand the special use of the word 'past' in the above definitions. To a forecaster, the past includes all periods for which reasonably final values are available. Future time, on the other hand, includes time that has passed for which we do not yet have reasonably complete and accurate data, as well as time not yet encountered. Some time series of interest to tourism forecasters may run three to six months behind actual time, so that we may not know what happened to tourism demand in 1999 until 2001. This produces the odd (to non-forecasters) habit of forecasting periods that have passed us by but for which relevant measures are not available. This is the use of 'future values' that is implicitly adopted in this book: if the measure has not been developed for it, then the time period lies in the future for forecasting purposes.

Additional terms will be defined as they arise in this book. The glossary at the end of the book is designed to provide a complete listing of important terms used herein and their definitions.

Uses of tourism demand forecasts

Tourism demand forecasts can be helpful to marketers and other managers in reducing the risk of decisions regarding the future. For example, tourism marketers use demand forecasts to:

- set marketing goals, either strategic or for the annual marketing plan
- explore potential markets as to the feasibility of persuading them to buy their product and the anticipated volume of these purchases
- simulate the impact of future events on demand, including alternative marketing programmes as well as uncontrollable developments such as the course of the economy and the actions of competitors.

Managers use tourism demand forecasts to:

- determine operational requirements, such as staffing, supplies, and capacity
- study project feasibility, such as the financial viability of building a new hotel tower, expanding a restaurant, constructing a new theme park or offering airline service to a new destination.

Planners and others in public agencies use tourism demand forecasts to:

- predict the economic, social/cultural, environmental consequences of visitors
- assess the potential impact of regulatory policies, such as price regulation and environmental quality controls
- project public revenues from tourism for the budgeting process
- ensure adequate capacity and infrastructure, including airports and airways, bridges and highways, and energy and water treatment utilities.

In short, sound tourism demand forecasts can reduce the risks of decisions and the costs of attracting and serving the travelling public.

It is difficult to imagine the business of tourism or indeed any sector of capitalism existing without forecasting to deal with the risks inherent in saving and investing. Bernstein (1996: 22) goes so far as to maintain: 'The successful business executive is a forecaster first: purchasing, producing, marketing, pricing, and organizing all follow.'

Consequences of poor forecasting

Every organization develops either implicit or explicit forecasts about the factors that affect its future success. If no explicit forecasting is done, then the organization's implicit forecasts can often be inferred from its actions. If a hotel hires more housekeeping personnel, then it is probably expecting an increase in its numbers of guests. If an airline lays off flight attendants, then it may well expect passenger demand to decline despite the absence of any formal forecasting process.

Most often, a business may make no change in its marketing or operations, implicitly forecasting no change in demand in the next month, quarter or year. This is a naive approach to the future that may well produce dire consequences. Table 1.1 lists some of these consequences.

Table 1.1   Uses of demand forecasts and consequences of poor forecasting

Uses of demand forecasts	*Consequences of poor forecasting*
Setting marketing goals	Over- or under-budgeting for marketing
Exploring potential markets	Marketing to wrong segments, ignoring the right ones
Simulating impacts on demand	Incorrect marketing mix, e.g., setting prices too high
Determining operational requirements	Excess labour, or customer unhappiness with limited service
Examining the feasibility of a major investment in plant or equipment	Wasted financial resources, difficulty in financing interest payments
Predicting economic, social and environmental consequences	Environmental and social/cultural degradation; inflation or unemployment
Assessing potential impact of regulatory policies	Business losses, unemployment, price inflation
Projecting public revenue	Budget deficits
Planning for adequate capacity and infrastructure	Traffic congestion, delays and accidents

Special difficulties in tourism demand forecasting

The nature of tourism demand presents a number of special challenges to the forecaster that do not afflict those in other industries.

Historical data are often lacking

Most forecasting methods require a minimum of five or ten years of data for forecasting. Some require more. Yet few cities or other destinations have such series. In the USA, consistent estimates of foreign visitor expenditures are available only from 1984, while the annual series hotel/motel room-nights sold and revenues at the national and regional levels begin in 1987.

A review of the 1999 edition of the World Tourism Organization's *Compendium of Tourism Statistics* identified 173 independent countries reporting out of 190 such nations in the world. Of these 173 countries, thirteen did not report an annual measure of international tourists (that is, overnight visitors). Thirty-one countries had no annual series of international tourism receipts, and forty-eight did not estimate international travel expenditures annually. One-half had no measure of international departures, and nearly one-half did not count visitor nights in hotels and similar establishments.

Tourism demand can be volatile

Visitor volumes fluctuate with the seasons and over annual periods, and often produce wide variations. Figure 1.2 shows percentage changes in U.S. international airline passenger-miles monthly over the year-earlier period

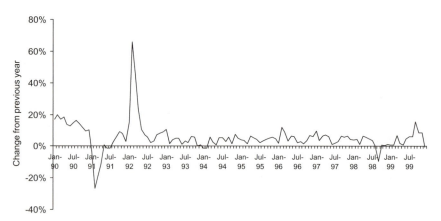

Figure 1.2 U.S. international airline traffic, monthly percentage change, 1990–99
Source: Air Transport Association of America

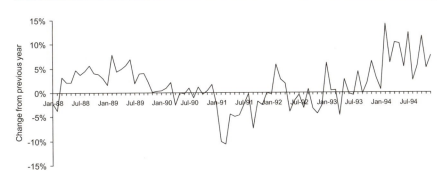

Figure 1.3 Hotel/motel room–night demand in the Los Angeles metropolitan area, monthly percentage change, 1984–94
Source: Smith Travel Research

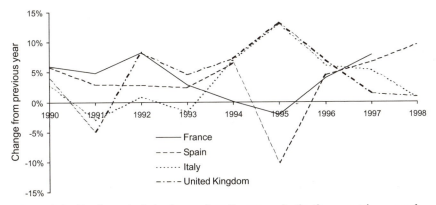

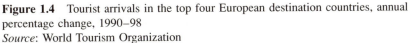

Figure 1.4 Tourist arrivals in the top four European destination countries, annual percentage change, 1990–98
Source: World Tourism Organization

during the early 1990s. Figure 1.3 presents similar measure for hotel room-nights sold in Los Angeles for a recent period. Figure 1.4 shows the percentage variation in international visitors to the top four European nation destinations. The more volatility there is in an activity, the more difficult it is to discern patterns that can help us forecast futures.

Tourism demand is sensitive to catastrophic influences

Part of the long-term volatility of tourism demand is due to the variety of shocks to the tourism system from external events. The worldwide petroleum shortages in 1973–4 and 1979–80 depressed international and domestic tourism in many countries. The Chernobyl nuclear accident in 1986 coupled

13

with the US–Libya conflict and resulting terrorism reduced US resident travel to individual European countries by one-quarter to two-thirds during that summer (Brady and Widdows, 1988: 10; Witt, Newbould and Watkins, 1992: 37). The Gulf War in 1991 depressed international tourism. Hurricanes, earthquakes, floods and epidemics have devastated visitor volumes in many parts of the world, as well.

In the U.S.A., reports of crimes against foreign visitors to Florida reduced volumes from Germany and Sweden by one-third in 1994 from the previous year (Florida Department of Commerce, 1995: 35). And Muslim militants' attacks on foreign visitors in Egypt are credited with depressing tourism receipts by 20 per cent in 1993 (Holman, 1993).

These are sporadic events that are virtually impossible to forecast, and their potential effects on tourism are even more obscure. Yet the forecaster must try to deal with them all.

Tourism behaviour is complex

Consumers travel for a multitude of reasons: relaxation, visiting friends and relatives, viewing sports, participating in sports, outdoor recreation, sightseeing, health, religious pilgrimages, and more. Business people travel to make sales calls, attend corporate meetings, attend conferences and conventions, inspect plant and equipment, lobby government officials, present press conferences, conduct trade missions, and other purposes. Moreover, the same person travelling for business today can be planning his or her family's vacation trip tomorrow, but with vastly different motives and resources.

Each of these trip purposes may show different patterns over time and be affected by different factors. If all trip purposes are aggregated into a single tourism demand series, the conflicting patterns may prevent determining the best forecasting models and obtaining the most accurate forecasts. For example, a study of various methods of forecasting international visitor arrivals in New Zealand found more accurate results were obtained by distinguishing series of holiday, visit friends/relatives, business and 'other' trip purpose series and independently forecasting them (Turner, Kulendran and Pergat, 1995). Witt and Witt (1992b: 8) reached a similar conclusion. However, in many cases, disaggregated tourism demand data may be lacking.

Visitors patronize a myriad of business establishments: airlines, taxis, railroads, hotels, bed and breakfast establishments, travel agents, tour operators, amusement parks, museums, spas and other health resorts, performing arts, and petrol service stations, to name a few. As forecasters, we have no clear concept of the 'travel product' a particular consumer seeks, and how the components affect his or her decisions to purchase complements and substitutes.

Further, there is no consensus on a sound theoretical foundation for tourism demand. We are not even certain how the family makes its vacation travel choices, as complex as they are as to timing, budgets, transport modes and places visited.

Finally, unlike most consumer products, most sales do not occur in a buyer's home area. Rather, visits to Paris may originate in London, Prague, Montreal, New York, Tokyo or Martinique. Consequently, we need to consider conditions in a number of widely dispersed areas as they affect demand for a place, an establishment, or a transport service.

There is a wide choice of forecast variables

Automobile industry forecasters must wrestle with hundreds of models from a dozen or so manufacturers. There may be hundreds of retailers of shoes in a country, with hundreds of styles of shoe. However, there is no question about the variables to be forecast: either units sold or sales revenue.

The world of tourism demand is not so simple. In attempting a tourism demand forecast, we must choose from among at least six variables that measure tourism demand, listed in Table 1.2.

It may be self-evident that a hotel company wants to forecast visitor-nights while an airline is interested in passenger-kilometres. Country, city, and other local destinations may focus on visitors, visitor-nights or visitor expenditures. Moreover, terminology changes by user. What are *visitors* to destinations, parks and attractions are *passengers* to transportation companies, *guests* to

Table 1.2 Alternative measures of tourism activity

Unit of measure	Activity measured
Visitors	Number of people travelling away from home
Visitor parties	Groups of people travelling away from home together
Visitor-nights	Total nights visitors spend away from home
Visitor-miles/kilometres	Distance travelled while away from home
Visitor expenditures	Total money spent purchasing goods and services related to the trip
Market size	Number of people travelling away from home once or more in a year

hotels and a resorts, and *customers* to restaurants and rental car companies. This plethora of measures of and terms for tourism demand has constrained the growth of a consistent body of knowledge built upon prior research. For example, forecast models for projecting passenger-miles cannot help most theme park operators very much.

Reviewing eighty-five international tourism demand forecasting models, Crouch (1994a) found that nearly two-thirds of them defined demand in terms of arrivals or departures. One-half of them measured demand in terms of expenditures and receipts. Other measures were used quite infrequently (ibid.: 43). This pattern may not hold in domestic tourism demand models, or those focused on the markets for an individual facility, such as a resort or attraction.

Witt, Newbould and Watkins (1992: 39) found that 'forecasting domestic tourist flows is considerably easier than forecasting international tourist flows' over a one-year horizon. They surmise the reasons to be the lack of exchange rate effects and international political upheavals. However, this observation is based on only one application: monthly visitor arrivals in Las Vegas from 1973 to 1988.

Sheldon (1993: 14) maintains that visitor expenditure is the only one of these measures that can directly translate into economic impact. However, these expenditures are difficult to derive and 'may have a high degree of error' (ibid.: 19). This helps explain why her comparison of eight forecasting methods in simulating international arrivals in six countries produced higher relative errors than similar tests on visitor arrivals data.

Future patterns of any human activity are more or less obscure to those living in the present. But these peculiarities of tourism demand forecasting make discerning the road ahead even more problematic. They require a number of rather difficult decisions to be made before the search for appropriate forecasting methods is begun.

In sum, tourism demand is a ubiquitous and growing phenomenon throughout the world today. Those public and private organizations that seek to serve and manage this demand need to reduce the risk of future failures. This risk is intensified by the special characteristics of tourism demand and supply. The successful manager will seek ways to reduce this risk by organizing knowledge about the past to better discern the future, the essence of tourism demand forecasting.

Organization of this book

Thirteen methods of applied tourism forecasting are discussed in the following pages. Chapter 2 briefly describes these methods and discusses means of evaluating the results of tourism forecasting efforts.

Chapter 3 details the forecasting process that ensures that the forecaster conducts a comprehensive survey of forecasting techniques available and that time and money resources are conserved in the process.

Chapter 4 presents the simplest methods of quantitative forecasting. These 'time series models' do not deal with causes and effects but rather try to simulate historical demand data for extrapolation into the future.

Chapter 5 presents more sophisticated methods for capturing the essence of a tourism demand series' past course. These have proved relatively popular in tourism demand forecasting.

Chapter 6 discusses the Box–Jenkins technique, a complex time series analysis method that has proved popular in business and economic forecasting and now in tourism forecasting, as well.

Chapter 7 explores regression analysis, primarily used to investigate relationships of certain explanatory variables to a tourism demand series. Quantification of these relationships serves to suggest causes of tourism's course, and equations for producing future values.

Chapter 8 presents an elaborate modelling technique for simulating the complexities of the real world. After being virtually ignored for a decade, there are now several expressions of this approach available for producing tourism forecasts.

Chapter 9 discusses four qualitative forecasting techniques that have proved useful in forecasting tourism demand in both the short term and the long term.

Finally, Chapter 10 draws on the experience of a number of tourism forecasters over the last decade or so to suggest future trends in forecasting this demand.

Note

1 Forecasting should not be confused with *prophecy*, which is foretelling the future by means of divine revelation. Prophecy does not depend upon arranging and analysing information about the past. But it is far less accessible to those forecasting tourism demand.

For further information

Archer, B. (1994). Demand forecasting and estimation. In *Travel, Tourism, and Hospitality Research: A Handbook for Managers and Researchers* (J. R. Brent Ritchie and C. R. Goeldner, eds) 2nd edition, pp. 105–14, Wiley.

Bernstein, P. L. (1996). *Against the Gods: The Remarkable Story of Risk*, chs 1 and 2. Wiley.

Calantone, R. J., di Benedetto, C. A. and Bojanic, D. (1987). A comprehensive review of the tourism forecasting literature. *Journal of Travel Research*, **26** (2), Fall, 28–39.

Coates, J. F. and Jarratt, J. (1989). *What Futurists Believe*. Lomond.

Cornish, E. (1977). *The Study of the Future*. World Future Society.

Naisbitt, J. (1994). *Global Paradox*. Morrow.

WTO publications

United Nations and World Tourism Organization (UN and WTO) (1994). *Recommendations on Tourism Statistics*. United Nations Department for Economic and Social Information and Policy Analysis.

World Tourism Organization (WTO) (1995a). *Concepts, Definitions and Classifications for Tourism Statistics: Technical Manual No. 1*. WTO.

World Tourism Organization (WTO) (1995b). *Collection of Tourism Expenditure Statistics: Technical Manual No. 2*. WTO.

World Tourism Organization (WTO) (1995c). *Collection of Domestic Tourism Statistics: Technical Manual No. 3*. WTO.

World Tourism Organization (WTO) (1995d). *Collection and Compilation of Tourism Statistics: Technical Manual No. 4*. WTO.

World Tourism Organization (WTO) (1999). *Tourism Satellite Account (TSA): The Conceptual Framework*. WTO.

2

Alternative forecasting methods and evaluation

Choosing an appropriate forecasting model is something like fitting a glove. There is some effort involved because one size does not fit all. Most people have five fingers on a hand, but some have more or fewer. Fingers vary in length and circumference. Some find wool linings itchy while others prefer these to any other.

It is relatively easy to tell when a glove fits properly. We can usually determine this before buying a pair. We do not have this luxury with a forecasting model. We cannot completely assess its ability to predict the future until that future has passed and we have had time to measure it. However, we can make some informed judgements at the initial stage of fitting the model to the information about the past at our disposal. Certain evaluation criteria help us weed out inappropriate techniques when considering which methods to begin with and which model to adopt for producing forecasts.

This chapter briefly discusses thirteen forecasting methods that have been applied to forecasting tourism demand. These will be explored in detail in the following chapters. Then, we examine various assessment criteria that, if properly applied and heeded, can save us a lot of headaches as we attempt to model tourism futures.

Types of forecasting methods

Business forecasting methods, and tourism methods among them, fall into two major categories: quantitative and qualitative. *Quantitative methods* organize past information about a phenomenon by mathematical rules. These rules take advantage of underlying patterns and relationships in the data of interest to the forecaster. Objective numerical measurements consistent over some historical period are required in these methods. These methods also assume that at least some elements of past patterns will continue into the future (Makridakis, Wheelwright and Hyndman, 1998: 9).

There are two major subcategories of quantitative methods: extrapolative and causal. *Extrapolative methods*, also called 'time series methods', assume that the variable's past course is the key to predicting its future. Patterns in the data during the past are used to project or extrapolate future values. Causal relationships are ignored.

The other subcategory of quantitative forecasting methods is *causal methods*. These attempt to mathematically simulate cause-and-effect relationships. Determining the causal variables (better called 'explanatory variables') that affect the forecast variable and the appropriate mathematical expression of this relationship is the central objective.

These methods have the advantage over time series methods of explicitly portraying cause-and-effect relationships. This is crucial in certain forecasting situations, such as when management wants to know how much impact on demand an increased advertising budget will have. Likewise, tourism policy forecasting requires causal models. However, these methods are more costly and time-consuming to construct than time series models, and are often considerably less accurate.

Qualitative methods are also called 'judgemental methods.' Past information about the forecast variable is organized by experts using their judgement rather than mathematical rules. These are not necessarily cheaper or easier to apply than quantitative methods, but they have the advantage of not requiring historical data series.

Figure 2.1 summarizes these classifications and lists the forecasting methods that are covered in this book.

A. Quantitative methods

    1. Extrapolative methods
        a. Naive
        b. Single moving average
        c. Single exponential smoothing
        d. Double exponential smoothing
        e. Classical decomposition
        f. Autoregression
        g. Box-Jenkins approach (ARIMA)

    2. Causal methods
        a. Regression analysis
        b. Structural econometric models

B. Qualitative methods
    1. Jury of executive opinion
    2. Subjective probability assessment
    3. Delphi method
    4. Consumer intentions survey

Figure 2.1 Types of forecasting methods

Forecasting methods and models

It is useful to understanding the various approaches to forecasting tourism's future discussed in this book to recognize the distinction between a *forecasting method* and a *forecasting model*.

> A forecasting **method** is simply a systematic way of organizing information from the past to infer the occurrence of an event in the future. 'Systematic' means following a distinct set of procedures in a prescribed sequence.

> A forecasting **model** is one expression of a forecasting method. More specifically, it is a simplified representation of reality, comprising a set of relationships, historical information on these relationships, and procedures to project these relationships into the future.

In the quantitative applications, a forecasting model may be a single equation or a group of related equations. In applying quantitative forecasting methods, it is the common practice to test several models incorporating the assumptions of a given method in order to find the most accurate one. This will be made clear in the following chapters.

Forecasting model evaluation criteria

Since there are a number of quantitative forecasting methods (for example, Figure 2.1), and each method can spawn from one to a score or more models, it is essential to have objective criteria by which to evaluate these. The following criteria are useful for evaluating your own models or those of others, and are not listed in order of importance. You will want to determine your own priorities.

- specified structure
- plausible structure
- acceptability
- explanatory power
- robustness
- parsimony
- cost
- accuracy.

Specified structure

Before you can evaluate your own model or someone else's, you must have the model's structure clearly detailed. There is a tendency among some to present forecasts as if derived from a 'black box', with input and output specified but no explanation of how the former are transformed into the latter. Advancement of scientific knowledge depends on replicating and building upon past research studies. In contrast, the black box approach obfuscates, preventing replication or even evaluation, and should be avoided in forecast modelling.

Plausible structure

Once you examine a model's structure, you can determine whether it is credible or not. A model that does not logically reflect the way the world works is not likely to produce accurate forecasts over significant periods. A common problem in using regression analysis for forecasting is when the relationships in the forecasting model defy common sense, such as when the equation indicates that demand for airline seats increases as fares are raised.

Acceptability

This is a pragmatic criterion. Is the model acceptable to management, or does it violate managers' paradigms or concepts of what constitutes a valid model?

There is not much point in applying a forecasting model that management finds unacceptable in its assumptions.

Explanatory power

In some cases, it is essential to explain the important relationships at work in producing the forecast values. When this is a requirement, the question becomes, does the forecasting model under study explain as much as management wants to know?

Robustness

A forecasting model is robust if its forecasts are little affected by the extreme values in the historical series. These extreme values are called 'outliers' because they lie outside of the range of most of the other values. For example, air travel across the north Atlantic was depressed by the Gulf War in January–February 1991 (see Figure 1.2). You would want to avoid a forecasting model that magnifies these effects in the forecasts it produces for subsequent months.

Some forecasting models may be extremely sensitive to outliers, that is, their forecasts change significantly if the outliers are removed. Others, however, are robust and their forecasts are resistant to the presence or absence of extreme historical values.

Parsimony

William of Ockham (1300–49) was a Franciscan cleric and philosopher. He proclaimed a logical principle known as Ockham's Razor: 'What can be done with fewer is done in vain with more' (Van Doren, 1991: 126, 209). The parsimony criterion argues for the simpler model over the more complex one when other important criteria are similar between the two. The more complex the model, the more costly it is to operate and the more likely that errors will occur in its construction and use. If you plan to spend time and money to develop a complex tourism-forecasting model, you should carefully evaluate its anticipated advantages over a simpler one. Ockham's Razor can shave time and money off of the forecasting process and may help you achieve better accuracy, as well.

Cost

Since time is always a scarce resource and money usually is, management generally prefers models that require less of both.

Accuracy

If the primary purpose of building a forecasting model is to clearly discern the future of a phenomenon, then the most important criterion of all is how accurately a model does this. That is, how closely do the estimates provided by the model conform to the actual events being forecast. There are at least three dimensions of accuracy: error magnitude accuracy, directional change accuracy and trend change or turning point accuracy. Moreover, there are at least three time frames where a forecasting model's accuracy can be explored: over all of the past data available when building the model, over the recent past of these data and over a period beyond the data set used to construct the model ('post-sample accuracy'). These aspects of accuracy are discussed in a following section.

Forecast measures of accuracy

Tourism demand forecasting is important to the tourism manager and to those that depend on that manager. More accurate forecasts reduce the risks of decisions more than do less accurate ones. In a brief survey of tourism demand forecasters and users of such forecasts, Witt and Witt (1992a: 154–61) found 'that accuracy is the most important forecast evaluation criterion'.

There are three measures of accuracy commonly found to be useful to tourism managers, and each of these is discussed in turn (further discussion of these can be found in Witt and Witt, 1992a: 124–34):

- error magnitude
- directional change
- turning point.

Error magnitude accuracy

The most familiar concept of forecasting accuracy is called 'error magnitude accuracy', and relates to forecast error associated with a particular forecasting model. This is defined as:

$$e_t = A_t - F_t \tag{2.1}$$

where t = some time period, such as a month, quarter or year
         e = forecast error
         A = actual value of the variable being forecast
         F = forecast value.

If the actual value is greater than the forecast value at time, t, then the forecasting error is positive. If less than the forecast value, then the forecasting error is negative.

Any model designed to forecast human behaviour will suffer from forecasting errors. Such errors are due to at least three factors that sometimes interact:

1 *Omission of influential variables.* No forecasting model can include all of the variables that affect the one being forecast. Moreover, even if such a model could be built, it is quite unlikely the forecaster could accurately estimate the true relationships between these and the forecast variable. Some events that affect visitor flows between England and France, for example, are simply random. These include the weather, transportation equipment failures and labour strikes, to name but a few salient ones.

2 *Measurement error.* We cannot measure visitor flows or other variables representing tourism demand completely accurately. Moreover, the variables that affect demand may be mismeasured as well. This is because some variables of interest are inherently unmeasurable (e.g. the attractiveness of a destination) and some are difficult to measure due to data collection difficulties (e.g. visitor expenditures).

3 *Human indeterminacy.* Human beings do not always act in rational ways, or even always in their own best interests. They often ignore budget constraints when planning a vacation. Patterns of behaviour do not last: a couple will visit the same destination every summer for years and then suddenly turn to an alternative. Humans get sick and must cancel planned trips, or schedule new ones to receive emergency health treatments. There is always a degree of randomness in human behaviour and this shows up in forecast errors.

There are quite a few ways to summarize the error magnitude accuracy of a forecasting model. Some of these compute measures of absolute error, and are thus subject to the units and time period over which the model is tested. They are often difficult to interpret and compare across different models.

Mean absolute percentage error

Other error magnitude measures compute percentage errors relative to the values in the historical series. These allow you to compare several different models across different time periods. One of the most useful of these, due to its simplicity and intuitive clarity, is the mean absolute percentage error, or *MAPE*:

$$\text{MAPE} = \frac{1}{n} * \left(\frac{|e_t|}{A_t} \right) * 100 \tag{2.2}$$

where n = number of periods
   e = forecast error (see Equation 2.1)
   A = actual value of the variable being forecast
   t = some time period.

The MAPE is a sum of the absolute errors for each time period divided by the actual value for the period, this sum is divided by the number of periods to obtain a mean value. Then, by convention, this is multiplied by 100 to state it in percentage terms. This is a simple measure permitting comparison across different forecasting models with different time periods and numbers of observations, and weighting all percentage error magnitudes the same. Lower MAPE values are preferred to higher ones because they indicate a forecasting model is producing smaller percentage errors.

Moreover, its interpretation is intuitive. The MAPE indicates, on the average, the percentage error a given forecasting model produces for a specified period. One author has suggested the following interpretation of MAPE values:

- less than 10 per cent is highly accurate forecasting
- between 10 and 20 per cent is good forecasting
- between 20 and 50 per cent is reasonable forecasting
- greater than 50 per cent is inaccurate forecasting (Lewis, 1982: 40).

Such a standard can be quite misleading because it ignores the change characteristics of the time series being forecast. If a time series increases at a mean rate of 2 per cent per year in the past, then a forecasting model with a MAPE of 8 per cent is not very useful: achieving the 'highly accurate' label is irrelevant to the case.

The essence of quantitative forecasting is identifying the particular patterns of a given time series – its personality. Applying forecasting accuracy standards that ignore this personality is tantamount to treating all wild animals as if they were hamsters: you will have severe problems with the tigers.

A better set of standards for assessing the accuracy of a forecasting model in simulating its time series is based on the 'naive' forecasting model. The simple version of this model (sometimes called 'Naive 1') forecasts the next period's value to be the same as this period's. If your tourism demand series is monthly or quarterly, then its seasonality requires you to set a period's value as equal to the same period one year earlier, the 'seasonal naive model'. Finally, you could forecast the growth rate for the next period's value as equal to the growth rate for this period over the previous period. Witt and Witt (1992) called this the "Naive 2 model".

We can compare the MAPE's or other measure of forecasting accuracy of a proposed forecasting model and the relevant naive model (Mentzer and Bienstock, 1998: 30). If our proposed model shows poorer forecasting accuracy than the naive approach, it is wasteful to develop it, and may even produce misleading results. To set the standards for evaluating the MAPE of a forecasting model, compute the MAPE for a naive model, compare the two, and apply the following guidelines:

- a model with a MAPE less than one-half of the naive MAPE indicates a highly accurate forecasting model
- a model MAPE equal to between 50 and 100 per cent of the naive MAPE indicates a reasonably accurate forecasting model
- a model MAPE equal to more than the naive MAPE is a poor forecasting model: you would be better off using the simpler, cheaper naive model and achieving the lower forecasting error.

Finally, note that the MAPE should be applied to the final, untransformed series you are ultimately planning to forecast. MAPE will not work with transformed series, such as first differences, where there is a chance that one or more values will be zero, or close to zero. In the former case, the MAPE cannot be computed because zero shows once or more in the denominator of Equation 2.2. In the latter, where one or more values are close to zero, the MAPE tends to explode in magnitude.

Theil's U-statistic

Theil's U-statistic provides an objective measure of the accuracy of a forecasting model relative to the Naive 1 model for the same data series (Makridakis, Wheelwright and Hyndham, 1998: 49–50). Formally,

$$U = \sqrt{\frac{\sum \left(\dfrac{F_{t+1} - A_{t+1}}{A_t} \right)^2}{\sum \left(\dfrac{A_{t+1} - A_t}{A_t} \right)^2}} \tag{2.3}$$

where F = forecast value
A = actual value of the variable being forecast
t = some time period.

The numerator of Equation 2.3 resembles Equation 2.1 for estimating the MAPE of a forecasting model, while the denominator is similar to the equation for estimating the MAPE of the Naive 1 model. The number of periods ('*n*' in Equation 2.1) in the numerator and denominator cancel each other out. The interpretation of the ranges of the U-statistic are as follows:

U = 1:   Naive 1 is as good as the forecasting model being evaluated

U < 1:   the forecasting model is better than the Naive 1 approach, and this superiority increases as the U-statistic gets smaller

U > 1:   the Naive 1 model produces a more accurate forecast of the data series than the forecasting model under scrutiny, so there is no reason to employ it.

Root mean square percentage error

Another measure of error magnitude accuracy useful over all time series and quantitative forecasting methods is the root mean square percentage error, or *RMSPE*:

$$\text{RMSPE} = \sqrt{\frac{\left(\dfrac{e_t}{A_t}\right)^2}{n}} * 100 \tag{2.4}$$

where n = number of periods
        e = forecast error
        A = actual value of the variable being forecast
        t = some time period.

This measure also computes an average error in terms of percentages and can be compared to actual rates of change in the historical data series. However, it penalizes larger errors more than small ones. This may be important if you can live with continuing but small errors from your forecasting model but cannot accept several large ones. For example, in staffing a hotel, it may not matter to you if the number of guests checking in on a day exceeds your forecast by 10 per cent because the existing staff can handle this. However, if check-ins occasionally turn out to be 50 per cent more than forecast, your customers and your staff will suffer during such periods. You would prefer the RMSPE measure of forecasting error to choose the model that most avoids these large mistakes.

Note that, as discussed in relation to the MAPE above, the RMSPE approach to error evaluation should only be applied to the final, untransformed demand series you are trying to forecast. This reduces the chances that values of zero or close to zero will end as the A_t term in Equation 2.4, producing useless results.

Figure 2.2 presents a case where these two measures of percentage error magnitude provide divergent signals of forecasting model accuracy. The actual visitor series is artificial for a fictitious destination. It shows a constant trend until 1995, when a major festival doubles the number of visitors.

Two forecast models have been employed to forecast the actual visitor data. Forecast model 1 simulates the trend of visitation quite well, and produces the lower MAPE. However, it completely misses the 1995 visitor spike. Forecast model 2 does not simulate the trend as well. Its MAPE is higher than forecast 1. But it does capture most of the 1995 visitor spike. By the RMSPE measure of error magnitude, it is superior to forecast 1 because the latter is heavily penalized for its 1995 forecast error in the RMSPE calculation.

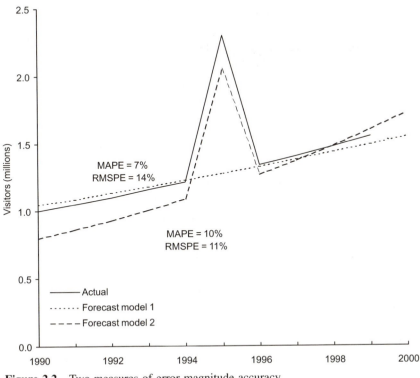

Figure 2.2 Two measures of error magnitude accuracy
Source: author

If you are more interested in capturing the overall trend, forecast model 1 is the better as indicated by its lower MAPE. On the other hand, if you are more interested in avoiding occasional large forecasting errors such as occurred with model 1 in 1995, then the RMSPE indicates model 2 is superior for your purposes.

This author believes the MAPE to be the better all-around indicator of forecasting accuracy than the RMSPE. MAPE is easier to calculate, is easier to understand and can be used to compare a forecasting method across a number of series. In the latter case, the RMSPE will indicate that a method is less accurate for time series with large values compared to those with small values. Finally, the RMSPE will heavily penalize a method with one very bad forecast caused by a shock such as a catastrophic storm or terrorist attacks on tourist facilities.

Perhaps the choice between MAPE and RMSPE as the best measure of error magnitude accuracy is not critical for most tourism demand series. In a comparison of various methods for forecasting international travel demand among countries, Witt and Witt (1992a: 122) found that both measures indicated approximately the same ranking of models. However, neither MAPE nor RMSPE is a useful indicator of two *other* concepts of forecasting accuracy.

Assessing post-sample accuracy

In seeking a forecasting model with the smallest MAPE or other measure of accuracy over the historical series, we may be tempted to reduce forecast error to near zero by developing a model sufficiently complex to explain even random errors. This is called 'overfitting a model' (Makridakis, Wheelwright and Hyndham, 1998: 45). While this may be temporarily satisfying, it is unlikely to produce a model that is accurate in predicting the future of the series. To guard against the urge to overfit, we should hold out one or more periods of the most recent data we have during the specification phase of our forecasting process (see Chapter 3 for more detail on this phase). We then develop a number of models based on the data series we are attempting to forecast, and then test them against our hold-out data.

An effective application of post-sample forecast accuracy measurement is to hold the most recent three or more periods of data out, develop alternative forecast models, apply each to forecasting each of these periods (called 'ex post forecasts'), compute the MAPEs or other measure of accuracy for each model and compare these values. The model with the lowest MAPE or other measure then has demonstrated it is the best for forecasting future values of the data series (that is, ex ante forecasts). This is what we are really looking for in a forecast model.

Holding out a set of values in a time series that does not have many to begin with (a common enough occurrence in tourism demand forecasting) is painful. You are effectively excluding the most recent information your historical time series has to offer. Regression analysis is flexible enough to offer a third way. Evaluate alternative models in ex post forecasting to determine the most appropriate form of the model and its explanatory variables. Then re-estimate the final model employing all available values of the time series and use this to produce forecasts of the true future. You will have even more confidence in your final model if the coefficients do not significantly change from those found in the test model.

Prediction intervals

So far, we have discussed forecasting as producing a single value for each future period we are interested in. However, whatever value we produce, it is only one likelihood among a number of possible values that will actually occur when the future unfolds. We can conceive of a range of possible values that we are quite certain will include the actual value produced by time. This range of values has been called the 'prediction interval' for each period we are forecasting. A leading business forecasting textbook succinctly details the advantages of publishing prediction intervals for our forecasts:

> It is usually desirable to provide not only forecast values but also accompanying uncertainty statements, usually in the form of *prediction intervals*. This is useful because it provides the user of the forecasts with 'worst'- or 'best'-case estimates and with a sense of how dependable the forecast is, and because it protects the forecaster from the criticism that the forecasts are 'wrong'. Forecasts cannot be expected to be perfect, and intervals emphasize this (Makridakis, Wheelwright and Hyndman, 1998: 52).

Statisticians view prediction intervals as a purely statistical concept, based on the mean squared errors of the historical series. One expression of the prediction interval for a forecast h periods after our historical series of n values is (Makridakis, Wheelwright and Hyndman, 1998: 54):

$$F_{n+h} = \pm z \sqrt{MSE_h} \tag{2.5}$$

$$MSE_h = \frac{1}{n-h} * \sum_{t=h+1}^{n} \left(e_t^h\right)^2 \tag{2.6}$$

where F_{n+h} = prediction interval h periods after the last value in the historical series

z = probability of the prediction interval including the actual value

MSE_h = mean squared error of the forecast value h periods after the last value in the historical time series

n = number of values in the historical time series

h = number of periods after the last value of the historical time series

e^h = error for a time period raised to the h power

t = some time period.

An example can help make this clear. Table 2.1 shows the error computed for each of twenty periods in a historical time series using a specific forecasting model (column B). Assume we want to compute the prediction interval three periods after the end of this series (that is, $h = 3$). Column C shows the error

Table 2.1 **Computation of the errors of a hypothetical forecast model for a prediction interval three periods after the time series ends**

A. Time period	B. Error (i.e., $e_t = A_t - F_t$)	C. Error cubed (i.e., $h = 3$)	D. Error cubed squared
1	1	1	1
2	5	125	15 625
3	−2	−8	64
4	−4	−64	4 096
5	−6	−216	46 656
6	7	343	117 649
7	2	8	64
8	−1	−1	1
9	3	27	729
10	−2	−8	64
11	5	125	15 625
12	6	216	46 656
13	5	125	15 625
14	−4	−64	4 096
15	7	343	117 649
16	2	8	64
17	6	216	46 656
18	−5	−125	15 625
19	−2	−8	64
20	3	27	729
Sum over relevant time periods			432 048

for each historical period cubed since $h = 3$. Column D shows the Column C values squared.

By Equation 2.6, we only sum the values in Column D beginning with the $h + 1$ period or time period 4, as indicated by the box. This sum is shown at the bottom of column D.

Finishing the computation in Equation 2.6:

$$\text{MSE}_3 = \frac{1}{20 - 3} * 432\,048 = 25\,415 \qquad \text{(2.6 cont.)}$$

The z term incorporates our level of confidence, taken from the normal distribution. If we want to be 95 per cent confident the prediction interval will contain the true value, $z = 1.960$. At a stringent 99 per cent level, $z = 2.576$. If we can settle for being 90 per cent confident, then $z = 1.645$. Say we choose to be 95 per cent confident, then

$$F_{20+3} = \pm 1.96 \sqrt{25\,415} = 159 \qquad \text{(2.7)}$$

If our forecast for period 13 is 1000, then we can be 95 per cent confident the actual value will be between $1000 - 159$ and $1000 + 159$, or between 841 and 1159.

Such prediction intervals only have meaning for statistical models, that is, models that incorporate some random error. They do not apply to deterministic forecasting models, such as the time series methods discussed in Chapters 4 and 5.

Directional change accuracy

Sometimes, the most important information we wish about the future is whether there will be more or fewer visitors next year than this year. This can help, for example, in deciding whether or not to increase transport capacity or staffing.

A directional change error, sometimes called 'tracking error,' occurs when a forecasting model fails to predict the actual direction of change for a period. Table 2.2 indicates the occasions of such errors, indicated by the E marks. The diagonal of the A marks indicates occasions when a forecasting model accurately identifies a change in direction.

There is a measure of directional change accuracy that indicates a model's success in forecasting whether a variable will be higher or lower than its previous value.

Table 2.2   Occasions of forecast model directional change accuracy

Actual data show	Forecast model predicts:		
	Increase	*No change*	*Decrease*
Increase	A	E	E
No change	E	A	E
Decrease	E	E	A

Notes:
A = model accurately forecasts direction of change.
E = model does not accurately forecast direction of change.

The equation for this measure is

$$\text{DCA} = \frac{\sum \text{FD}_t}{\sum \text{AD}_t} * 100 \qquad (2.8)$$

where   DCA = directional change accuracy in per cent
　　　　FD　= directional change accurately forecast
　　　　AD　= directional change actually occurring
　　　　t　　= some time period.

Figure 2.3 offers an application of this measure of directional change accuracy. This chart shows actual annual visitor volume at the John F. Kennedy Center for the Performing Arts in Washington, D.C., and a simple forecast model's values. When an A appears, the model has correctly forecast the directional movement. Where an E is shown, the forecast model has failed to predict the next period's change correctly.

Altogether, the actual series shows ten periods of decline and the model correctly predicted seven of these. The actual series rose six times, and the model forecast two of these. According to Equation 2.8, nine movements were correctly forecast out of sixteen occurring, for a directional change accuracy of 56 per cent.

Trend change accuracy

Turning point or trend change error is a subset of change of direction error. It occurs when a forecasting model fails to predict a turning point when one occurs, or predicts a turning point when none occurs.

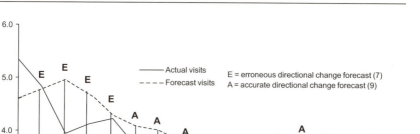
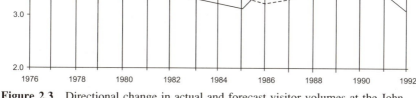

Figure 2.3 Directional change in actual and forecast visitor volumes at the John F. Kennedy Center, annually, 1976–92
Source: U.S. National Park Service and author

A trend change or *turning point* is defined as at least two periods showing an *upward trend* over an initial period, and the next period showing a downward change:

$$\text{upward trend} = A_{t-2} < A_{t-1} < A_t$$
$$\text{and turning point} = A_t > A_{t+1}$$
$$\text{or no turning point} = A_t < A_{t+1},$$

or at least two periods showing a *downward trend* from an initial period and the next period showing an upward change:

$$\text{downward trend} = A_{t-2} > A_{t-1} > A_t$$
$$\text{and turning point} = A_t < A_{t+1}$$
$$\text{or no turning point} = A_t > A_{t+1}.$$

Thus, four consecutive data points are required to define turning points and enable us to calculate trend change error. The latter is equal to the percentage of turning points and no turning points forecast accurately. A simple practice is to divide the number of turning points and no turning points accurately forecast by the total number of turning points and no turning points actually occurring, and multiplying this quotient by 100 to place it in percentage terms.

In Figure 2.4, the vertical lines indicate a change in trend (that is, a turning point) in the actual time series. If there is a turning point, it is located at the third point of the four required to identify it. For example, in 1979, after declining through the 1976–8 period (three data points), visitor volume increased (that is, changed direction). This created a turning point in 1978. The forecast series failed to do the same, and this is marked by an E. Then visitor volume declined each year until 1986, when it changed direction again. The forecast model also failed to identify this 1987 turning point. Finally, after rising over the 1985–8 period, the actual series fell in 1989, creating the last turning point at 1988. The forecast model disregarded this, as well, missing all four turning points.

The forecast model correctly predicted eight out of ten of the 'non-turning points' in the series, indicated by A in Figure 2.4. So, this model's overall score in correctly predicting turning points is the sum of zero turning points forecast plus eight non-turning points actually predicted, divided by fourteen possible predicted turning points, or 57 per cent.

These turning points can be viewed as the peaks or troughs of business cycles. If a tourism manager can forecast these turning points far enough in advance, the company can reduce the risk of major capital investments and other financial decisions. If you discern a downward turn on the horizon after a rising trend in a certain visitor segment, you can reduce resources directed to that segment and use them to attract growing segments.

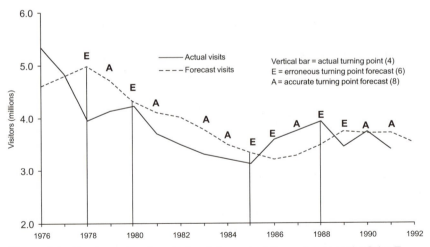

Figure 2.4 Turning points in actual and forecast visitor volumes at the John F. Kennedy Center, annually, 1976–92
Source: U.S. National Park Service and author.

Value of graphical data displays

It is hard to exaggerate the importance of viewing a data series to forecasting it properly. Each time series has a personality, and displaying the series helps make this explicit as no other method can. Makridakis, Wheelwright and Hyndman (1998: 23) maintain: 'The single most important thing to do when first exploring the data is to visualize the data through graphs.'

A *time plot* is a graph that displays a time series related to its periods at equally spaced intervals. These may be days, weeks, months, seasons, quarters or years. Figure 2.5 shows a time plot of U.S. domestic airline traffic annually as a line chart. (This is usually preferable to a bar chart because it emphasizes the time sequence of the values.) We can more clearly discern the progress of this series here than by simply viewing a table of the values: after slow growth through 1982, airline traffic accelerated through 1990, declined for a year, and then resumed its upward trend.

Figure 2.5 also includes the eight elements essential to understanding any graphical data display:

- name of the series (chart title)
- periods charted (in this case, calendar years)
- time period covered (1980–99)
- name of the units of the series (vertical axis title)
- series units shown (value labels on the vertical axis)
- time units (value labels on the horizontal axis)
- source of the time series (at bottom left)
- data measure (the line or 'curve' representing the data).

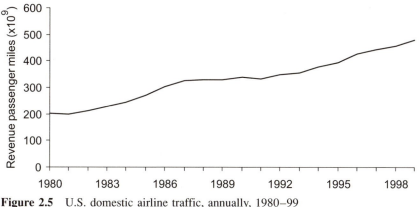

Figure 2.5 U.S. domestic airline traffic, annually, 1980–99
Source: Air Transport Association of America

This information gives the reader a clear understanding of the series charted and where it came from. Moreover, it helps the forecaster to distinguish different series and the same series over different time periods (for example, months instead of years).

Sometimes, it is helpful to identify the actual values in the curve charted by either including the numbers or horizontal and vertical lines at each value on the horizontal and vertical axes. In addition, the values charted need not be the actual values of the time series. They may be the time series transformed or redefined as changes each period, percentage changes, indexed to some base year, or logarithms of the time series.

Of course, we can show more than one series on a single chart, as in Figures 2.3 and 2.4. Make sure you include a legend to separate the different series represented.

The other graphical display most useful in forecasting is the *scatter diagram*, which shows two time series at each point in time as a single point. Figure 2.6 shows the scatter diagram for U.S. real gross domestic product and U.S. airline traffic. Note that each point corresponds to a single year. Note also that there appears to be a clear relationship between the two series: As gross domestic product (GDP) rises, so does airline traffic. The only exception is the 1981–2 period.

Since the scatter diagram plots two series, the units may not be consistent. These are clearly stated, however, as the horizontal and vertical axis labels.

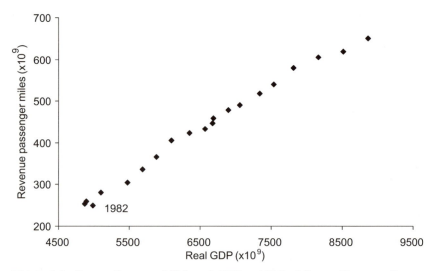

Figure 2.6 Scatter diagram of U.S. real GDP and U.S. airline traffic, annually, 1980–99
Source: Air Transport Association of America

Note also that the origin does not denote zero for either series. This is to avoid a large empty space and compressing the points to fit into a relatively small portion of the chart space.

Computer software

The forecasting methods discussed here require the use of a personal computer or a mainframe computer. There are a number of software programs designed for the personal computer that embody the forecasting methods discussed in the following chapters. Statistical Package for the Social Sciences (SPSS) and Statistical Analyses System (SAS) are two of the most widely known, but there are a host of others being released or upgraded monthly. You should check with your computer software resource supplier for an up-to-date assessment of what is available.

However, be aware that current spreadsheet programs available for the personal computer, such as Microsoft® Excel or Lotus 1–2-3, have built-in statistical programs that suffice for many forecasting applications, such as correlation and linear regression analysis. Since these programs also include graphical display programs, you can enter your time series, chart the data and explore forecasting methods all on the same computer display screen.

Assessing data quality

Every forecasting model designed to simulate human behaviour will produce forecasting errors. Some of these are due to the difficulty of measuring phenomena accurately, both the activity we wish to forecast and factors that may affect that time series. Before we begin to apply various forecasting methods, we need to assess the quality of our time series. The following discussion applies both to the time series we wish to forecast and to time series we are considering for use in explaining the course of our forecast series in a causal model.

Missing data

We need complete time series over the period we wish to study, that is, there is a data point corresponding to each time unit. Most quantitative forecasting methods will not work on time series with missing data points. If the points are missing at the very beginning of the series, then we can simply deal with the shorter series. If data are missing within the time series, and we do not wish to discard earlier data, then we must replace the missing data with estimates.

One procedure is to search for other time series that are highly correlated with the one we are trying to complete. Then we regress the longest complete segment of our series on the correlated one to obtain a regression equation that can 'forecast' data points for the missing periods. Another popular method used to supply missing data is the linear time trend regression discussed in Chapter 7.

Correlation and regression are discussed more fully in Chapter 7. If the data are seasonal, then you need to use only the same months, quarters, etc. in the years in your regression model.

The simplest method is to interpolate the missing data point, that is, set the missing value equal to the mean of the data points on either side of it in time. If you are dealing with seasonal data, use the same months in adjoining years to interpolate.

Discontinuous series

The U.S. Department of Commerce maintains a time series of U.S. receipts from international travellers from 1964 to 1999. However, as indicated in Figure 2.7, a new estimating methodology was instituted in 1987, producing a new time series beginning with 1984.

It is clear that there are two different time series at work here: 1964 to 1987 and 1984 to 1999. Yet it is published as a single time series, with a marked jump in 1984. Using this series for forecasting will incorporate this jump as a change in traveller behaviour rather than a change in estimation methodology.

The careful forecaster has two choices. One is to deal only with the consistent time series of 1984 to the present. The other is to try to 'backcast'

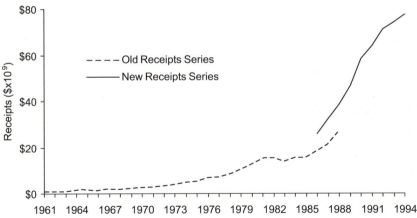

Figure 2.7 U.S. international travel and passenger fare receipts, old and new annual series, 1961–94
Source: U.S. Department of Commerce

40

from the new series back to earlier years. We should avoid, however, simply shifting the old series up by an amount to splice it in with the new. Such a splicing assumes that the old methodology captured traveller behaviour as well as the new one, an assumption we have no grounds to make.

Data anomalies

An 'anomaly' is a deviation from an established pattern. In time series, these extreme values are commonly called 'outliers'. They are extreme values that deviate unusually far from the pattern established by our time series. The values for January to April, 1991, in Figure 1.2 (Chapter 1) are outliers in the international airline traffic series, as are the February and March values in 1992.

You can identify such anomalies through your graphical data displays. They will also be evident when you produce forecasts of your time series and some values fall unusually far from your forecast line.

Most outliers can be explained. Catastrophic events such as unusually harsh weather, wars and terrorism can depress tourism demand for a short period. Special events such as the quadrennial Olympic Games can artificially boost visitor volume for two weeks to a month. You should look for such explanations before dealing with outliers.

If there is no explanation, and you suspect the anomalous value is due to measurement error, then you will want to correct the offending value. The technique suggested above for filling in missing data can be used here. However, if there is an explanation, most statistical experts argue against adjusting the outlier in any way. To do so is to eliminate information that is useful in understanding how extreme events affect your time series. Such information can be incorporated in your forecasting model.

Number of data points

Generally, the more observations we have in our time series, the more likely our forecasting method will capture the patterns of the activity we are trying to forecast.

Some forecasters suggest that you need five data points for each one you are trying to forecast. If you want to forecast two years ahead, you need ten years in your time series, according to this rule. If you want to forecast each of twelve months ahead, you need at least five complete years of monthly data to do so adequately. However, this should be viewed as a minimum. Some quantitative forecasting methods require significantly more data points to provide reliable estimates.

Data precision

Most tourism demand data can be stated in terms of thousands or millions of visitors, and millions or thousands of millions of visitor expenditure units. As a practical matter, dealing with data with six or more digits obscures interpretation. We are usually interested in what will happen in the next year or so, and the changes we are interested in are captured only in the first three or four digits. Moreover, the more digits we are attempting to maintain in a database, the more apt we are to make data entry errors.

On the other hand, if we represent forecast variable in only one or two digits, we limit the amount of variation that will show up in our time series. Quantitative forecasting methods examine such variation for patterns useful in predicting the future.

A useful middle course is to round off your series to four digits. This allows the variability in the series to express itself, keeps the maximum rounding error to five one-hundredths of 1 per cent, and does not strain our ability to catch data entry errors very much. This minimal loss of precision is not likely to affect the accuracy of your forecasts.

By the four-digit rule, you may round off the number, 1 234 567, to the nearest thousand and enter 1235. But you should avoid rounding off a number such as 678 910 to the nearest thousand, because this would produce the three-digit number, 679. (Instead, round it off to four digits as 678.9 thousand.) The reason for this is that the maximum rounding error for a three-digit number is nearly one-half of 1 per cent. If you are forecasting a series where the annual percentage changes are small, this rounding error could significantly distort your forecasts.

Reasonable data

Graphing your time series will indicate whether its course appears reasonable or not. Tourism demand has risen since the Second World War for most countries, and its time series should reflect this. On the other hand, if catastrophes have intervened, declines in the series should be evident.

Most tourism demand fluctuates substantially as seasons change. You should see these changes in monthly or quarterly data. The number of distinctive seasons will vary according to the location of the demand. Some tropical destinations have two seasons, while those in moderate northern and southern latitudes experience four.

If your time series do not appear to follow a reasonable path, you should enquire about measurement errors among those who collected, compiled or transcribed the data.

Sound data collection

Tourism demand data can be compiled from administrative reports. Most transportation data are based on such reports of actual counts of tickets sold, passengers carried, etc. Theme parks, museums and other attractions also produce administrative records useful to the tourism forecaster. Commercial lodging places in most countries are required to keep careful records of the number of guests and length of stay. The only questions here are, are the data transcribed properly, and are they complete?

Some tourism demand data are estimated through sample surveys. To be representative of the larger population to which they refer, such surveys must ensure that every member of the population has a known, non-zero chance of being included. For a thorough discussion of the elements of valid tourism surveys, see WTO (1995d).

The careful forecaster will inquire into how the data to be used was collected and processed, to understand what measurement anomalies may be present and how much of the variation through time is due to sampling error.

Finally, a technique sometimes used in tourism demand estimation is direct observation. By counting the number of passengers getting off an airline flight, you can develop a time series of the number of passengers carried on the flight. It is common to estimate tourism by personal motor vehicle by counting vehicles and ascribing some average number of passengers per vehicle.

If such observation is used to develop your time series, you should seek to clearly understand how measurement errors might have crept into it. Observer fatigue, limited observation under bad weather conditions, observer carelessness and other events may significantly affect the data reported yet not reflect the behaviour of the phenomenon you are trying to measure.

Summary

There is a substantial history of tourism demand forecast modelling. This suggests that successfully dealing with the special characteristics of tourism demand over time is not a trivial task. Questions of definitions and classifications and the appropriate measure of demand must be resolved first before tackling the art of model-building.

There are two main classes of business-forecasting models: quantitative and qualitative. Within these, there are a number of viable alternatives the forecaster can use. Fortunately, there are tested criteria for evaluating forecasting models and for testing their accuracy in three areas: error magnitude, directional change and trend change accuracy. Research has indicated that no single tourism demand forecasting method is superior in all of these three accuracy measures, although success in forecasting turning points is often accompanied by success in predicting directional changes (Witt and Witt, 1995: 471).

Indeed, we cannot safely maintain that quantitative forecasting techniques exceed qualitative ones in terms of accuracy and usefulness. Bernstein (1996: 6) notes the 'persistent tension' between those who assert the best decisions are based on quantification and numbers, and those who argue that subjective approaches are superior 'is a controversy that has never been resolved'. We do not resolve it here, but rather indicate the conditions, objectives and resources under which a quantitative approach is more likely to produce useful forecasts than qualitative ones, and vice versa. Chapter 3 provides advice on choosing between quantitative and qualitative forecasting methods.

Accuracy is the most popular single criterion for judging tourism demand forecasting models, and can be measured in several ways. The MAPE is the most versatile, self-evident, and simplest to determine of these.

Graphically displaying a time series of the past and future helps immeasurably to model it and evaluate a model's output. Such displays will make problems with past measures evident and suggest ways of dealing with them. Moreover, charts of time series prove quite useful in narrowing the field of potential forecasting methods to try.

For further information

Archer, B. (1994). Demand forecasting and estimation. In *Travel, Tourism, and Hospitality Research: A Handbook for Managers and Researchers* (J. R. Brent Ritchie and C. R. Goeldner, eds) 2nd edition, pp. 105–14, Wiley.

Calantone, R. J., di Benedetto, C. A. and Bojanic, D. (1987). A comprehensive review of the tourism forecasting literature. *Journal of Travel Research*, **26** (2), Fall, 28–39.

Levenbach, H. and Cleary, J. P. (1981). *The Beginning Forecaster: The Forecasting Process through Data Analysis*, chs 1 and 6. Lifetime Learning.

Makridakis, S., Wheelwright, S. C. and Hyndman, R. J. (1998), *Forecasting: Methods and Applications*. 3rd edition, ch. 1. Wiley.

Witt, S. F. and Witt, C. A. (1992). *Modeling and Forecasting Demand in Tourism*, chs 1, 6 and 8. Academic Press.

Witt, S. F. and Witt, C. A. (1995). Forecasting tourism demand: a review of empirical research. *International Journal of Forecasting*, **11** (3), September, 447–75.

3

The tourism forecasting process

Simply put, forecasting is a *process* designed to predict future events. In the realm of tourism demand, an event may be the number of visitors to a destination, the number of room-nights sold in a hotel or a group of hotels, the number of passengers flying between two points or the number of brochures requested by potential visitors. A valid forecast event has two character-istics: a specific time and a specific outcome. These outcomes are often precise volumes of demand. However, they may be stated as ranges or even qualitative conditions, such as visitor demand is forecast to be greater next year than this year.

This chapter presents a tourism demand fore-casting *programme* in its sequential steps, describes a strategy for determining in advance the methods most likely to provide successful forecasts and outlines evaluation procedures for the model chosen for implementation. It also presents the steps for conducting a forecasting *project*, that is a single set of forecasts at a point in time, rather than the continuing set of forecasts over time that the forecasting programme provides. Since historical data are critical to most forecasting methods, criteria for judging the quality of data available to the forecaster are also discussed.

The forecasting programme

Here the objective is to establish a system for periodically producing forecasts required by management, termed a tourism demand forecasting programme. Figure 3.1 presents the four major phases of developing this forecasting programme, focusing on building a system that will be used repeatedly over a year or more to produce forecasts.

```
1.  Design phase

2.  Specification phase

3.  Implementation phase

4.  Evaluation phase
```

Figure 3.1   The forecasting programme

The *design phase* guides the forecaster in choosing the appropriate forecasting method to employ. This phase examines the problem, the resources and the relationships that help determine a preliminary choice of method.

The *specification phase* includes determining the relationships that will comprise the appropriate forecasting model and selecting an appropriate model.

The *implementation phase* comprises employing the selected model to generate forecasts and preparing these forecasts for presentation to management.

The *evaluation phase* covers monitoring the forecasts over time to determine if adjustments should be made in the forecasting model, and making the appropriate adjustments to secure the most accurate series of forecasts.

The following sections detail the steps comprising each of these phases of the forecasting process.

The design phase

This initial stage of the forecasting process guides the forecaster in selecting the appropriate forecasting method to use. A forecasting method is an individual technique for projecting future events. This is distinct from a forecasting model, which is an individual application of a given method. For example, we might test a number of regression models to determine the most reliable, but we are only examining applications of one method: regression analysis.

The forecasting methods most useful in tourism forecasting are listed in this chapter, and described in detail in Chapters 4–9.

Figure 3.2 lists the steps in the design phase. Each of these is discussed below.

```
A.  Define the problem.

B.  Determine user needs.

C.  Determine variables to be forecast.

D.  Determine resources available.

E.  Hypothesize relationships.

F.  Determine data availability.

G.  List available forecasting methods.

H.  Apply preliminary selection criteria.

I.  Make a preliminary selection of method.
```

Figure 3.2   1 Design phase

The first step in the design phase is to *define the problem*. This will often be done by the forecaster's supervisor or a higher official. The problem should be stated as clearly as possible, avoiding jargon and mathematical language at this stage. And the problem should involve some future event, so that forecasting is the appropriate tool for suggesting solutions.

Figure 3.3 indicates some of the types of problems a tourism forecaster may be asked to resolve.

After defining the problem, the next step is to *determine user needs*. Precisely what information will the manager require to resolve the problem? Over what future period? By what time unit (day, week, month, year, etc.)? Broken out by what market segments or some other classification?

A. Feasibility of offering passenger service on a new airline route.

B. Expected hotel room sales for budgeting purposes.

C. Number of restaurant personnel needed during a weekend.

D. Appropriate goals for a theme park's marketing plan.

E. Potential demand from a new market segment.

F. Expected effects of a lodging tax increase on room-nights sold.

G. Anticipated government revenue from a lodging tax increase.

H. Economic, social/cultural, or environmental consequences of increased visitor volume.

I. Adequacy of tourism infrastructure capacity ten years from now.

Figure 3.3 Representative tourism forecasting problems

Once you have gathered these views, you can determine the variables to be forecast. You must translate user needs into one or more events that can be measured and predicted. If, for example, your hotel's director of sales needs to know by how much business will rise next year, you can translate this into the variables room-nights sold and room revenue.

The next step is to *determine the resources available* to you for your forecast. These resources include money for purchasing data and computer software, and time for completing and presenting the forecast.

Next, you need to *hypothesize relationships*. Staying with the hotel sales example, what are the major factors in the marketplace that have a strong influence on the hotel's room sales? Such factors might be competitors' room rates, your hotel's room rates, airline service into your area and the state of the economy in your generating markets. You should write down how each of these factors is expected to influence demand for your product. For example, if your competitors cut room rates, this would most likely have an adverse impact on your demand. Articles in professional journals and the advice of your colleagues can help you isolate these.

Economic theory can be helpful to you in listing expected relationships. The following economic principles suggest relationships you should consider in your forecasting. Each of these is *ceteris paribus*, that is, all other factors are held constant:

■ Raising the price of your product will tend to reduce your demand; lowering the price will increase demand.

■ If a competitor increases the price of a product similar to yours, this will tend to increase the demand for your product; the opposite occurs if a competitor reduces the price.

■ Increasing the quality of your product, that is, the value as perceived by the consumer, in the absence of a co-ordinate increase in price, will tend to increase the demand; reducing the quality without reducing the price will reduce demand.

■ If a tourism operator increases the price of a product that is usually consumed jointly with yours (called a 'complementary product'), this will tend to reduce the demand for your product (e.g. increasing petrol prices reduces demand for car rentals).

■ Reducing consumers' costs of obtaining information about your product will tend to increase demand for your product; this is a salutary effect of marketing programmes.

■ Reducing consumers' costs of reserving and purchasing your product will increase the demand; efforts to improve distribution are helpful here.

■ Rising business or personal income after taxes will tend to increase the demand for most tourism products; falling income after taxes will have the opposite effect.

■ An increase in the supply of a product similar to yours without a price increase will tend to reduce the demand for yours.

Sometimes, you do not need to include any explanatory variable other than time, and there is a collection of forecasting techniques (called 'time series methods') for applying this assumption to your past data. These are discussed in Chapters 4–6.

The next step is to *determine data availability.* In forecasting your hotel's room-nights sold next year, you have an in-house historical series of appropriate data. But you may need to include the size of the local market for hotel rooms, average room rates, major special events expected, airline fares, the economic situation in your major generating markets, among others. Chapter 7 discusses these explanatory variables more fully.

Next, you should *list available forecasting methods.* This book presents a number of these used in forecasting tourism demand. (See Figure 2.1 in Chapter 2 for the list.) Your own list would include those for which you have computer software or which you feel comfortable applying through computer spreadsheet analysis.

Next, from this list you should *apply preliminary selection criteria* in order to narrow the list of available methods down to a few key approaches likely to produce the most reliable forecasts. These are preliminary in the sense that their ability to forecast accurately within your historical data series while observing the principles, restrictions and assumptions of the method will ultimately determine which method you finally select for use.

One strategy to narrow the choices down to one of four major groups of methods is to follow the guide in Figure 3.4. In the discussion of extrapolation, or time series, methods, additional guidelines will be provided to make advance selection of the methods likely to provide the most reliable forecasts.

Objective data (criterion 1 in Figure 3.4) are numerical measures of the past activity you are trying to forecast produced by objective measurement techniques rather than someone's opinion or subjective judgement.

The *forecast horizon* (criterion 2) refers to the most distant time period you are trying to forecast. Extrapolative techniques have often proved less successful in providing accurate long-range forecasts than causal methods (that is, regression analysis and structural econometric models).

Large changes in the environment (criterion 3) denotes future forces likely to change relationships among the forecast variables and the factors that

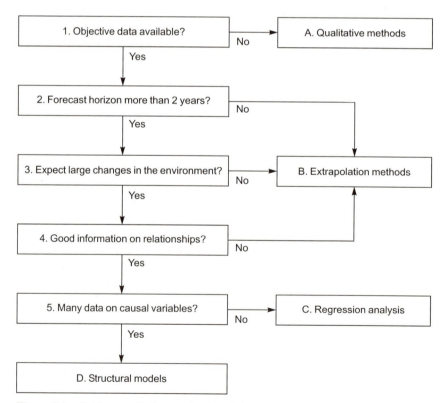

Figure 3.4   Guide to preliminary selection of the most appropriate forecasting method

influence them. These include major economic expansions and recessions, tax and regulatory policies, price inflation, availability of key commodities such as petroleum, and terrorist threats and attacks, among others.

Good information on relationships (criterion 4) refers to how much is known about which variables affect the variable you are trying to forecast, and how they do so. For example, prices and income are two variables that often explain changes in visitor flows from one country to another. Economic theory suggests that as prices (airfares, hotel rates, exchange rates, etc.) rise, the flow slackens or declines. And as income rises, the flow increases or accelerates. Our knowledge of this theory encourages us to use a forecasting method that embodies these relationships.

It is important to note here that part of this answer is whether we need to explain what is causing changes in the variable we are trying to forecast. In policy forecasting, for example, it is essential to understand the process that is producing changes in visitor demand. In this case, we cannot rely on extrapolation methods (method B), because they, by definition, do not include any causal factors.

Finally, *many data on causal variables* (criterion 5) refers to how long the time series are on the factors that influence your forecast variable. A rule of thumb often proposed for causal methods such as regression analysis and structural models is that you need at least five historical data points for every period ahead you plan to forecast. For example, if you plan to forecast tourism arrivals in your country from abroad for each of the next three years, you need at least fifteen years' of historical data on these arrivals.

You have now enough information to *make a preliminary selection of forecasting method*. The major decision is whether to choose a *qualitative* forecasting method (as discussed in Chapter 9) or a *quantitative* method, including extrapolation methods (method B in Figure 3.4), regression analysis (method C) and structural econometric models (method D). Once you have done this, you proceed to the second phase of the forecasting process.

The specification phase

The second stage in the forecasting process is the specification phase. The objective here is to determine the best forecasting *model* based upon historical data patterns and relationships. We begin by detailing the specification of a quantitative method, as outlined in Figure 3.5.

If you have chosen to use one of the causal quantitative methods (regression analysis or structural econometric models), the first step in the specification phase is to *specify relationships* between the variable you wish to forecast and the variables that you believe affect it. For example, economic theory and

A. Specify relationships if a causal method.

B. Collect, prepare and verify input data.

C. Select the starting model and programme it.

D. Estimate model parameters.

E. Verify their reasonableness.

F. Determine the model's accuracy in the past.

G. Test other models.

H. Compare their accuracies, abilities to predict turning points or trends, and choose the best model.

I. Document results to date.

Figure 3.5 2.1 Quantitative method specification phase

research suggests that the cost of airline tickets inversely affects the demand for airline travel. As ticket costs rise, air travel demand declines. This is a relationship you may want to investigate in this phase.

Sometimes the explanatory variables affecting your activity may affect one another. For example, for airlines and hotels, the amount of capacity available tends to inversely affect fares and rates. Fares and rates, in turn, affect the demand for your service. Consequently, you should investigate these complex relationships in selecting your best forecasting model.

The next step is to *collect, prepare and verify input data.* You may need to purchase one or more time series. If so, try to obtain them in an electronic medium that you can directly read into your computer. If you can obtain data only in paper copy form, someone must then enter it into a computer database. Make sure you verify that these data have been entered correctly.

Next, *select the starting model and programme it.* This model is the one that appears initially to provide the best forecasts. Programme it into your computer software by following the rules of your particular statistical program or spreadsheet.

Next, *estimate the model parameters. Parameters* in this use are factors that define the actual relationships in the equation or equations that comprise your forecasting model. A given set of parameters constitutes a specific forecasting model.

You must now *verify the reasonableness* of these parameters, that is, verify that the parameters in your forecasting equation are sensible or logical. If you find, for example, that your price variable is positively correlated with the demand you are trying to forecast, this is not reasonable. It suggests that as you increase room rates, your demand for rooms increases. Economic theory argues against this relationship, except in rare cases.

Or you might find that your price and income variables have relatively small parameters, indicating each of these has little impact on visitor demand. This does not appear reasonable given the preponderance of research indicating these are important variables in most tourism demand forecasting situations.

If you are using regression analysis, another aspect of this verification is checking the validity of your model. This is discussed more fully in Chapter 7.

If your model does not produce reasonable or valid parameters, then you must discard it and try another.

Once you are satisfied with the parameter values, you should *determine the model's accuracy in the past*. Here, you use the model to forecast values over the period for which you have actual values for the forecast variable, and compare the model's estimates with these actual values. This is called 'backcasting,' or making 'within-sample predictions'. Optimally, you want a forecasting model that accurately simulates the past. If it does not, then it is difficult to have much confidence in its ability to forecast the future.

There are several ways to assess a forecasting model's success in backcasting. Here, you employ the measures of accuracy discussed in Chapter 2, such as the MAPE or the RMSPE. Here, it is preferable to test out-of-sample forecasts (ex post forecast) accuracy as described in Chapter 2. You may also assess the model's success in predicting turning points or changes in trend.

Once you have tested your initial model, try a different model that appears reasonable, following the same steps. And when you have tested a set of models, you can *compare their accuracies and choose the best model* based on this comparison. This is rather straightforward. You want to use the model that most accurately forecasts the actual values you have in your historical series.

The final step in the specification phase is to *document the results to date*. Write down the details on all of the models you tested and why you chose the one that you did for actual forecasting use. This documentation will prevent you from wasting time testing models you have already reviewed, and answering questions from your managers about potential forecasting models.

Qualitative forecasting methods utilize experts to provide forecasts. Figure 3.6 outlines the specification phase of this set of forecasting methods.

The first step is to *specify the method to be implemented*. Four qualitative forecasting methods are described in Chapter 9. All of these require that a panel of experts be composed.

> A. Specify the method to be implemented.
>
> B. Detail how the experts will be selected.
>
> C. Indicate what phenomena will be covered.
>
> D. Document the plan.

Figure 3.6   2.2 Qualitative method specification phase

Next, *detail how the experts will be selected*. As explained in Chapter 9, these experts may be business colleagues, other professionals and managers, or consumers.

The third step is to *indicate what phenomena will be covered*. These topics must be turned into carefully worded questions that will elicit reasoned responses from the experts.

Finally, *document the plan* by writing down in detail the procedures to be followed. Review these carefully to avoid allowing researcher opinions to bias the results.

The implementation phase

Implementation is the third phase in the forecasting process, as outlined in Figure 3.7. Here, the forecast is actually produced, documented and presented.

The first step is to *obtain the forecast*. If using a quantitative method, you input the values into your model that are necessary for reaching your forecasting horizon. If using a qualitative method, you develop the forecast out of the responses received from your experts.

The next step is to *make subjective adjustments, if necessary* in the forecast. For example, the last several values of your historical series may all be lower than your forecast model results for these periods. To present your forecast values for the future without adjustment is to guarantee they will be

> A. Obtain required forecasts.
>
> B. Make subjective adjustments, if necessary.
>
> C. Document the model and its results.
>
> D. Present forecasts to management.

Figure 3.7   3 Implementation phase

inaccurate. Appendix 3 presents a technique for modifying your model's results to reflect recent history accurately.

The third step in the implementation phase is to *document the model and its results*. Here you write up how you carried out the design phase, specification phase and implementation phase of the forecasting process. This should include models that were tested and rejected and the reasons why, as well as any subjective adjustments made. Having complete documentation can prevent you from testing again models you have already examined and rejected.

Finally, the forecaster *presents the results to management*. Details on this step are discussed in Chapter 9.

The evaluation phase

The final stage in the forecasting process is the evaluation phase, as outlined in Figure 3.8.

The evaluation phase begins with the step to *monitor forecast accuracy*, that is track the relationship between actual values as the future unfolds, and forecast values. A popular method for tracking forecasts against actual values is presented in Chapter 10. If your model does not simulate future values relatively accurately as time unfolds, the next step is to *determine the causes for any deviations*. If your review of causes indicates that your forecast values are likely to over- or under-estimate future values of your variable, then you may choose to *revise the forecast*.

Or you may find evidence that the trend or causal relationships have changed and you then must *determine if your parameters have changed*. That is, whether the coefficients or equations no longer reflect what is actually happening as the future unfolds.

Finally, after considering all the evidence, you may decide *to generate a new forecast from the existing model or, alternatively, develop a new model*.

A. Monitor forecast accuracy.

B. Determine the causes for any deviations.

C. Revise the forecast, if warranted.

D. Determine if parameters have changed.

E. Generate a new forecast from the existing model or develop a new model.

Figure 3.8   4 Evaluation phase

·The forecasting project

Sometimes an organization does not invest in a formal demand forecasting programme but still has the need for forecasts from time to time. Or, alternatively, an academic or other researcher may undertake a forecasting project to test theories or provide more information about the shape of tourism futures. For example, Frechtling (2000) prepared long-term forecasts of outbound travel from twenty major tourism generating countries. These were intended to suggest the tendencies of these markets and to distinguish those with highest growth potential from those with the least at the turn of the twenty-first century. Other forecasting projects are summarized in the Applications section of each of the following chapters.

A forecasting *project* is essentially ad hoc, designed for a specific need, required in a relatively short period of time and unlikely to be repeated in the near future. This does not mean, however, that it should be improvised or impromptu. If a forecasting project is undertaken to reduce the risk of decision-making, then care and effort should be invested in it so that it meets this challenge.

Under this assumption, it would be wise for the forecaster to follow the first three phases of the forecasting programme in Figure 3.1. He or she might want to abridge some of these in the interests of timely results, but not ignore any completely. However, the evaluation phase (phase 4) is not appropriate because the models developed are not intended to be continually adjusted over time. Rather, if later you plan to undertake a forecasting project in the future similar to one in the past, you should begin by evaluating the results of the earlier programme in light of what actually occurred as part of the design phase of your project.

Finally, note that post-sample forecasting accuracy becomes even more important in the specification phase of a forecasting project (see Chapter 2). We should evaluate the relative accuracies of various models in forecasting the final three or more periods, depending on the number of observations we have. Since we will only take one shot at producing forecasts, we should adopt the model that best forecasts future values.

Summary

Like all serious attempts to discern futures, the tourism demand forecasting process should follow four sequential steps:

1 Design.
2 Specification.

3 Implementation.
4 Evaluation.

The design phase guides you in choosing the appropriate forecasting method to use. The diagram in Figure 3.4 can help you make a preliminary selection of the most fruitful forecasting method to follow. These methods are detailed in the chapters that follow.

The specification phase includes determining the relationships that will comprise the appropriate forecasting model and selecting an appropriate model. The implementation phase comprises employing the selected model to generate forecasts and preparing these forecasts for presentation to management. Finally, the evaluation phase covers monitoring the forecasts over time to determine if adjustments should be made, and making the appropriate adjustments to secure the most accurate forecasts.

Following these steps ensures that the forecaster systematically develops a valid strategy for solving his or her forecasting challenge. This helps ensure that you do not waste time and money in determining the shapes of the tourism futures you are interested in.

For further information

Armstrong, J. S. (1985). *Long-range Forecasting: From Crystal Ball to Computer*. 2nd edition, ch. 3. Wiley.

Levenbach, H. and Cleary, J. P. (1981). *The Beginning Forecaster: The Forecasting Process through Data Analysis*, pp. 1–40. Lifetime Learning.

Makridakis, S., Wheelwright, S. C. and McGee, V. (1983). *Forecasting: Methods and Applications*. 2nd edition, ch. 16. Wiley.

Moore, T. W. (1989). *Handbook of Business Forecasting*, chs 1 and 2. Harper & Row.

Saunders, J. A., Sharp, J. A. and Witt, S. F. (1987). *Practical Business Forecasting*, ch. 1. Gower.

4

Basic extrapolative models and decomposition

Extrapolative or time series forecasting methods use only past patterns in a data series to extrapolate the future from the past. These implicitly assume that the course of a variable, such as tourism demand, over time is the product of a substantial number of unknown forces that give the series a momentum. This momentum can be captured in a model reflecting one of several time series methods.

A *time series forecasting model* relates the values of a time series to previous values of that time series, its errors, or other related time series (Makridakis, Wheelwright and Hyndman, 1998: 616).

The advantage of time series methods is that they are, for the most part, relatively simple to apply, requiring no more than a data series and a computer spreadsheet program. The exception is the Box–Jenkins approach, which requires a computer program specifically designed to prepare the analyses.

In this chapter, we examine the following basic time series methods:

■ naive
■ single moving average.

In addition, we will explore an approach to dealing with time series with recurring seasonal patterns.

In Chapter 5, the following time series forecasting methods are discussed:

■ single exponential smoothing
■ double exponential smoothing
■ autoregression.

Chapter 6 presents the Box–Jenkins approach, the most sophisticated process for developing a quality forecasting model using time series methods.

Since forecasts derived from such methods depend so heavily on past patterns in the data, a premium is placed on examining the shape of the historical data series to be forecast. Graphical presentation is indispensable to this process. Through portraying the course of the time series over the past, we can tentatively determine the best extrapolative method to apply (the design phase). Then we test different models and determine the best one for forecasting our future (the specification phase).

Patterns in time series

There are five data patterns to look for in building time series forecasting models. Identifying the type of time series we have helps us make an initial choice as to best extrapolative method to use in the design phase of our forecasting process:

■ seasonality
■ stationary
■ linear trend
■ non-linear trend
■ stepped series.

Each of these patterns will be discussed in turn. Figures 4.1–4.6 display each of these patterns in tourism data.

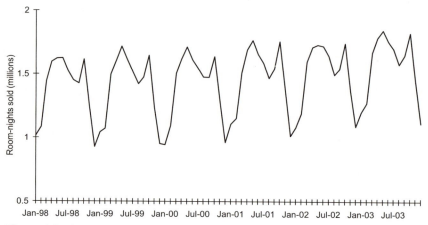

Figure 4.1 Seasonal series of hotel/motel room demand in the Washington, D.C., metropolitan area, monthly, 1994–99
Source: Smith Travel Research

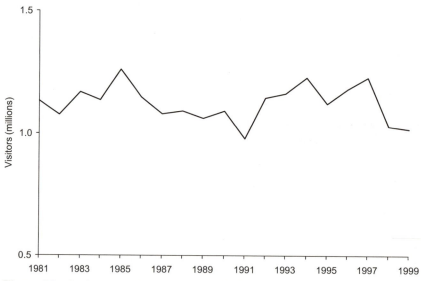

Figure 4.2 Stationary series of visitors to the White House, Washington, D.C., annually, 1981–99
Source: U.S. National Park Service

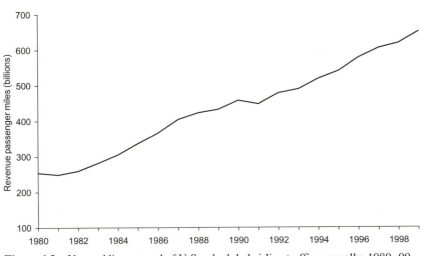

Figure 4.3 Upward linear trend of U.S. scheduled airline traffic, annually, 1980–99
Source: Air Transport Association of America

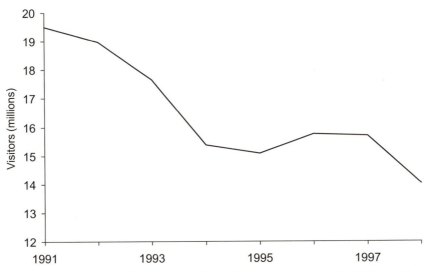

Figure 4.4 Downward linear trend of Canadian resident visits to the U.S.A. and
Mexico, annually, 1991–98
Source: Statistics Canada

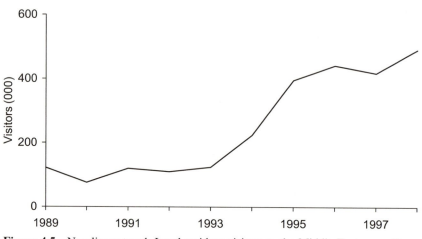

Figure 4.5 Non-linear trend: Israel resident visitors to the Middle East, annually, 1989–98
Source: World Tourism Organization

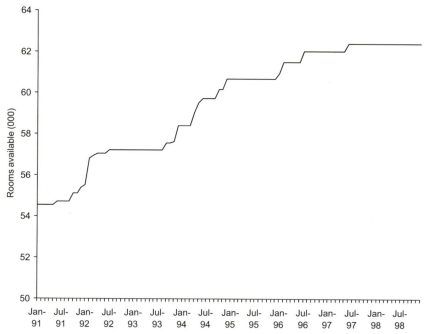

Figure 4.6 Stepped series of hotel/motel room supply in New York city, monthly, 1987–94
Source: Smith Travel Research

Seasonal patterns

The first data pattern we look for in a historical series of our data is the seasonal pattern or 'seasonality'.

> **Seasonality** refers to movements in a time series during a particular time of year that recur similarly each year (Moore, 1989: 49).

The seasonal pattern is due to climate and weather, social customs and holidays, business customs, and the calendar. Those that relate specifically to tourism demand are shown in Table 4.1.

Calendar effects are significant in assessing tourism's seasonality. The fact that February usually only has twenty-eight days makes it the low month in most tourism demand series.

These seasonal patterns occur regularly and often obscure the underlying trends we are trying to forecast. Consequently, it is wise to remove seasonality from a weekly, monthly, quarterly or any other sub-annual series. This produces a 'seasonally adjusted' series that is better suited for forecasting. However, once you are satisfied with a forecast of your seasonally adjusted series, then you add seasonality back into the series, since most managers are interested in what values will actually occur in a future month or quarter.

There are also certain events that do not occur regularly every year, but recur regularly over a period of years. Such periodic events that produce

Table 4.1 Causes of seasonality in tourism demand

Cause of seasonality	Tourism examples
Climate/weather	Summer vacations, snow-skiing, fall foliage tours, popularity of tropical destinations in the winter, cruise line departures, ocean resort demand
Social customs/holidays	Christmas/new year holidays, school breaks, travel to visit friends and relatives, fairs and festivals, religious observances, pilgrimages
Business customs	Conventions and trade shows, government assemblies, political campaign tours, sports events
Calendar effects	Number of days in the month; number of weekends in the month, quarter, season or year

regular increases in tourism demand for certain destinations include the U.S. presidential inauguration in Washington, D.C. (January of each year after a year evenly divisible by four, for example, 1985, 1989, 1993 and 1997), and the Passion Play at Oberammergau, Germany (years ending in zero).

The fact that February has twenty-nine days every fourth year will add a small increase to that month's tourism figures. (This increase should average about $1 \div 28 = 3.6$ per cent.) Moreover, much leisure travel is centred on weekends and these are not distributed equally among the months or among years. The normal pattern is for a month to have four complete weekends and two or three months in a year will have five weekends. However, the following years have four months with five weekends, an unusual event: 1995, 2003, 2005 and 2011. The year 2000 is nearly unique in that it includes *five* months with five complete weekends, for a total of fifty-three complete weekends. The last time this happened was 1972, and it will not happen again until 2028.

The regularity of the impact of such super-annual recurrent events on tourism demand should be taken into account in tourism forecasting. Methods for dealing with such regular 'supra-annual' events are discussed in Appendix 2.

Figure 4.1 shows the monthly demand for hotel/motel rooms in terms of room-nights sold in the Washington, D.C., metropolitan area over four recent years. It is clear that there are seasonal patterns in the data: May and October usually vie for peak month, while December, January and February compete for the trough. The series rises from this low each year throughout the spring to its May peak, and then falls gradually during the summer to a trough in September. Hotel/motel demand rises sharply in October (a big month for meetings and conventions) and then declines steadily to December.

If it exists, seasonality is easily recognizable from a graph of sub-annual data. Another, more quantitative, way of identifying seasonality is to examine the autocorrelation function for a period up to one-year's worth of sub-annual periods (for example, twelve periods for monthly data). This technique is covered in Chapter 6 in the discussion of the Box–Jenkins approach.

We will discuss traditional techniques for dealing with this seasonality later in this chapter.

Other data patterns

Stationarity means a time series fluctuates rather evenly around a horizontal level. In statisticians' parlance, it is *stationary* in its mean, that is, the mean of the series is constant over time. Figure 4.2 presents such a tourism demand series. This is the easiest data pattern to deal with in forecasting.

Linear trend is illustrated in Figures 4.3 and 4.4. These show time series rising or falling at a rather steady rate each period. Many tourism demand series follow a rising linear trend.

Non-linear trend has a rate of increase that varies in a regular way over the time series. Figure 4.5 shows a series that appears to follow an S-shape, a familiar pattern in forecasting and represented by the logistic curve or Gompertz's equation. This pattern shows rapid growth at the beginning of the series, levels off to a saturation point, and then declines.

Stepped series are unusual in tourism demand. A stepped series occurs when there is a saturation point, such as a capacity constraint, that is periodically adjusted. For example, the number of cruise visitors allowed to disembark in Bermuda would be a constraint on such tourism. Whenever the government changes this limit, the series would rise (or fall) to another plateau, assuming the island remains as popular with cruise lines as it does currently. Figure 4.6 displays the rooms available in the New York city metropolitan area and reflects new lodging properties opening for business and hotel construction pauses 1989–94. This, of course, is not a tourism demand series; rather, it represents tourism supply. If demand for New York city hotel/motel rooms was at capacity over a period of years, then a stepped demand series would result.

These four basic data patterns suggest the appropriate time series forecasting methods to employ on a seasonally adjusted series.

Time series forecasting methods

In the balance of this chapter and in the next two chapters, we examine seven different extrapolation methods for forecasting time series, in order of their complexity, beginning with the simplest.

The naive forecasting method

The naive forecasting method simply states that the value for the period to be forecast is equal to the actual value of the last period available. More formally,

$$\text{Naive 1 model:} \quad F_t = A_{t-1} \tag{4.1}$$

where   F = forecast value
         A = actual value
         t = some time period.

Equation 4.1 is also called the 'random walk model,' because it embodies the idea that a series is random, that is, exhibits no discernible trend or other pattern. More precisely, the *change* in a series value from the present one to the next, future, one is random. So the last value is the best forecast of the next value. Values before the last one in the time series are of no use in forecasting the next, future, one (Landsburg, 1993: 189–90).

This is the simplest forecasting model. As such, it is frequently used as a benchmark to compare other forecast models against. It is not unusual for more elaborate models to produce higher MAPEs than the naive model, and are thus not worth the time and money to operate. Witt and Witt (1992a: 99–123) present a number of these situations among international tourism demand series and conclude that more complex forecasting models are less accurate than the naive model for many series.

There are two other versions of the naive concept that are sometimes used as a benchmark forecast. We can define the 'Naive 2' forecast value as the current value multiplied by the growth rate between the current value and the previous value. This might be a useful benchmark for a series that trends upward or downward.

$$\text{Naive 2 model:} \quad F_t = A_{t-1} * \frac{A_{t-1}}{A_{t-2}} \tag{4.2}$$

where F = forecast value
       A = actual value
       t = some time period.

The 'seasonal naive' can be used with seasonal data and postulates that the next period's value is equal to the value of the same period in the previous year. So, for example, the seasonal naive value for July 1999 is equal to the actual value for July 1998.

$$\text{Seasonal naive model:} \quad F_t = A_{t-m} \tag{4.3}$$

where F = forecast value
       A = actual value
       t = some time period
       m = number of periods in a year (for example, four quarters, twelve months).

Single moving average

Sometimes the last value does not seem 'typical' of our time series. We might obtain a better forecast for the next period by averaging the last several values.

This is the single moving average (SMA) method of extrapolation and is second in simplicity only to the naive method.

We can average any number of periods to produce a forecast through the SMA model. The general equation for the single moving average is:

$$F_t = \frac{A_{t+1} - A_{t+2} - A_{t-n}}{n} \qquad (4.4)$$

where   F = forecast value
         A = actual value
         t = some time period
         n = number of past periods.

The SMA method allows some past values to determine forecast values, and all have the same influence on the forecast value. For example, we might use the average of the previous three values to serve as our forecast for the next period. Or we might use the previous four values or six values or any number than can be accommodated by our time series.

Figure 4.7 shows single moving averages for three, six and twelve periods on the seasonal series of hotel/motel room demand in the Washington, D.C., metropolitan area. It is clear that the more past values included in the single moving average, the smoother it becomes. This is because the more values (the higher n is), the less influence any one value has on the average; rather, the values tend to offset each other to provide a smooth forecast series.

If a time series shows wide variations around a trend, then the longer the single moving average the better it will pick up the trend. In Figure 4.7, for example, the twelve-month SMA clearly shows the series trend, while the shorter SMAs do not. However, long SMAs are slow to pick up recent changes in trend because so many past values are affecting it. The SMA method is more accurate in forecasting a series with very little variation around its trend than one with significant seasonality or volatility.

Table 4.2 compares the accuracy of the three naive models and three simple moving average models for forecasting hotel/motel room demand in Washington, D.C. We assess the relative accuracy of these forecasting models by comparing how low each model's mean absolute percentage error (MAPE) is.

It is clear the SMA models are not good forecasting models. Neither are the Naive 1 and Naive 2 models. The seasonal naive model, however, produces relatively accurate forecasts, but still misses the actual value by about 4 per cent on the average. Any other model we develop should be compared to the seasonal naive model, to see if it can improve on that model's accuracy.

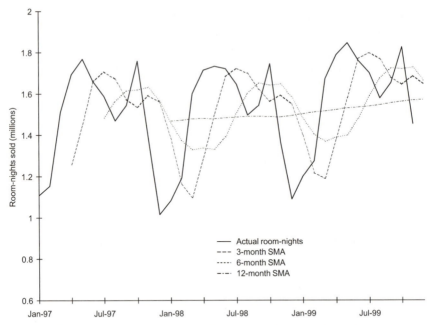

Figure 4.7 Single moving averages of Washington, D.C., hotel/motel room demand, monthly, 1997–99 *Source*: Smith Travel Research and author

Table 4.2 Comparison of accuracies of naive and simple moving averages in forecasting Washington, D.C., hotel/motel room demand, monthly, 1996–9

Method/model	MAPE
Naive	
Naive 1	12%
Naive 2	14%
Seasonal naive	4.2%
Simple moving average	
3-month	16%
6-month	18%
12-month	15%

Accounting for seasonal patterns

The room demand series in Figure 4.1 contains a pattern that appears to repeat itself every year: *seasonality*. Many forecasting methods have difficulty simulating this regularity. One approach is to only use models that do recognize seasonal patterns to forecast our time series. This approach is discussed in Chapter 5 with regard to double moving average models, and in Chapter 6 as a function of the Box–Jenkins approach.

Another approach for dealing with seasonality is for the forecaster to build a forecasting model to simulate it and use this to remove seasonality from the data series we wish to forecast. By this process, we quantify a relatively stable recurring pattern in the time series, remove it and then focus on forecasting the more complex seasonally adjusted series. An added advantage of explicitly describing the seasonal pattern is that we can study it over time to see if it is shifting, either on its own or in response to specific marketing initiatives. For example, airlines and seasonal resorts often introduce marketing programmes to build up low periods of demand. By quantifying the seasonal pattern in our demand series, we can see if they are working. Or we can monitor the impact of the introduction of year-round schooling or the decline in households with children to see if this is shifting the seasonal demand for our product.

One straightforward method of systematically dealing with seasonality and forecasting is the *classical decomposition* approach. This uses a single moving average to remove seasonality from a series we wish to forecast and then considers a number of methods for forecasting the remaining series. There are other ways to deal with seasonality, which will be discussed in the context of specific forecasting methods.

Decomposition

The classical decomposition approach attempts to decompose a time series into four constituent parts: trend, cycle, seasonal and an irregular component. These are defined, as follows:

> The **trend component** is the long-term movement of the time series and can often be approximated by a linear model.

> The **cyclical component** is a wave-like movement around the long-term trend that varies in amplitude and duration, but normally lasts for several years or more from a peak to the following peak and shows more variation than the seasonal component.

> The **seasonal component** represents a pattern in a time series that is repeated over fixed intervals of time up to a year in length.

> The **irregular component** is the error term and is usually assumed to be random with a constant variance.

Figure 4.8 charts an artificial time series of the number of monthly visitors to 'Pleasantville', an imaginary destination. The series appears to follow a weak upward trend until April 1998, and then a stronger trend thereafter. Seasonality is not evident, nor is a cyclical pattern clear.

However, Figure 4.8 is actually the product of the trend, cycle, seasonal and irregular components shown in Figures 4.9–4.12. Classical decomposition

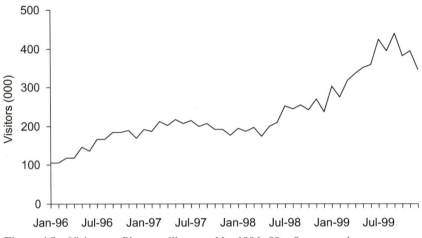

Figure 4.8   Visitors to Pleasantville, monthly, 1996–99   *Source*: author

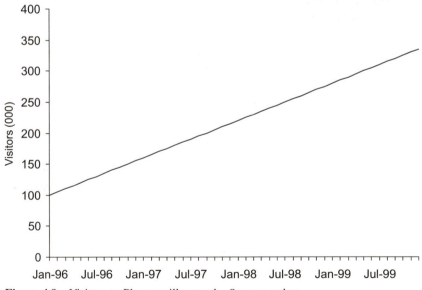

Figure 4.9   Visitors to Pleasantville: trend   *Source*: author

decomposes a time series such as monthly visitor volumes in Pleasantville (Figure 4.8) in its component parts (shown in Figures 4.9–4.12).

While there are several possible ways to apply decomposition, the method presented here has been widely used and is called the 'ratio-to-moving

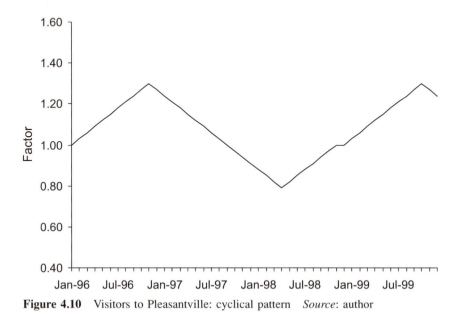

Figure 4.10   Visitors to Pleasantville: cyclical pattern   *Source*: author

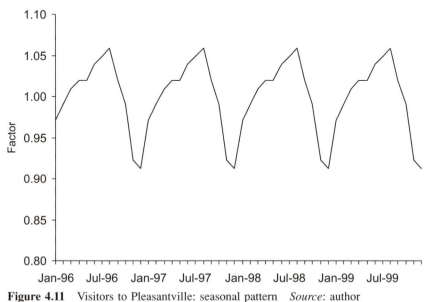

Figure 4.11   Visitors to Pleasantville: seasonal pattern   *Source*: author

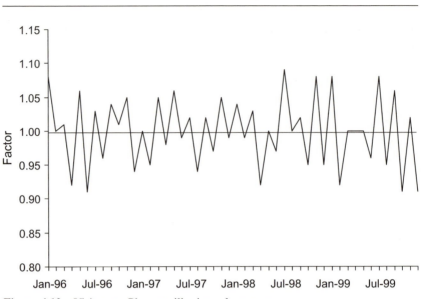

Figure 4.12　Visitors to Pleasantville: irregular pattern

averages classical decomposition method'. It assumes a multiplicative relationship among the components as follows:

$$A_t = T_t * C_t * S_t * I_t \tag{4.5}$$

where　A = actual value in the time series
　　　　T = the trend component
　　　　C = the cyclical component
　　　　S = the seasonal component
　　　　I = the irregular component
　　　　t = some time period less than one year (usually a month or a quarter).

The challenge of decomposition is to distinguish these components, develop forecasts for each and then recombine them to produce forecasts of the actual values useful to managers.

The first step in this decomposition method is to isolate the seasonal and irregular factors through the ratio-to-moving-averages method. We begin by developing a moving average series as long as the number of data points our time series has in a year. For example, if we are examining a monthly series, then we would compute a twelve-month moving average. If we are dealing with quarterly data, than we would produce a four-quarter moving average.

Such moving averages represent the trend-cycle ($T_t \times C_t$) components of Equation 4.5 because they contain no seasonal effects by definition, and little or no randomness since the irregular component period tends to cancel itself out when averaged over a number of periods. We will employ monthly data in this exercise, so a twelve-month moving average represents the trend-cycle components of the time series.

The following example demonstrates the steps in this decomposition method.

Figure 4.13 shows monthly hotel/motel room-nights sold in the Washington, D.C., metropolitan area for the years 1996 through 1999.[1] It is clear that there is a seasonal pattern in these data. This is highlighted in Figure 4.14, which simply stacks the monthly data by years.

The seasonal patterns are rather consistent over these years. An exception appears in January 1997, which shows higher room demand relative to the subsequent February than in earlier years. This is due to the presidential inauguration that year which boosted hotel occupancies towards their limit for a week to ten days that January. It is wise to deal with such a periodic 'supra-annual' event before quantifying the seasonality of a time series. Procedures for doing so are discussed in Appendix 2.

To quantify the seasonal pattern, we set up a spreadsheet as in Table 4.3, with the periods identified in the first column and the data points in the second. Next, compute the twelve-month moving average: this begins in

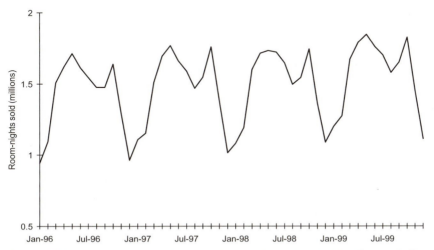

Figure 4.13 Seasonal series of hotel/motel room demand in the Washington, D.C., metropolitan area, monthly, 1996–99
Source: Smith Travel Research

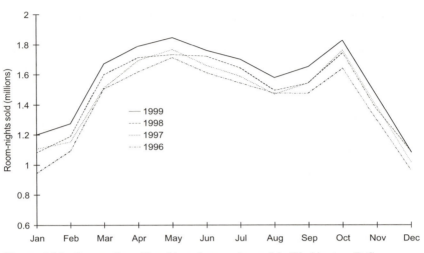

Figure 4.14 Seasonality of hotel/motel room demand in Washington, D.C., monthly, 1996–99
Source: Smith Travel Research

December 1996, at the end of the first twelve-month period. For example, the average of the first twelve months is 1407, which is placed in the 'Dec-96' cell in the third column.

This moving average ends at the data point shown in the third column. We need to transform this moving average so that each monthly value is at its centre. That is, for example, the twelve-month moving average for January 1997 has that month as its centre. Unfortunately, the centre of twelve values is halfway between the sixth and the seventh values. This is halfway between June and July for the first twelve-month moving average.

Fortunately, there is a simple way of centring the moving average on an actual month. The centre of the first twelve months of data (January–December 1996) is half way between June and July 1996. The centre of the next twelve-month moving average (February 1996–January, 1997) is half way between July and August 1996. The average of these two values would be centred on July 1996.

Consequently, the first value in the fourth column of Table 4.3 is the average of the first two values in the third column. This two-month moving average is repeated for each of the data points available. The result is a centred twelve-month moving average for July 1996–June 1999.

Returning to Equation 4.5, we can see what we have accomplished. When we divide each actual data point by the centred twelve-month moving average, we isolate the seasonal and irregular components, as follows:

Table 4.3   Hotel/motel room demand in Washington, D.C., and seasonal ratios, 1996-9

1. Month-year	2. Room-nights sold (000)	3. 12-month moving average	4. Centred 12-month moving average (T × C)	5. Seasonal ratios (S × I)
Jan-96	944			
Feb-96	1095			
Mar-96	1506			
Apr-96	1618			
May-96	1713			
Jun-96	1613			
Jul-96	1545		1414	1.093
Aug-96	1476		1423	1.038
Sep-96	1475		1426	1.035
Oct-96	1640		1429	1.147
Nov-96	1293		1434	0.902
Dec-96	963	1407	1439	0.670
Jan-97	1108	1420	1442	0.768
Feb-97	1154	1425	1444	0.799
Mar-97	1511	1426	1447	1.045
Apr-97	1694	1432	1454	1.165
May-97	1767	1437	1463	1.208
Jun-97	1661	1441	1469	1.131
Jul-97	1589	1444	1470	1.081
Aug-97	1469	1444	1470	0.999
Sep-97	1545	1449	1476	1.047
Oct-97	1759	1459	1480	1.188
Nov-97	1381	1467	1480	0.933
Dec-97	1015	1471	1481	0.686
Jan-98	1082	1469	1486	0.728
Feb-98	1192	1472	1489	0.800
Mar-98	1600	1479	1490	1.074
Apr-98	1714	1481	1489	1.151
May-98	1733	1478	1488	1.165
Jun-98	1722	1483	1490	1.155
Jul-98	1645	1488	1498	1.098
Aug-98	1495	1490	1507	0.992
Sep-98	1543	1490	1513	1.020
Oct-98	1744	1489	1519	1.148
Nov-98	1363	1487	1527	0.892
Dec-98	1089	1493	1533	0.710
Jan-99	1200	1503	1537	0.781
Feb-99	1273	1510	1543	0.825
Mar-99	1672	1516	1551	1.078
Apr-99	1789	1522	1559	1.147
May-99	1846	1532	1566	1.179
Jun-99	1760	1535	1571	1.120
Jul-99	1700	1540		
Aug-99	1578	1547		
Sep-99	1652	1556		
Oct-99	1826	1562		
Nov-99	1453	1570		

$$\frac{A_t}{T_t * C_t} = S_t * I_t \qquad\qquad (4.6)$$

where A = actual value in the time series
  T = the trend component of the series
  C = the cyclical component
  S = the seasonal component
  I = the irregular component
  t = some time period less than one year.

That is, by dividing each value by the twelve-month centred moving average, we isolate the seasonal-irregular ($S_t \times I_t$) component. This is the series in the last column of Table 4.3 entitled '5. Seasonal ratios (S × I)'.

These seasonal ratios are arrayed in part B of Table 4.4 by month. Their average for each month is shown in the sixth column entitled, 'Raw seasonal factors'. These ratios represent the seasonality pattern of the monthly data. For example, hotel/motel room-nights sold in January is, on the average, only 75.9 per cent of the average monthly room sold for a year. February is over 80 per cent. August is the month that comes closest to representing average monthly room demand at only 1 per cent above the monthly average for a full year. December is the lowest month for room demand (68.9 per cent of the average) while May is the highest month (18.4 per cent above the average).

These seasonal ratios are 'raw' in the sense that they do necessarily sum to an even twelve. They must or they will add an upward boost or downward drag to the forecast series. We force them to sum to twelve by dividing their raw sum into twelve and multiplying the resulting 'adjustment factor' by each of the raw seasonal factors. This produces the final column of '7. Adjusted seasonal factors'. In this case, the adjustment made a small increase in the June raw factors.

By averaging the seasonal ratios in part A of Table 4.4, we not only isolate the seasonal pattern, we dispose of the irregular component as well. Since this component is assumed to be random, its mean is zero. In averaging the seasonal ratios, we assume the irregular pattern approximates this mean.

The next step is to produce a seasonally adjusted series. Part A of Table 4.4 recounts the actual room-nights sold from Table 4.3, arrayed by month for ease of explanation. By dividing each of these monthly values by the appropriate adjusted seasonal factors in column 7 of part B, we obtain a series stripped of its seasonal component shown in part C as described in Equation (4.6).

Consequently, each of the values in part C can be interpreted as embodying the trend-cycle component of the series. This series is shown in Figure 4.15 compared with the actual series with seasonality included. The seasonally

Table 4.4   Producing a seasonally adjusted series of hotel/motel room demand in Washington, D.C.

A. Hotel/motel room-nights sold in Washington, D.C. (000)

	1996	1997	1998	1999
Jan	944	1108	1082	1200
Feb	1095	1154	1192	1273
Mar	1506	1511	1600	1672
Apr	1618	1694	1714	1789
May	1713	1767	1733	1846
Jun	1613	1661	1722	1760
Jul	1545	1589	1645	1700
Aug	1476	1469	1495	1578
Sep	1475	1545	1543	1652
Oct	1640	1759	1744	1826
Nov	1293	1381	1363	1453
Dec	963	1015	1089	1113

B. Seasonal ratios and seasonal factors

	Seasonal ratios				6. Raw seasonal factors	7. Adjusted seasonal factors
	1996	1997	1998	1999		
Jan		0.768	0.728	0.781	0.759	0.759
Feb		0.799	0.800	0.825	0.808	0.808
Mar		1.045	1.074	1.078	1.066	1.066
Apr		1.165	1.151	1.147	1.154	1.154
May		1.208	1.165	1.179	1.184	1.184
Jun		1.131	1.155	1.120	1.135	1.136
Jul	1.093	1.081	1.098		1.091	1.091
Aug	1.038	0.999	0.992		1.010	1.010
Sep	1.035	1.047	1.020		1.034	1.034
Oct	1.147	1.188	1.148		1.161	1.161
Nov	0.902	0.933	0.892		0.909	0.909
Dec	0.670	0.686	0.710		0.689	0.689
				Total	11.999	12.000
			Adjustment factor		1.0001	

C. Seasonally adjusted hotel/motel room-nights sold in Washington, D.C. (000)

	1996	1997	1998	1999
Jan	1243	1459	1425	1581
Feb	1354	1427	1475	1575
Mar	1413	1418	1502	1569
Apr	1402	1468	1485	1550
May	1447	1493	1464	1559
Jun	1420	1463	1516	1550
Jul	1417	1457	1508	1559
Aug	1462	1455	1481	1563
Sep	1427	1495	1492	1598
Oct	1412	1515	1502	1572
Nov	1422	1519	1499	1599
Dec	1399	1474	1582	1616

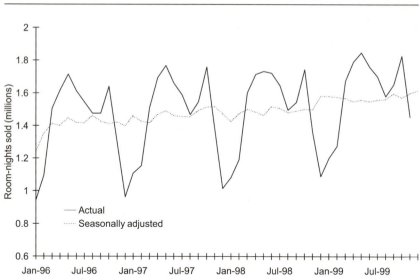

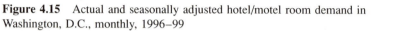

Figure 4.15 Actual and seasonally adjusted hotel/motel room demand in Washington, D.C., monthly, 1996–99

adjusted series of room-nights sold shows no seasonal pattern. It appears to indicate a weak upward trend, which is confirmed by examining the positions of the monthly room-night curves in Figure 4.14. Each successive year sits a little bit higher than the previous one, with the exception of 1998, which shows weak demand in May and duplicates 1997 for the September–November period.

This information is useful for the next step: developing a forecasting model for the trend-cycle series. We could attempt to distinguish the trend from the cyclical components of this series, but this would do us little practical good. While it is relatively simple to develop a good forecasting model for a time series trend, cyclical patterns are very difficult to forecast well due to their varying amplitude and duration. (For a discussion of this problem, see Makridakis, 1990: 71–2.)

Consequently, the next step is to forecast the trend-cycle series. There are a number of time series methods discussed in this chapter and the next, all of which may be used to forecast the seasonally adjusted (that is, trend-cycle) series. In addition, regression methods may be used, as well (Chapter 7). For the present, we will use the SMA method as an example of applying the decomposition process. In practice, you would experiment with more complex forecasting methods to find the one that best tracks your time series.

Table 4.5 contains several SMA forecasts of the historical time series of hotel/motel room-nights sold in the Washington, D.C., area, along with forecasts for January 2000, the first future period. Note that a simple moving average forecast appears the next period after the time span of the SMA. For

Table 4.5   Hotel/motel room demand in Washington, D.C., seasonally adjusted (SA) actual and forecast series, monthly, 1996–9

1. Month-year	2. Actual SA series	Simple moving average forecasts			
		3-month	4-month	6-month	12-month
Jan-96	1243				
Feb-96	1354				
Mar-96	1413				
Apr-96	1402	1337			
May-96	1447	1390	1353		
Jun-96	1420	1421	1404		
Jul-96	1417	1423	1421	1380	
Aug-96	1462	1428	1421	1409	
Sep-96	1427	1433	1437	1427	
Oct-96	1412	1435	1431	1429	
Nov-96	1422	1434	1429	1431	
Dec-96	1399	1420	1431	1427	
Jan-97	1459	1411	1415	1423	1402
Feb-97	1427	1427	1423	1430	1420
Mar-97	1418	1429	1427	1424	1426
Apr-97	1468	1435	1426	1423	1426
May-97	1493	1438	1443	1432	1432
Jun-97	1463	1459	1451	1444	1435
Jul-97	1457	1474	1460	1455	1439
Aug-97	1455	1471	1470	1454	1442
Sep-97	1495	1458	1567	1471	1447
Oct-97	1515	1469	1467	1471	1447
Nov-97	1519	1488	1480	1479	1456
Dec-97	1474	1509	1496	1484	1464
Jan-98	1425	1503	1501	1486	1470
Feb-98	1475	1473	1483	1480	1467
Mar-98	1502	1458	1473	1484	1471
Apr-98	1485	1467	1469	1485	1478
May-98	1464	1487	1472	1480	1480
Jun-98	1516	1483	1481	1471	1477
Jul-98	1508	1488	1492	1478	1482
Aug-98	1481	1496	1493	1491	1486
Sep-98	1492	1502	1492	1493	1488
Oct-98	1502	1494	1499	1491	1488
Nov-98	1499	1492	1496	1494	1487
Dec-98	1582	1498	1493	1500	1485
Jan-99	1581	1528	1519	1511	1494
Feb-99	1575	1554	1541	1523	1507
Mar-99	1569	1580	1559	1539	1516
Apr-99	1550	1575	1577	1551	1521
May-99	1559	1565	1569	1559	1527
Jun-99	1550	1559	1563	1569	1535
Jul-99	1559	1553	1557	1564	1537
Aug-99	1563	1556	1554	1560	1542
Sep-99	1598	1557	1558	1558	1548
Oct-99	1572	1573	1567	1563	1557
Nov-99	1599	1578	1573	1567	1563
Dec-99	1616	1590	1583	1573	1571
Jan-00	1596	1596	1585	1574	
	MAPE	1.67%	1.67%	1.63%	2.19%

example, the three-month SMA forecast for 'Apr-96' is the three-month average for January–March, 1996, not February–April, although this exists. Using the SMA as a forecast requires us to compute it for the latest months we have and then appoint it the forecast for the first future month.

Table 4.5 also includes the MAPEs for each of these series. They do not differ very much, and are moderate compared to the compound monthly percentage change (2.43 per cent over this period). However, they are all better than our best naive model, which was seasonal naive with an MAPE of 4.2 per cent (from Table 4.2).

Figure 4.16 charts these forecast series, along with the original seasonally adjusted series of room demand. None of the series captures directional change well, and turning points are not captured at all.

We will test other models on this series in the next chapter, to see if we can obtain more accurate forecasts. However, to continue our decomposition example, we need to choose a 'best' SMA model and return seasonality to the forecasts of this model. The six-month SMA model shows the smallest MAPE in Table 4.5, so this is chosen.

Table 4.6 shows how seasonality is returned to our forecast of the seasonally adjusted series of hotel/motel room demand in Washington, D.C. The '2. Seasonal factors' column contains the adjusted seasonal factors displayed in column 7, in part B of Table 4.4. They are repeated every twelve

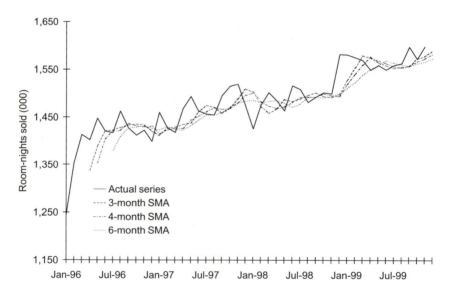

Figure 4.16 Seasonally adjusted hotel/motel room demand in Washington, D.C., and simple moving average forecasts, monthly, 1996–99
Source: Smith Travel Research and author

Table 4.6 Computation of SMA seasonal forecast series and actual series of hotel/motel room demand in Washington, D.C., monthly, 1996–9

1. Month-year	2. Seasonal factors	3. 6-month SMA	4. Seasonal forecast	5. Actual series
Jul-96	1.091	1380	1505	1545
Aug-96	1.010	1409	1422	1476
Sep-96	1.034	1427	1475	1475
Oct-96	1.161	1429	1660	1640
Nov-96	0.909	1431	1301	1293
Dec-96	0.689	1427	983	963
Jan-97	0.759	1423	1080	1108
Feb-97	0.808	1430	1156	1154
Mar-97	1.066	1424	1518	1511
Apr-97	1.154	1423	1642	1694
May-97	1.184	1432	1695	1767
Jun-97	1.136	1444	1640	1661
Jul-97	1.091	1455	1587	1589
Aug-97	1.010	1454	1468	1469
Sep-97	1.034	1459	1508	1545
Oct-97	1.161	1471	1709	1759
Nov-97	0.909	1479	1345	1381
Dec-97	0.689	1484	1022	1015
Jan-98	0.759	1486	1128	1082
Feb-98	0.808	1480	1197	1192
Mar-98	1.066	1484	1581	1600
Apr-98	1.154	1485	1714	1714
May-98	1.184	1480	1752	1733
Jun-98	1.136	1471	1670	1722
Jul-98	1.091	1478	1612	1645
Aug-98	1.010	1491	1506	1495
Sep-98	1.034	1493	1543	1543
Oct-98	1.161	1491	1731	1744
Nov-98	0.909	1494	1358	1363
Dec-98	0.689	1500	1033	1089
Jan-99	0.759	1511	1147	1200
Feb-99	0.808	1523	1231	1273
Mar-99	1.066	1539	1640	1672
Apr-99	1.154	1551	1791	1789
May-99	1.184	1559	1846	1846
Jun-99	1.136	1569	1782	1760
Jul-99	1.091	1564	1706	1700
Aug-99	1.010	1560	1575	1578
Sep-99	1.034	1558	1611	1652
Oct-99	1.161	1563	1815	1826
Nov-99	0.909	1567	1425	1453
Dec-99	0.689	1573	1084	1113

MAPE = 1.63%

months (that is, all the January factors are the same, all the February factors are the same, etc.) because they are assumed to remain constant.

The third column of Table 4.6 contains the six-month SMA forecasts from the fifth column of Table 4.5. They begin with July 1996 because the first six months of the year are used up in the moving average model. To return appropriate seasonality to our forecast series, we multiply the forecasts in column 3 by the seasonal factors in column 2 to obtain the seasonal forecast series in column 4. The last column of Table 4.6 is the actual time series of room demand in Washington, D.C.

Figure 4.17 compares our forecast series to the actual time series of Washington, D.C., room demand. For the most part, our forecast tracks the original series well. It misses one direction change (September 1996) out of forty-one possible directional movements in the actual series, for directional change accuracy of nearly 98 per cent.

There is one last point to consider before moving on to more complex extrapolative models. This is whether we should compare the MAPEs of competing models on the seasonally adjusted series or on the original series with seasonality included.

It is this latter series that we are trying to forecast, so the most prudent approach is to perform our error magnitude accuracy analysis on all forecast

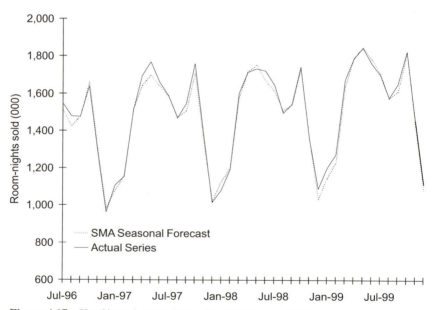

Figure 4.17 Hotel/motel room demand in Washington, D.C., actual and forecast series, monthly, 1996–99
Source: author

models with seasonality returned. This is true whether we are using MAPE, or RMSPE or some other measure of accuracy.

When the seasonal pattern is quite regular, however, the MAPEs will not differ for a model between the seasonally adjusted and the original series with seasonality. This is true in the present case of Washington, D.C., hotel/motel room demand. The seasonality in this series is so regular that we can compute the MAPE of the seasonally adjusted series and be confident this will indicate the most accurate model on this criterion on the seasonal series, as well. Indeed, the MAPEs for both the seasonal series and the seasonally adjusted series are the same: 1.63 per cent. This has the additional advantage of saving time: we do not need to go the extra step of adding seasonality back into our forecast series before comparing error magnitude accuracies.

Assessing the stability of the seasonal factors

The equality of the MAPEs for both the seasonal and seasonally adjusted series indicates the seasonal factors do not change appreciably over the series sample. Figure 4.18 depicts the seasonal factors computed over the entire

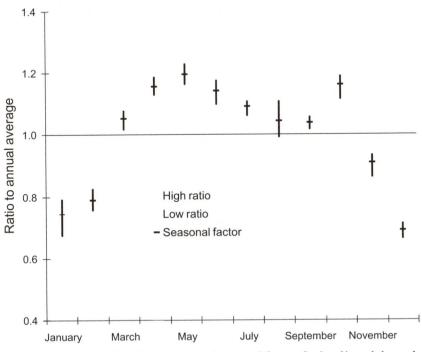

Figure 4.18 Seasonal ratio ranges around seasonal factors for hotel/motel demand in Washington, D.C., monthly, 1987–99. *Source*: author

series of hotel/motel demand for the Washington, D.C., area and the highest and lowest seasonal ratios produced in any year. January, with its occasional presidential inauguration, and August show the highest variability. September and December indicate the lowest seasonal variability. Further study would indicate whether there is a trend in January and August hotel/motel demand, or whether these appear to be random changes in monthly demand over the last twelve years.

Applications

Miller, McCahon and Miller (1991) found that simple moving average and single exponential smoothing models could accurately forecast daily meals ('covers') served in two restaurants. The models worked better when the seasonal patterns were first removed, and for forecasting the most popular menu items as a group.

Conclusion

The simplest extrapolative forecasting methods are the naive method and the simple moving average method. These are seldom used on their own to produce forecasts of tourism demand, but rather are the foundation for

---

1. Isolate the seasonal component and nullify the irregular component:
   a. Compute the 12-month or 4-quarter moving average ending at each observation in the time series for the final period of the first year and each successive period.
   b. Centre this series on each value possible.
   c. Compute the ratio of each period's value to its moving average.
   d. Average these ratios and force the resulting seasonal factors to sum to 12 (monthly series) or 4 (quarterly).
   e. Compute seasonally adjusted values for each period.

2. Forecast the cycle/trend series over the historical series using various methods and choose the best model based on:
   a. error magnitude accuracy, or
   b. directional change accuracy, or
   c. turning point accuracy, or
   d. some combination of these.

3. Use the best model to forecast the future periods of interest.

4. Return seasonality to the forecast series.

Figure 4.19 Steps in applying the classical decomposition forecasting approach

developing and applying more sophisticated models. The naive models are especially useful as benchmarks for evaluating more complex forecasting techniques.

Classical decomposition is a straightforward approach to distinguishing the seasonal cycle-trend and irregular components of a time series in order to develop reasonable forecasts. The advent of powerful spreadsheets on personal computers has made this method especially easy to apply. Figure 4.19 provides a summary of the steps in this forecasting method.

Note

1 It is best to use all of the time series we have in forecast modelling, which, in this case, goes back to January, 1987. However, in the interests of clear exposition and space economy, this series has been shortened to cover only the monthly periods of 1996 to 1999 here.

For further information

Clifton, P., Nguyen, H. and Nutt, S. (1992). *Market Research: Using Forecasting in Business*, pp. 223–49. Butterworth-Heinemann.

Cunningham, S. (1991). *Data Analysis in Hotel and Catering Management*, pp. 184–201. Butterworth-Heinemann.

Levenbach, H. and Cleary, J. P. (1981). *The Beginning Forecaster: The Forecasting Process through Data Analysis*, ch. 8. Lifetime Learning.

Makridakis, S., Wheelwright, S. C. and Hyndman, R. J. (1998), *Forecasting: Methods and Applications*. 3rd edition, ch. 3. Wiley.

Mentzner, J. T. and Bienstock, C. C. (1998). *Sales Forecasting Management*, pp. 42–52. Sage.

Moore, T. W. (1989). *Handbook of Business Forecasting*, chs 3 and 4. Harper & Row.

5

Intermediate extrapolative methods

In Chapter 4, we introduced the extrapolative or time series methods of forecasting. We explored the use of the most basic extrapolative models: the naive and its variations, and SMA models. We then examined seasonality and took advantage of the regularity of this pattern over years through the classical decomposition approach.

Decomposition estimates the average magnitude of seasonal patterns, removes them from the time series and provides us with a trend-cycle, or seasonally adjusted, series. We can then test a number of alternative quantitative forecasting models on this series, including extrapolative methods. We look for the model that best simulates our data series, using the criterion of error magnitude, directional change, turning point, or some combination of these. This should be the best candidate for forecasting future periods. Once we have determined this model, we can produce the forecasts we need and return seasonality to the forecast series.

Alternatively, we could try to deal with the seasonal series directly. We would be disregarding any analysis of the seasonal patterns but this may not be important to us. We would then simply produce forecasts of future seasonal values without regard to the structure of the seasonal process.

In this chapter, we examine intermediate extrapolative forecasting methods, specifically:

- single exponential smoothing
- double exponential smoothing
- triple exponential smoothing
- autoregression.

These methods are intermediate in their complexity among time series forecasting methods. Single exponential smoothing can be used to forecast from stationary time series, while double exponential smoothing is designed for series showing a linear trend or a trend with seasonality removed. Triple exponential smoothing can be used for series including both trend and seasonal components. Autoregression in this context uses regression analysis to model a series' trend. A technique for producing such a trend, even from seasonal data, will be introduced.

Intermediate time series methods are somewhat more complex than their basic brethren, but can still be handled in modern computer spreadsheets. However, as complexity rises, more data are required in the time series models to obtain satisfactory results. Consequently, we will use the complete time series available to us of hotel/motel room demand for the Washington, D.C., metropolitan area, that is monthly data from January, 1987 to December, 1999.

Single exponential smoothing

In trying to forecast a future period, the simple moving average method gives equal weight to all of the past values included in it. For example, each of the values in a three-month moving average model has a weight of one-third in determining the forecast. On the other hand, those values excluded from an SMA model (in this case, values four periods or more back) do not have any effect on the forecast at all. The single exponential smoothing (SES) method allows us to vary the importance of recent values to the forecast and includes all of the information past values can provide us.

The logic of the SES is evident in its general equation:

$$F_t = F_{t-1} + \alpha(A_{t-1} - F_{t-1}) \tag{5.1}$$

where F = forecast value
α = smoothing constant between 0 and 1
A = actual value
t = some time period.

Equation 5.1 says that the forecast for the period, t, is equal to the forecast for the previous period (t–1) plus a portion of the error the forecasting model produced for that previous period (remember that error is defined as the actual value for a period less the forecast value for that period: see Equation 2.1 in Chapter 2).

The portion of the previous period's error to be included in next period's forecast is set by the forecaster and is called the 'smoothing constant.' By convention, the Greek letter alpha (α) is used to represent this constant. The smoothing constant must take a value between zero and one. If it equals zero, then the SES model always forecasts the same value: the initial forecast value. If the smoothing constant equals one, then the SES model reverts to the naive model, because the forecast values on the right-hand side of Equation 5.1 cancel each other out.

The practice in SES modelling is to try the range of possible values for the smoothing constant in one-tenth or fifty one-hundredths increments to find the one that minimizes the MAPE or some other measure of forecasting error over the past series. This minimum error model is the best SES model for the series. Bear in mind that the higher the smoothing constant, the more weight it gives to the last value in the time series. The lower this constant, the more weight it gives to all of the values prior to the last one, which are summarized in the F_{t-1} term in Equation 5.1.

This is clear in Equation 5.2, which reorganizes Equation 5.1 and simplifies computation.

$$F_t = \alpha A_{t-1} + (1 - \alpha)F_{t-1} \tag{5.2}$$

We can place these F_t forecast values in the third column of a spreadsheet, with the dates in the first column and the time series itself in the second.

Single exponential smoothing will only work on stationary series with no seasonality. Consequently, you should consider it for dealing with annual data, or monthly or quarterly time series where seasonality has been removed. Figure 5.1 shows the seasonally adjusted series of hotel/motel room demand in the Washington, D.C., metropolitan area developed by the ratio-to-moving-averages method discussed in Chapter 4's treatment of classical decomposition. While there is no seasonal pattern left, it is clear that the series in Figure 5.1 trends upwards. That is, it is not stationary in its mean.

We can achieve stationarity of a trended series by differencing it. Figure 5.2 shows the first differences of our seasonally adjusted room demand series (the solid line). It appears stationary, and thus can provide a satisfactory SES forecast series.

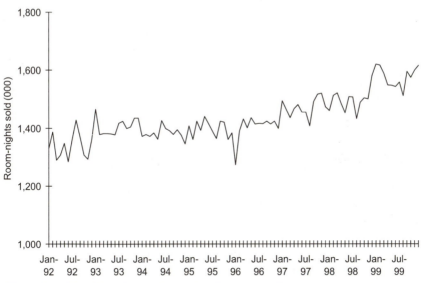

Figure 5.1 Hotel/motel room demand in Washington, D.C., seasonally adjusted, monthly, 1992–99
Source: Smith Travel Research and author

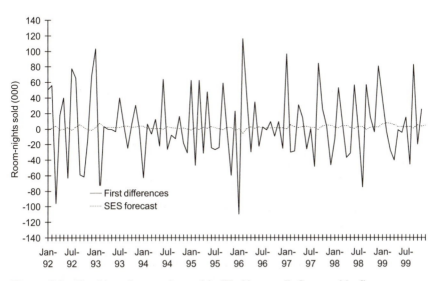

Figure 5.2 Hotel/motel room demand in Washington, D.C., monthly first differences, seasonally adjusted, 1992–99
Source: author

There is one issue left to resolve: how to start the SES forecast series. Each period's forecast requires a forecast for the previous period. However, the first period in the series does not have a forecast value associated with it.

The process of providing a forecast value for the first period is called 'initialization'. Initialization is an important consideration in SES modelling. In some time series, especially one with a large variance around its (stationary) mean, the forecast value chosen for the first period of the SES series will influence all future period forecasts significantly. This is especially true if the smoothing constant is small.

A number of initialization processes have been proposed. None of the alternatives has a superior theoretical foundation, so the principle of parsimony can be applied here with impunity.

The simplest value for the first F_{t-1} is the first *actual* value we have: an application of the naive forecasting method. The next simplest is to average the first three or four values in the series to obtain the initial forecast: an application of the simple moving average method.

Based on experience, the best approach to initialization appears to be the steps shown in Figure 5.3. This assumes you have set up your SES forecast model to produce forecasts based on varying values of the smoothing

---

1. Use the first actual value as the forecast value for the first period.

2. Vary your smoothing constant in one-tenth or fifty one-hundredth increments between 0 and 1 to find the value with the smallest MAPE, and record the constant and MAPE.

3. Change the initial forecast value to be the moving average of the first three periods.

4. Vary the smoothing constant to see if you can achieve a smaller MAPE, and record it and your constant if you do.

5. Change the initial forecast value to be the four-period moving average.

6. Vary your smoothing constant to see if you can achieve a smaller MAPE than found in step 4.

7. Choose the initial forecast value and smoothing constant combination that achieves the lowest MAPE: this is your best SES model.

Figure 5.3 Steps in obtaining the best SES model by varying the smoothing constant and the initial value

constant, with the MAPE or some other measure of error magnitude programmed to vary with the constant, as well (the MAPE is assumed to be the error magnitude measure in the figure).

Employing this differenced series of the seasonally adjusted room-nights sold by Washington, D.C., hotels and motels, we achieved the lowest MAPE (1.77 per cent) with a smoothing constant of 0.05 and initialized by the differenced series' first actual value. The SES forecast series is shown in Figure 5.2. It has indeed smoothed the series of first differences. It produces a forecast for January 2000 of 5. Table 5.1 illustrates how this forecast of first differences is used to obtain a forecast of the actual value for January.

Table 5.1 Turning the SES model forecast of January 2000 first difference into a final forecast

	January 2000 seasonally adjusted series			
1. December 1999	*2. SES forecast first difference*	*3. Seasonally adjusted forecast*	*4. Seasonal factor*	*5. Seasonalized forecast*
1615	5	1620	0.741	1201

Column 1 contains the last value in the seasonally adjusted historical series of hotel/motel room demand in thousands. The second column contains the SES forecast first difference for January 2000. The third column is simply the sum of the first two columns: the forecast first difference is added to the previous actual value to obtain a forecast of the seasonally adjusted series for January 2000.

Column 4 shows the seasonal adjustment factor for January for hotel/motel room demand from Table 4.4, part B, column 7. Column 5 is the product of this factor and the seasonally adjusted forecast in column 3. It is our best SES forecast of hotel/motel room-nights sold in January 2000.

Figure 5.4 recounts the steps in applying the single exponential smoothing model as detailed above.

The advantages of the SES are its simplicity and ability to fit stationary time series well. Its disadvantages are that it cannot deal with series showing any sort of trend or seasonality. Moreover, achieving stationarity in the mean may be a difficult chore with some time series. Finally, the SES can only

1. Make sure there is no seasonality in the series to be forecast; remove seasonality by decomposition, if necessary

2. Confirm by sight that it is stationary; achieve stationarity by first or second differencing, if necessary.

3. Set up a spreadsheet with the time period in the first column and the non-seasonal, stationary historical data in the second column.

4. Program the SES equation in the third column, with the smoothing constant in a separate cell at the top.

5. Program computation of the absolute percentage errors in the fourth column, with the MAPE as the mean of the column.

6. Apply the steps to choosing the optimum smoothing constant and initial value presented in Figure 5.3.

7. If a smoothing constant of one produces the minimum MAPE, adopt the naive forecasting method instead.

8. Using the best SES model, produce a forecast for the next period.

9. Add non-stationarity to this estimate, if necessary.

10. Return the seasonality to the forecast series, if necessary.

Figure 5.4   Steps in using an SES model to forecast

forecast one period ahead of the time series. Fortunately, we have another extrapolative method that offers more flexibility in dealing with series without seasonality: double exponential smoothing.

Double exponential smoothing: dealing with a linear trend

Second order or double exponential smoothing was developed to deal with time series showing a linear trend over time, such as the seasonally adjusted series of hotel/motel room demand in Washington, D.C., shown in Figure 5.1. In essence, a DES model computes a smoothed level and trend at each data point. These values for the last point in the time series can be used to forecast one or two points ahead in the future.

A number of DES models have been proposed but the simplest and one of the easiest to apply is Brown's one-parameter adaptive method.

The equations for this DES model are:

Level: $L_t = \alpha A_t + (1 - \alpha)(L_{t-1} + b_{t-1})$ (5.3)

Trend: $b_t = \alpha(L_t - L_{t-1}) + (1 - \alpha)b_{t-1}$ (5.4)

Forecast: $F_{t+h} = L_t + hb_t$ (5.5)

where L = level of the series
$\quad\quad\quad\alpha$ = level and trend smoothing constant between 0 and 1
$\quad\quad\quad$A = actual value
$\quad\quad\quad b$ = trend of the series
$\quad\quad\quad t$ = some time period
$\quad\quad\quad h$ = number of time periods ahead to be forecast.

Equation 5.3 produces an estimate of the level of the series at time t, while Equation 5.4 denotes the slope of the series at that period. Equation 5.5 produces the forecast. The trend, b_t, is multiplied by the number of steps ahead you wish to forecast, h, and added to the base value, L_t.

Table 5.2 shows the detailed steps for computing a DES forecast for hotel/motel room demand for February 1999. The data for January 1999, developed

Table 5.2 Example of the computation of the double exponential smoothing forecast for hotel/motel room demand in Washington, D.C., for February 1999

1. Level	(α	×	A_t)	+	$(1 - \alpha)$	×	$(L_{t-1}$	+	$b_{t-1})$	=	L_t
Dec-98	0.2	×	1581	+	0.8	×	1493	+	0	=	1511
Jan-99	0.2	×	1619	+	0.8	×	1511	+	3	=	1536

2. Trend	α	×	$(L_t$	−	$L_{t-1})$	+	$(1 - \alpha)$	×	b_{t-1}	=	b_t
Dec-98	0.2	×	1511	−	1493	+	0.8	×	0	=	4
Jan-99	0.2	×	1535	−	1511	+	0.8	×	4	=	8

3. Forecast	L_t	+	$(h \times b_t)$	=	F_{t+1}	Forecast for
Dec-98	1511	+	(1×4)	=	1515	Jan-99
Jan-99	1535	+	(1×8)	=	1543	Feb-99

Note: Smoothing constant $\alpha = 0.2$
Source: author

according to the SES steps in Figure 5.4, are required to begin the process. Computation of the values for the 'Dec-98' rows is not shown but follow the same procedures. Note the Forecast rows assume $h = 1$ for one step ahead forecasts. In an actual spreadsheet, you would embody Equations 5.3, 5.4 and 5.5 in columns rather than the rows shown in Table 5.2.

You need to develop two initial estimates to begin the DES process. Makridakis, Wheelwright and Hyndman (1998: 159) suggest the following:

$$\text{Level initialization:} \quad L_1 = A_1 \tag{5.6}$$

$$\text{Trend initialization:} \quad b_1 = A_2 - A_1 \tag{5.7}$$

A variation on this DES method is Holt's linear method (Makridakis, Wheelwright and Hyndman, 1998: 158). Here, the smoothing constant, α, in the level equation (5.3) is replaced by an independent smoothing constant, β, in the trend equation (5.4). These two values are varied between zero and one to produce the equation with the lowest MAPE or other measure of error. This, of course, increases the effort since there are sixty-four combinations of α and β just accounting for the eight values to the tenths decimal place available for testing, not including zero and one. But this does allow for more variation in the smoothing constants.

In summary, the advantages of the DES method are that it is relatively simple, captures linear trends up or down well and can forecast several periods ahead (unlike the SES method). Its disadvantages are that it cannot track non-linear trends well, fails to simulate a stepped series well and cannot deal with seasonality. Finally, in common with all time series methods, it does not incorporate any causal relationships that may be important to management.

Figure 5.5 summarizes the steps in a DES forecasting model.

Applications of double exponential smoothing

Sheldon (1993) tested eight models for forecasting international visitor expenditures in six developed countries and found that DES was the second most accurate model in terms of MAPE. The most accurate model was the Naive 1 model of no change from the previous year.

Martin and Witt (1989) compared the accuracy of seven forecasting methods for simulating visitor flows among twenty-four origin-destination pairs and, like Sheldon, found that exponential smoothing was the second most accurate model in terms of MAPE, after Naive 1.

1. Make sure there is no seasonality in the series to be forecast; remove seasonality by decomposition, if necessary.

2. Confirm by sight that the series follows a linear trend; if it does not, the DES method will not produce acceptable accuracy.

3. Set up a spreadsheet with the time period in the first column and the historical data in the second column.

4. Program the Level equation (5.3) in the third column, with the smoothing constant in a separate cell at the top.

5. Program the Trend equation (5.4) in the fourth column, referring to the same smoothing constant.

6. Program the Forecast equation (5.5) in the fifth column.

7. Program computation of the absolute percentage errors for each period in the sixth column, with the MAPE as the mean of this column.

8. Set your initial values for Level and Trend following Equations 5.6 and 5.7.

9. Vary your smoothing constant in one-tenth or fifty one-hundredth increments between 0 and 1 to find the value with the smallest MAPE, and record the constant and MAPE.

10. Choose the DES model with the minimum MAPE.

11. Using this DES model produce forecasts for future periods by varying h in the Forecast equation for the last value in your time series.

12. Return seasonality to this forecast series.

Figure 5.5 Steps in developing and applying a DES forecasting model

Triple exponential smoothing: dealing with a linear trend and seasonality

The SES and DES cannot be used on series that include seasonal patterns. This is not a drawback if you want to model the seasonal structure of your series and then apply forecasting methods to the seasonally adjusted series. However, you may want to use an extrapolative series on a tourism demand series that includes seasonal patterns, say to save time or because you are not interested in the seasonal patterns per se.

The Holt-Winters' trend and seasonality method employs triple exponential smoothing: one equation for the level, one for the trend and one for the seasonality. The equations associated with each of these elements are as follows (Makridakis, Wheelwright and Hyndman, 1998: 165):

$$\text{Level:} \quad L_t = \alpha\, \frac{A_t}{S_{t-s}} + (1 - \alpha)(L_{t-1} + b_{t-1}) \tag{5.8}$$

$$\text{Trend:} \quad b_t = \beta(L_t - L_{t-1}) + \left(1 - \beta\right)b_{t-1} \tag{5.9}$$

$$\text{Seasonal:} \quad S_t = \gamma\, \frac{A_t}{L_t} + (1 + \gamma)S_{t-s} \tag{5.10}$$

$$\text{Forecast:} \quad F_{t+h} = (L_t + hb_t)S_{t-s+h} \tag{5.11}$$

where   L = level of the series
α = level smoothing constant between 0 and 1
A = actual value
s = number of seasonal periods in a year (for example, four quarters, twelve months)
b = trend of the series
β = seasonal smoothing constant between 0 and 1
S = seasonal component
γ = seasonal smoothing constant between 0 and 1
t = some time period
h = number of time periods ahead to be forecast.

As in the Brown DES adaptive smoothing model above, Equation 5.8 estimates the level of the series at time, t, but with the addition that the actual value is divided by the seasonal number, S, to remove seasonality as we did with the twelve-month moving average in the decomposition process above. The trend equation (5.9) denotes the trend at this period and mirrors the trend equation (5.4) in the Brown's/Holt's method. But a third equation (5.10) estimates a factor at time, t, multiplied by the result of the level and trend equations to produce the forecast equation (5.11).

Initialization is more complex than for the earlier DES models. Values must be sought for L_s, b_s and S_s, that is, at the end of the first complete season. One recommended approach is the following (Makridakis, Wheelwright and Hyndman, 1998: 168):

Initial level $\quad L_s = \dfrac{A_1 + A_2 + \cdots + A_s}{s}$ (5.12)

Initial trend $\quad b_s = \dfrac{1}{S}\left(\dfrac{A_{s+1} - A_1}{s} + \dfrac{A_{s+2} - A_2}{s} + \cdots + \dfrac{A_{s+s} - A_s}{s}\right)$

(5.13)

Seasonal indices for the first year

$$S_1 = \dfrac{A_1}{L_s}, S_2 = \dfrac{a_2}{L_s}, \cdots, S_8 = \dfrac{A_s}{L_s}$$ (5.14)

The level is initialized in Equation 5.12 by the average of the first season of values. The trend is initialized in Equation 5.13 by the average of each of the s estimates of trend over the first season. Finally, the seasonal indices are initially set as the ratio of the first year's values to the mean of the first year, L_s, in Equation 5.14.

Figure 5.6 presents the steps in applying the Holt-Winters triple exponential smoothing model.

---

1. Set up a spreadsheet with the time period in the first column and the historical data in the second column.

2. Program the Level equation (5.8) in the third column, with its smoothing constant (α) in a separate cell at the top.

3. Program the Trend equation (5.9) in the fourth column, with its smoothing constant (β) at the top.

4. Program the Seasonal equation (5.10) in the fifth column, with its smoothing constant (γ) at the top.

6. Program the Forecast equation (5.11) in the sixth column.

7. Program the computation of the absolute percentage errors for each period in the seventh column, with the MAPE as the mean of this column.

8. Set your initial values for Level, Trend and Seasonal components following Equations 5.12, 5.13 and 5.14.

9. Vary your smoothing constants in one-tenth increments between 0 and 1 to find the combination of values with the smallest MAPE, and record the constants and MAPE.

10. Choose the model with the minimum MAPE.

11. Using this DES model produce forecasts for future periods by varying h in the Forecast equation for the last value in your time series.

Figure 5.6 Steps in developing and applying the Holt–Winters' triple exponential smoothing forecasting model

Table 5.3 Example of the computation of the triple exponential smoothing forecast for hotel/motel room demand in Washington, D.C., for February 1999

1. Level	α	$\times$	$(A_t$	$\div$	$S_{t-s})$	$+$	$(1-\alpha)$	$\times$	$(L_{t-1}$	$+$	$b_{t-1})$	$=$	L_t
Dec-98	0.25	$\times$	(1089	$\div$	0.68)	$+$	0.75	$\times$	(1490	$+$	2.0)	$=$	1517
Jan-99	0.25	$\times$	(1200	$\div$	0.74)	$+$	0.75	$\times$	(1517	$+$	3.2)	$=$	1547

2. Trend	β	$\times$	$(L_t$	$-$	$L_{t-1})$	$+$	$(1-\beta)$	$\times$	b_{t-1}	$=$	b_t
Dec-98	0.05	$\times$	(1517	$-$	1490)	$+$	0.95	$\times$	2.0	$=$	3.2
Jan-99	0.05	$\times$	(1547	-	1517)	$+$	0.95	$\times$	3.2	$=$	4.6

3. Seasonal	γ	$\times$	$(A_t$	$\div$	$L_t)$	$+$	$(1-\gamma)$	$\times$	S_{t-s}	$=$	S_t
Dec-98	0.35	$\times$	(1089	$\div$	1517)	$+$	0.65	$\times$	0.68	$=$	0.69
Jan-99	0.35	$\times$	(1200	$\div$	1547)	$+$	0.65	$\times$	0.74	$=$	0.74

4. Forecast	$(L_t$	$+$	h	$\times$	$b_t)$	$\times$	S_{t-s+h}	$=$	F_{t+1}	*Forecast for*
Dec-98	(1517	$+$	1	$\times$	3.2)	$\times$	0.74	$=$	1125	Jan-99
Jan-99	(1547	$+$	1	$\times$	4.6)	$\times$	0.79	$=$	1226	Feb-99

Note: Smoothing constants:
$\alpha = 0.25$
$\beta = 0.05$
$\gamma = 0.35$

Table 5.3 provides an example of the application of Holt-Winters to hotel/motel room demand in the Washington, D.C., area, a series with demonstrated seasonality (see Figure 4.1).

Applications of triple exponential smoothing

Chu (1998c) tested six forecasting methods in forecasting monthly visitor arrivals in ten Asian-Pacific nations over the 1975–94 period: Naive 1, Naive 2, time trend regression, sine wave regression, autoregressive/moving average (ARIMA) and Holt-Winters. Using the MAPE as his measure in eighteen-month ex post forecasts, he found Holt-Winters models were second only to ARIMA in producing superior forecasts for nine of the ten countries, and led ARIMA in forecasting New Zealand visitor arrivals.

Turner, Kulendran and Fernando (1997a) compared six different methods for forecasting quarterly tourism flows to each of Japan, Australia and New Zealand from seven originating countries over the 1978–95 period. They grouped the quarters into four 'periodic series' for each origin-destination pair and applied Holt's exponential smoothing method and the autoregressive method to the series to develop ex post forecasts. They tested these against Winters's exponential smoothing method and the Box–Jenkins ARIMA for the straight seasonalized series. They found the models applied to the periodic series generally proved less accurate in ex post forecasting than the ARIMA model or the naive model applied to the seasonalized series. The Winter's models proved generally less accurate than the Naive 1 model for the seasonalized series.

Prediction intervals for extrapolative models

As noted in Chapter 2, extrapolative models do not allow prediction intervals to be generated because they are deterministic, that is, do not allow random error to enter into the forecasts. However, it is useful to have some indication of a range of feasible future values, such as the maximum and minimum percentage changes that have occurred in the time series. For example, the 1987–99 hotel/motel demand series for Washington, D.C., shows the maximum year-over-year change was 17.4 per cent and the minimum was –6.2 per cent. These were both for Januarys, which we recognized are subject to wide swings. They could form appropriate bounds around your forecast for a future January.

If you are forecasting for February 2000 from this series with a Holt-Winters model and your forecast is 1.3 million, you can set prediction intervals around it of +10.9 per cent and –6.2 per cent of the February 1999 value (that is, 1.19 to 1.41 million). These are the maximum percentage changes that have occurred in the past for months other than January.

The autoregressive method

It is not unusual for a tourism series to show a strong relationship between the current period's value and the observation for the previous period's or those for several previous periods. Autoregressive models attempt to exploit this momentum effect, and they have the flexibility of being able to follow non-linear trends. 'Autoregressive' refers to the fact that the current period's value is regressed on some collection of past values from the same time series, usually no more than four or five. Regression analysis is discussed in detail in Chapter 7, and refers to developing a mathematical expression of the relationship of one dependent variable to one or more independent variables.

An autoregressive model follows the form:

$$F_t = a + b_1 A_{t-1} + B_2 A_{t-2} + \cdots + b_n A_{t-n} \qquad (5.15)$$

where   F = forecast value
$\quad\quad\quad$ a = estimated constant
$\quad\quad\quad$ b = estimated coefficient
$\quad\quad\quad$ A = actual value in the time series
$\quad\quad\quad$ t = some time period
$\quad\quad\quad$ n = number of past values included.

The constant and coefficients as well as which past values to be included are determined by *stepwise regression.* This is an application of regression analysis (Chapter 7) where independent variables are added to the forecast equation one at a time and retained if they increase the equation's explanatory power (measured by MAPE, the F-statistic or the coefficient of determination) and have coefficients that are significantly different from zero (measured by the *t*-statistic).

Autoregression is best applied to a seasonally adjusted series. If you are dealing with sub-annual (for example, monthly or quarterly) data, the first step is to produce such a series from the time series you have, such as by the decomposition method (Chapter 4). Next, program regression analysis in your spreadsheet. Make sure it produces a measure of explanatory power for each set of variables included (MAPE, F-statistic, etc.).

To program this in a computer spreadsheet, enter your time periods and time series in the first and second columns, respectively. In the third column, enter the time series but lagged one period. That is, the value next to February 1987 should be the original time series value for January 1987. Copy these lagged data through the rest of the column.

Similarly, the fourth column should have the column two time series lagged by two periods: the original January data point would appear in the March 1987 position. Repeat this by column for as many lagged variables as you want to test in your autoregression models. Then, when you run the spreadsheet regression program, you can easily identify the combination of explanatory variables you wish to include.

In our case of modelling hotel/motel room demand in the Washington, D.C., areas, there are seven possible combinations of the time series lagged one, two and three months (for example, first lagged value only, first and second lagged values, all three lagged values, first and third lagged values). Six of these models indicated all of the estimated coefficients were significantly different from zero through analyses of *t*-tests. One produced insignificant coefficients, indicating the associated independent variable was not significant and the equation was misspecified (discussed further in Chapter 7).

The models with significant coefficients are listed in Table 5.4 by their independent variables, along with their MAPEs. Regressing the differenced seasonally adjusted series of hotel/motel room demand on values one period earlier and two periods earlier produced the largest coefficient of determination (R^2) adjusted for degrees of freedom, a common measure of the fit of a regression equation (see Chapter 7 for more details). It also produced the lowest measure of error magnitude, but not significantly lower than the other two autoregressive models with significant regression equations.

In summary, the autoregressive model exploits the idea that the last several values of a time series may be a good basis for forecasting the next value. Since it can produce non-linear trend estimates, it is well suited for any series

Table 5.4 **Comparison of autoregressive models on seasonally adjusted hotel/motel demand in Washington, D.C., significant at 0.05 on the F-test**

Explanatory variables	Adjusted R^2	MAPE
A_{t-1}, A_{t-3}	0.84	2.2%
A_{t-1}, A_{t-2}	0.83	2.3%
A_{t-1}	0.82	2.3%
A_{t-2}, A_{t-3}	0.80	2.5%
A_{t-3}	0.75	2.6%
A_{t-3}	0.75	2.7%

1. If necessary, remove seasonality from the historical time series.

2. Regress the seasonally adjusted series against earlier values in a stepwise fashion (see Chapter 7):
   a. Regress the actual values against combinations of the past four or five values.
   b. Examine coefficients for significance by their t-statistics.
   c. Assess all models where all coefficients are significantly different from zero by examining their MAPEs over the historical series.
   d. Choose the model with the lowest MAPE as the forecast model.

3. Forecast the seasonally adjusted series over the future periods of interest.

4. Return seasonality to the forecast series.

Figure 5.7 Steps in developing and applying an autoregressive forecasting model

with a trend. However, since it is based on a set of previous values it can only forecast a few periods after the time series ends before it starts relying on its own forecast values as independent variables. This often degenerates into a horizontal trend after several periods and magnifies any errors in the early forecasts as well.

Figure 5.7 relates the steps in developing an autoregressive tourism forecasting model, as detailed above.

Prediction intervals for autoregressive models

The autoregressive method produces statistical models with stochastic elements. Consequently, you can fairly produce prediction intervals by the method in Chapter 2.

Comparing alternative time series models

At this point, we have examined six time series forecast methods:

1 Naive.
2 Single moving average.
3 Single exponential smoothing.
4 Double exponential smoothing.
5 Triple exponential smoothing.
6 Autoregressive.

Table 5.5 shows the actual hotel/motel demand series and two forms of the naive model for comparison (rows 1 and 2). Rows 3 to 7 present information on the best forecasting equation for each of the methods, based on lowest MAPE. The MAPEs are shown along with Theil's U-statistic for each of the forecasting models. Finally, forecasts are presented for January 2000 (column E) and the forecast error for this value (see row 8).

Note Theil's U for the seasonal naive model (row 2) indicates it is better *for forecasting the original series with seasonality* than the Naive 1 model. Otherwise, the MAPEs and Theil's U are consistent. The single exponential smoothing model shows up a bit worse than the naive approach on accuracy. However, it produces the most accurate forecast of the January 2000 value.

Generally, there is no clear relationship between the MAPEs over the time series and the forecast errors in column E. This emphasizes the importance of post-sample testing of prospective forecasting models. We would expect the SES model to produce the most accurate forecast for one month after the time series among these models. However, SES models do not produce reasonable forecasts farther out than one month.

Table 5.5   Comparison of time series models forecasting hotel/motel room demand in Washington, D.C., monthly, 1987–99

A. Method	B. Characteristics	C. MAPE	D. Theil's U-statistic	E. Jan-00 forecast (thousand room-nights)	F. Forecast error
1. Naive 1		2.3%	NA	1 197	1.6%
2. Seasonal naive		3.5%	0.302	1 200	1.3%
3. Simple moving average	12-month	1.9%	0.855	1 169	3.8%
4. Single exponential smoothing	$\alpha = 0.2$	2.3%	1.023	1 201	1.2%
5. Brown's one parameter adaptive method	$\alpha = 0.05$	2.1%	0.708	1 186	2.5%
6. Holt-Winters' trend and seasonality method	$\alpha = 0.25$, $\beta = 0.05$, $\gamma = 0.35$	2.3%	0.702	1 192	2.0%
7. Autoregressive	A_{t-1}, A_{t-3}	2.2%	0.982	1 188	2.3%
8. Actual value for Jan-00 = 1216 thousand room-nights sold					

Note: NA = not applicable.

This comparison indicates that it is possible to use a relatively straightforward extrapolative model such as the SES to improve on the naive model for forecasting this series. The two exponential smoothing models and the best autoregressive model all produced series with lower MAPEs than the naive model. The best simple moving average model did not.

Choosing a time series method

We have discussed six different time series methods for forecasting tourism demand. Each has advantages and disadvantages in dealing with particular time series. It is useful to have some guidance at the beginning of the forecasting project as to what method to first employ. Tables 5.6–5.9 can help

Table 5.6 Decision for choosing time series methods: stationary data

	1	2	3	4	5	6	7	8	9	10
Pattern										
Annual seasonality	N	N	N	Y/N	Y/N	Y/N	Y	Y	N	N
Non-annual seasonality	N	N	N	Y/N	Y/N	Y/N	N	N	Y	Y
Forecast horizon										
1 to 3 periods	Y	Y	N	Y/N	Y	N	Y	N	Y	N
4 to 12 periods	N	N	Y/N	Y/N	N	Y/N	N	Y/N	N	Y/N
13 or more periods	N	N	Y/N	XXX	N	Y/N	N	Y/N	N	Y/N
Series length										
< 10 points or 1 season	Y	N	Y/N	Y	N	N	N	N	N	N
< 20 points or 2 seasons	N	Y/N	Y/N	N	Y/N	Y/N	N	N	N	N
< 30 points or 3 seasons	N	Y/N	Y/N	N	Y/N	Y/N	N	N	N	N
> 30 points or 3 seasons	N	Y/N	Y/N	N	N	N	Y	Y	Y	Y
Naive	NS	NS	NS	NA	NA	NA	NA	NA	NA	NA
Classical decomposition	NA	NA	NA	NA	NA	NA	FC	FC	NA	NA
Single expon. smoothing	FC	FC	FC	NA	NA	NA	NA	NA	NA	NA
SES + seasonal differencing	NA	NA	NA	NA	FC	FC	FC	FC	FC	FC
Double expon. smoothing	NR	NR	NR	NA	NA	NA	NA	NA	NA	NA
Autoregressive	SU	NR	NA	NA	NA	NA	NA	NA	NA	NA
Autoregressive + seas. diff.	NA	NA	NA	NA	SU	NR	SU	NR	SU	NR

Key to codes

Y = yes; N = no; Y/N = yes or no; Y to one implies N to others; XXX = unwise to attempt.

FC = first choice; NA = not appropriate; NR = not recommended; NS = normally satisfactory; SU = sometimes useful.

Source: After Saunders, John A., Sharp, John A. and Witt, Stephen F. (1987), *Practical Business Forecasting*, p. 100. Used with permission.

Table 5.7 Decision for choosing time series methods: data with linear trend

	1	2	3	4	5	6	7	8	9	10
Pattern										
Annual seasonality	N	N	N	Y/N	Y/N	Y/N	Y	Y	N	N
Non-annual seasonality	N	N	N	Y/N	Y/N	Y/N	N	N	Y	Y
Forecast horizon										
1 to 3 periods	Y	Y	N	Y/N	Y	N	Y	N	Y	N
4 to 12 periods	N	N	Y/N	Y/N	N	Y/N	N	Y/N	N	Y/N
13 or more periods	N	N	Y/N	XXX	N	Y/N	N	Y/N	N	Y/N
Series length										
< 10 points or 1 season	Y	N	Y/N	Y	N	N	N	N	N	N
< 20 points or 2 seasons	N	Y/N	Y/N	N	Y/N	Y/N	N	N	N	N
< 30 points or 3 seasons	N	Y/N	Y/N	N	Y/N	Y/N	N	N	N	N
> 30 points or 3 seasons	N	Y/N	Y/N	N	N	N	Y	Y	Y	Y
Naive	NR	NR	NA	NA	NA	NA	NA	NA	NA	NA
Classical decomposition	NA	NA	NA	NA	NA	NA	FC	FC	NA	NA
Single expon. smoothing	NA	NA	NA	NA	NA	NA	NA	NA	NA	NA
SES + seasonal differencing	NA	NA	NA	NA	FC	FC	FC	FC	FC	FC
Double expon. smoothing	FC	FC	FC	NA	NA	NA	NA	NA	NA	NA
Autoregressive	SU	NS	NR	NA	NA	NA	NA	NA	NA	NA
Autoregressive + seas. diff.	NA	NA	NA	NA	NS	NR	NS	NR	NS	NR

Key to codes

Y = yes; N = no; Y/N = yes or no; Y to one implies N to others; XXX = unwise to attempt.

FC = first choice; NA = not appropriate; NR = not recommended; NS = normally satisfactory; SU = sometimes useful.

Source: After Saunders, John A., Sharp, John A. and Witt, Stephen F. (1987), *Practical Business Forecasting*, p. 100. Used with permission.

Table 5.8 Decision for choosing time series methods: data with non-linear trend

	1	2	3	4	5	6	7	8	9
Pattern									
Annual seasonality	N	N	N	Y/N	Y/N	Y/N	Y	Y	N
Non-annual seasonality	N	N	N	Y/N	Y/N	Y/N	N	N	Y
Forecast horizon									
1 to 3 periods	Y	Y	N	Y/N	Y	N	Y	N	Y
4 to 12 periods	N	N	Y/N	Y/N	N	Y/N	N	Y/N	N
13 or more periods	N	N	Y/N	XXX	N	Y/N	N	Y/N	N
Series length									
< 10 points or 1 season	Y	N	Y/N	Y	N	N	N	N	N
< 20 points or 2 seasons	N	Y/N	Y/N	N	Y/N	Y/N	N	N	N
< 30 points or 3 seasons	N	Y/N	Y/N	N	Y/N	Y/N	N	N	N
> 30 points or 3 seasons	N	Y/N	Y/N	N	N	N	Y	Y	Y
Naïve	NR	NR	NA	NA	NA	NA	NA	NA	NA
Classical decomposition	NA	NA	NA	NA	NA	NA	FC	FC	NA
Single expon. smoothing	NA	NA	NA	NA	NA	NA	NA	NA	NA
SES + seasonal differencing	NA	NA	NA	NA	FC	FC	FC	FC	FC
Double expon. smoothing	FC	FC	FC	NA	NA	NA	NA	NA	NA
Autoregressive	SU	NS	NR	NA	NA	NR	NS	NR	NA
Autoregressive + seas. diff.	NA	NA	NA	NA	NS	NR	NS	NR	NS

Key to codes

Y = yes; N = no; Y/N = yes or no; Y to one implies N to others; XXX = unwise to attempt.

FC = first choice; NA = not appropriate; NR = not recommended; NS = normally satisfactory; SU = sometimes useful.

Source: After Saunders, John A., Sharp, John A. and Witt, Stephen F. (1987), *Practical Business Forecasting*, p. 100. Used with permission.

Table 5.9 Decision for choosing time series methods: stepped data

	1	2	3	4	5	6	7	8	9	10
Pattern										
Annual seasonality	N	N	N	Y/N	Y/N	Y/N	Y	Y	N	N
Non-annual seasonality	N	N	N	Y/N	Y/N	Y/N	N	N	Y	Y
Forecast horizon										
1 to 3 periods	Y	Y	N	Y/N	Y	N	Y	N	Y	N
4 to 12 periods	N	N	Y/N	Y/N	N	Y/N	N	Y/N	N	Y/N
13 or more periods	N	N	Y/N	XXX	N	Y/N	N	Y/N	N	Y/N
Series length										
< 10 points or 1 season	Y	N	Y/N	Y	N	N	N	N	N	N
< 20 points or 2 seasons	N	Y/N	Y/N	N	Y/N	Y/N	N	N	N	N
< 30 points or 3 seasons	N	Y/N	Y/N	N	Y/N	Y/N	N	N	N	N
> 30 points or 3 seasons	N	Y/N	Y/N	N	N	N	Y	Y	Y	Y
Naive	NS	NS	NS	NA	NA	NA	NA	NA	NA	NA
Classical decomposition	NA	NA	NA	NA	NA	NA	NA	NA	NA	NA
Single expon. smoothing	NA	NA	NA	NA	NA	NA	NA	NA	NA	NA
SES + seasonal differencing	NA	NA	NA	NA	NS	NS	NS	NS	NS	NS
Double expon. smoothing	SU	SU	SU	NA	NA	NA	NA	NA	NA	NA
Autoregressive	NA	NA	NA	NA	NA	NR	NA	NA	NA	NA
Autoregressive + seas. diff.	NA	NA	NA	NA	NA	NR	NA	NA	NA	NA

Key to codes

Y = yes; N = no; Y/N = yes or no; Y to one implies N to others; XXX = unwise to attempt.
FC = first choice; NA = not appropriate; NR = not recommended; NS = normally satisfactory; SU = sometimes useful.

Source: After Saunders, John A., Sharp, John A. and Witt, Stephen F. (1987), *Practical Business Forecasting*, p. 100. Used with permission.

you in this process. They are an adaptation of ones found in Saunders, Sharp and Witt (1987). These four tables correspond to the four common patterns in time series discussed in Chapter 4 (shown in Figures 4.2–4.6):

1 Stationary.
2 Linear trend.
3 Non-linear trend.
4 Stepped series.

To make use of these tables, begin by viewing a chart of your series, such as the actual series in Figure 5.8 showing our familiar monthly room demand in the Washington, D.C., metropolitan area. In this case, we can reach the following conclusions:

■ type of series: linear trend
■ pattern: annual seasonality
■ series length: ninety-six observations.

In addition, assume we must forecast each of the first six months of 2000.
    Since we have a linear trend, we go to Table 5.7 'Data with linear trend'. Next, we look across the 'Annual seasonality' line under 'Pattern' and ignore

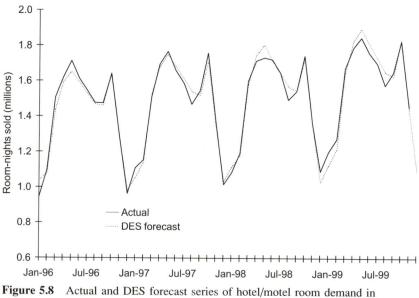

Figure 5.8 Actual and DES forecast series of hotel/motel room demand in Washington, D.C., monthly, 1996–99
Source: author

all columns with an 'N', since we do have annual seasonality. This eliminates the first three columns and the last two from consideration because they all assume no annual seasonality.

A point about terminology may be appropriate here. For most tourism uses, 'Non-annual seasonality' refers to weekly series where we focus on daily movements. For example, it is common for guest arrivals to peak on certain days of most weeks. For downtown hotels that cater to business travellers, this is likely to be Monday to Thursday, with fewer check-ins on Friday to Sunday. For resort hotels appealing to the leisure visitor, the peak days for arrivals are likely to be Friday and Saturday, with low periods Tuesday to Thursday. These are patterns that are repeated in a kind of seasonality, but which is not annual. Restaurants, airlines, rental car companies and attractions tend to show such non-annual seasonality as well. However, our series is a monthly, annual seasonality one.

Focusing on the remaining columns 4 to 8, we next move to 'Forecast horizon'. This has been set at six periods, so we look for columns with 'Y' in the middle line, '4 to 12 periods.' Columns 4, 6 and 8 qualify, while columns 5 and 7 drop out.

Finally, we move to the 'Series length' section. Our series is eight years long and we are working with monthly data, so we have ninety-six data points. This is the last row in the section '>30 points or 3 seasons'. Of columns 4, 6 and 8, only 8 has a 'Y' in it. Consequently, we read down this column to determine which are the methods most likely to produce a quality forecasting model. This suggests that classical decomposition and single exponential smoothing with seasonal differencing are first choices. We might also consider an autoregressive model with seasonal differencing as well.

Summary

The basic and intermediate time series methods discussed here have broad applications in tourism. They are quick, simple and cheap to operate and can account for trends and seasonality. They lend themselves to easy re-estimation as new data become available and can be operated with little statistical training.

According to Witt, Newbould and Watkins (1992: 38), exponential smoothing tourism forecasting models 'tend to perform well, with accuracy levels comparable to more complex and statistically sophisticated forecasting methods which require considerable user understanding to employ them successfully'. They further maintain that while this method is not prominent in forecasting literature, in actual practice it, along with the moving average method, is the most popular.

The major disadvantage of these methods is that they cannot take into account factors affecting the series other than its past values. They do not explain the relationships between such factors and the series of interest. Should events occur that can radically change tourism behaviour, such as pestilence, terrorism, entertainment mega-events or natural disasters, time series methods fail. However, they can indicate the values that should have been achieved in the absence of these catastrophes, and thus measure the magnitude of their impact on tourism.

For further information

Clifton, P., Nguyen, H. and Nutt, S. (1992). *Market Research: Using Forecasting in Business*, pp. 223–49. Butterworth-Heinemann.

Levenbach, H. and Cleary, J. P. (1981). *The Beginning Forecaster: The Forecasting Process through Data Analysis*, ch. 8. Lifetime Learning.

Makridakis, S. (1990). *Forecasting, Planning and Strategy for the 21st Century*, ch. 3. Free Press.

Makridakis, S., Wheelwright, S. C. and Hyndman, R. J. (1998), *Forecasting: Methods and Applications*, ch. 4, 3rd edition. Wiley.

Martin, C. A. and Witt, S. F. (1989). Accuracy of econometric forecasts of tourism. *Annals of Tourism Research*, **16**, 407–28.

Mentzner, J. T. and Bienstock, C. C. (1998). *Sales Forecasting Management*, pp. 53–78. Sage.

Moore, T. W. (1989). *Handbook of Business Forecasting*, chs. 3 and 4. Harper & Row.

Shim, J. K., Siegel, J. G. and Liew, C. J. (1994). *Strategic Business Forecasting*, ch. 6. Probus.

6

An advanced extrapolative method

In the previous two chapters, we discussed simple and intermediate time series methods. These are readily constructed in spreadsheets and require the grasp of relatively simple mathematical concepts. They are not, however, suited for dealing with the widest range of tourism demand time series. For example, they have difficulty capturing non-linear trends and cannot simulate cycles very well.

This chapter describes the most popular advanced extrapolative method. This method can handle a wider range of time series effectively and is growing in popularity in tourism demand forecasting.

The Box–Jenkins approach

While most of this book is a discussion of individual time series methods of tourism forecasting and specific expressions of these methods in models, we now turn to a forecasting *strategy* called the Box–Jenkins approach after its creators, George Box and Gwilyn Jenkins of Great Britain. This has become a popular approach due to its ability to handle any time series, its strong theoretical foundations, and its operational success.

The Box–Jenkins approach searches for the combination of two forecasting methods and their parameters that minimizes the error in simulating the past series. It then statistically checks this combination for validity. If the combination passes this test, it can be used in forecasting the series.

The two methods are *autoregression* and *moving average* (*note*: the latter is different from the moving average method discussed in Chapter 4). The Box–Jenkins approach is a process that makes use of these two methods to suggest the most appropriate form of the forecasting model and then tests this model's validity. The acronym, ARMA, is used to identify the autroregressive/moving average combined method.

The ARMA models can only deal with time series stationary in their means and variances. When approaching a time series that is not, differencing is used to achieve stationarity. That is, a first difference is computed by subtracting the first historical value in the time series from the second, and the second from the third, etc., and the resulting series examined for a stationary mean. If this does not appear, then the first differenced series is differenced again, and the resulting series inspected for stationarity.

The number of times a series must be differenced to achieve stationarity is indicated by its 'integration index'. For example, if the second differenced series described above achieves stationarity, then its integration index is 2. When this approach is used to develop a series to which an ARMA model can be applied, then the integration factor is included in the description of the model, and it is labelled an 'ARIMA' model for autoregressive/integrated/moving average model. We will deal more simply with the stationarity problem here and not discuss the full ARIMA model process. Fortunately, the ARMA process captures the important aspects of the Box-Jenkins approach.

The Box–Jenkins approach is appropriate for forecasting horizons of twelve to eighteen months and when at least fifty observations are available. It is not appropriate if there are repeated outliers at the end of the historical series. It is a complex and tedious process that does not lend itself to spreadsheet analysis. Rather, you should use a statistical package, such as Statistica™,[1] that performs the analysis.

There are five phases in applying the Box–Jenkins approach:

1 Preparation (achieving stationarity, removing seasonality).
2 Identification (examining autocorrelations, selecting a model).
3 Estimation.
4 Diagnostic checking.
5 Forecasting.

Preparation phase

The first step is to examine the series for stationarity and seasonality. The Box–Jenkins approach requires that the series to be forecast be stationary in its mean and variance, that is, its mean should not drift up or down over time as it does in series exhibiting linear trends, non-linear trends and steps (see Chapter 4).

Stationarity of the mean

Figure 6.1 shows the annual room-nights sold in the Washington, D.C., metropolitan area and the mean of this series as it progresses. Here, the mean is the moving average of all available data points at each period. For example, in 1988, the mean is the average of the values for 1987 and 1988, and for 1989, the mean is the average of the values for 1987–9. It is clear by examination of the time series plot that the mean trends upward and is not stationary.

Table 6.1 provides the actual data and the moving mean for Figure 6.1. The data here also indicate that this series is not stationary in the mean. This is confirmed by a *t*-test of the difference between the mean of the first half of the period (1987–93) and the last half (1994–9). The *t*-statistic indicates that we

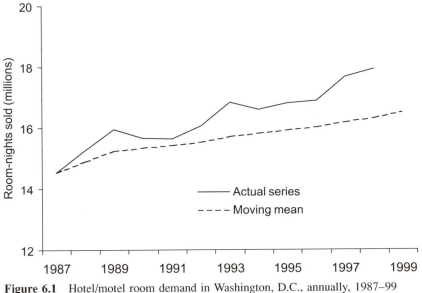

Figure 6.1 Hotel/motel room demand in Washington, D.C., annually, 1987–99
Source: Smith Travel Research and author

Table 6.1   Actual series, moving mean and first differences of Washington, D.C., hotel/motel room demand, annually, 1987–99 (millions)

1. Year	2. Actual series	3. Moving mean	4. First difference	5. Moving mean
1987	14.6	14.6		
1988	15.3	14.9	0.72	0.72
1989	15.9	15.3	0.67	0.70
1990	15.7	15.4	−0.28	0.37
1991	15.6	15.4	−0.02	0.27
1992	16.0	15.5	0.40	0.30
1993	16.8	15.7	0.80	0.38
1994	16.6	15.8	−0.24	0.29
1995	16.8	15.9	0.21	0.28
1996	16.9	16.0	0.08	0.26
1997	17.7	16.2	0.77	0.31
1998	17.9	16.3	0.27	0.31
1999	18.9	16.5	0.94	0.36

Source: Smith Travel Research and author.

can be over 99 per cent confident that the difference between the two samples is not zero. To achieve stationarity in the mean, as we must for applying the Box–Jenkins approach, the series is 'first-differenced', that is, a new series is created which is the difference between successive values of the original series. The *t*-statistic for the two halves of the differenced series (column 5 in Table 6.1) indicates their respective means are not significantly different from each other.

Table 6.1 shows the first differences and their moving mean in columns 4 and 5, respectively. It is clear that, after the first few periods, this achieves stationarity in the mean. It is this series that would be simulated by the Box–Jenkins approach and then forecast. If the first differenced series does not achieve a stationary mean, the remedy is to difference this series again to obtain a second-differenced series. In most cases, you need not go beyond second differencing to achieve a stable mean.

Stationarity of the variance

Some series are not stationary in their variance. That is, the size of their fluctuations grows over time, even if their mean is stationary. This is often true of long time series that grow at a significant rate. The fluctuations at the later data points tend to be larger than those at the early points. Many tourism time series fit this pattern, reflecting the dramatic increase in travel away from home throughout most of the world since the Second World War.

Figure 6.2 shows such a series: U.S. scheduled airline traffic for the years 1960–94. It is evident to the eye that the absolute fluctuations later in the series are greater than earlier. This is confirmed by an F-test of the ratio of the variance of the first twenty years to that of the latter years: there is a difference between the variances of the two series at the 0.05 level of significance.[2]

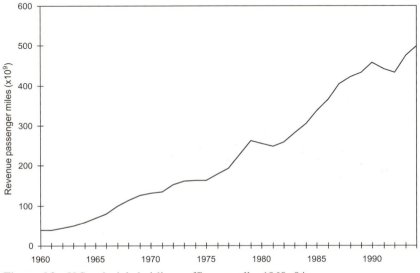

Figure 6.2 U.S. scheduled airline traffic, annually, 1960–94
Source: Air Transport Association of America

A common solution to non-stationarity in variance is to transform the series into logarithms. Figure 6.3. shows the logarithms of U.S. scheduled airline traffic for 1960–99.

The logarithmic transformation is most useful when the variance of the series is proportional to the mean level of the series and this mean increases or decreases at a constant percentage rate. This is not the case here. As a result, this transformation overcorrects the variance by moving it earlier in the series. The fluctuations from 1960 to 1970 are absolutely greater than those later in the logarithmic series. The F-test of the variances of the first and second halves of the time series confirms that the variances are not equal in this transformed series.

If the logarithmic transformation does not stabilize the series variance, then try transforming the original series into its square roots. The square root

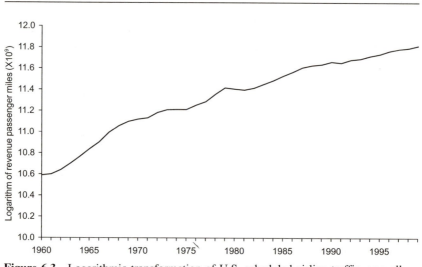

Figure 6.3 Logarithmic transformation of U.S. scheduled airline traffic, annually, 1960–99
Source: Air Transport Association of America

transformation of the airline traffic series is shown in Figure 6.4. It appears that the variance around the moving mean is constant over the period. This is confirmed by the F-test of the variances of the first and second halves of the series: there is no difference at the 0.05 level of significance.

An F-test of the variances of the Washington, D.C., hotel/motel demand series indicates the series is stable in its variance. Therefore, no transformation was needed to achieve stationarity of this series' variance.

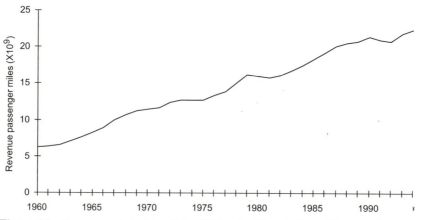

Figure 6.4 Square root transformation of U.S. scheduled airline traffic, annually, 1960–94
Source: Air Transport Association of America and author

In summary, check for stationarity of the variance of your series first. If this is lacking, transform the original series into logarithms or square roots to stabilize its variance. Then examine this transformed series for stability of its mean. If the mean is not stable (i.e., the transformed series indicates a trend), resolve this through first or second differencing of your transformed series. Make sure you address non-stationarity in the variance first, however. You want to complete your logarithmic or square root transformation before any differencing. This is because differencing frequently produces negative values, and you cannot transform a negative number into a logarithm or square root.

Seasonality

The autoregressive and moving average processes at the heart of the Box–Jenkins approach cannot work with seasonal data series such as most monthly or quarterly series of tourism demand. After the series has been transformed to achieve stationarity in both mean and variance, you should look for seasonal patterns in the resulting series. Identifying seasonality and dealing with it differ in the Box–Jenkins approach from that used in classical decomposition discussed in Chapter 4.

Identifying seasonality in the series to be forecast is done by examining the *autocorrelation coefficients*. Autocorrelation coefficients are similar to the coefficients estimated in the autoregressive method discussed in Chapter 5. But instead of regressing the current value of a series on a group of its past values, you compute the *correlations* for each relationship.

Formally, the autocorrelation coefficient, r, for any A_t and A_{t-n}, where n is the number of previous time periods you are interested in, is equal to:

$$r_{A_t, A_{t-n}} = \frac{\sum\limits_{t=k+1}^{n} \left(A_t - \overline{Y}\right)\left(Y_{t-k} - \overline{Y}\right)}{\sum\limits_{t=1}^{n} \left(A_t - \overline{Y}\right)^2} \tag{6.1}$$

where r = correlatión coefficient
        A = value in the time series
        $\overline{Y}$ = the mean of the time series
        t = any time period
        n = number of time periods previous to t.

For example, if n equals 1, then you are correlating each value with its immediate predecessor. If n equals 12, then you are correlating each value with its counterpart twelve periods earlier, or 'lagged' twelve periods.

The correlation coefficient, r, will vary between -1 and $+1$. The closer it is to ends of this range (that is, the farther it is from zero), the higher the correlation between the two values. If the correlation coefficient is nearly $+1$, then the two series move together: when one is much larger than its mean, the other one will tend to be larger than its mean. When one is far below its mean, then the other series will tend to be also.

The closer r is to -1, the more the two series move in opposite directions. If one series is much higher than its mean, then the other will be much lower, and vice versa.

Seasonality is identified in a sub-annual time series when there is significant autocorrelation at points $n = 4, 8, 12$, etc., for quarterly series, and $n = 12, 24, 36$, etc. for monthly series. Figure 6.5 shows the correlation coefficients for the Washington, D.C., hotel/motel room demand monthly series for $n = 1$ through 25 months.

An individual autocorrelation between data points at any given distance apart, such as any one shown in Figure 6.5, is deemed significant at the 95 per cent confidence level if its value falls outside of the following range:

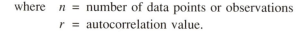

$$-\frac{1.96}{\sqrt{n}} < r < \frac{1.96}{\sqrt{n}} \tag{6.2}$$

where n = number of data points or observations
         r = autocorrelation value.

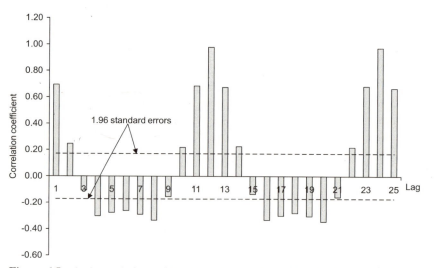

Figure 6.5 Autocorrelations of hotel/motel room demand in Washington, D.C., lagged one to twenty-five periods
Source: author

The dashed vertical lines indicate 1.96 standard errors on either side of zero. Thus, horizontal bars that do not exceed this line are not significantly different from zero at the 95 per cent confidence level (or 0.05 level of significance). Those autocorrelations that break this line (as most of them do) are significantly different from zero.

It is clear that the highest correlations in this figure are at $n = 12$ and 24. This indicates there is monthly seasonality. (We ignore the high correlation at a one-month lag: this is a common characteristic of monthly time series indicating that adjoining months share seasonal and trend characteristics.) There are also significant correlations for 'runs' of successive monthly spans, such as four to eight months. This suggests the series is not stationary in its mean, that is, the data show a trend.

Many tourism demand series will show both seasonality and trend. Indeed, a series without inherent seasonality will appear to be seasonal if it has a significant trend: for example, December's values will always be greater than the previous January's. It is suggested, therefore, to first remove the trend by first-differencing before tackling the seasonal pattern.

Figure 6.6 shows the autocorrelations for the first-differenced series of Washington, D.C., room-nights sold. This has removed the runs of four or more months of significant autocorrelations. However, the transformed series still emphasizes the seasonality of hotel/motel room demand by the high correlations at twelve and twenty-four previous months. The autocorrelation at twelve months is not far from a perfect correlation of 1.0.

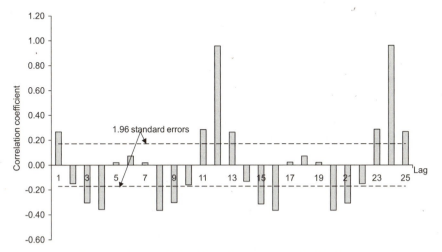

Figure 6.6 Autocorrelations of hotel/motel room demand in Washington, D.C., one-span differences
Source: author

Once seasonality is identified, it is removed by again differencing over the seasonal periods the first-differenced series. With monthly seasonality, these 'seasonal differences' (sometimes called 'long differences', or 'twelve-span differences') are computed by constructing a new series of the difference of a current period's value and the value lagged twelve periods back. Table 6.2 shows the computation for monthly Washington, D.C., hotel/motel demand for 1999. Note that a seasonal pattern remains after the first differencing: the largest absolute values in column 3 remain in the spring and fall. But the twelve-span differencing in column 5 appears to produce a random series.

Table 6.2   Computation of seasonal differences of first-differenced Washington, D.C., hotel/motel room demand, monthly, 1998–9

	Room-nights sold (000)			
1. Month-year	*2. Actual* (A_t)	*3. First differences* $(A_t{-}A_{t-1}) = FD_t$	*4. Year earlier first differences* $(A_{t-12}{-}A_{t-11}) = FD_{t-12}$	*5. Seasonal second differences* $(FD_t{-}FD_{t-12})$
Jan–98	1 017			
Feb–98	1086	69		
Mar–98	1443	357		
Apr–98	1598	155		
May–98	1624	26		
Jun–98	1626	2		
Jul–98	1527	−99		
Aug–98	1452	−75		
Sep–98	1428	−24		
Oct–98	1617	189		
Nov–98	1250	−367		
Dec–98	927	−323		
Jan–99	1043	116	26	
Feb–99	1072	29	69	−40
Mar–99	1497	425	357	68
Apr–99	1607	110	155	−45
May–99	1717	110	26	84
Jun–99	1615	−103	2	−105
Jul–99	1516	−99	−99	0
Aug–99	1424	−92	−75	−16
Sep–99	1475	51	−24	75
Oct–99	1646	172	189	−17
Nov–99	1236	−411	−367	−44
Dec–99	953	−283	−323	40

Source: Smith Travel Research (see Appendix 1)

Figure 6.7 presents the autocorrelations of the first-differenced series of Washington, D.C., room-nights from Figure 6.6 differenced again: this time, a span of twelve periods. This has removed all significant autocorrelations except for three lags: one month, two months, and twelve months.

It is not uncommon for autocorrelations to remain significant for the first one or two periods even after significant differencing. This recognizes that a monthly value is likely to be close to values for the first and second preceding months because they all embody some of the same seasonal and trend patterns. Such information is used to suggest the form of the autoregressive, moving average model.

For a series to be stationary, it is necessary for the autocorrelations to drop quickly into insignificance as the number of lags increases. This is true of our short- and long-differenced series in Figure 6.7: the autocorrelations drop below the 1.96 standard error bounds after the second lag, with one exception.

There is still a significant autocorrelation at the twelve-months span in the long-differenced series. However, it is now negative and has declined to a value of about 0.4. Further short and long differencing cannot improve on the autocorrelation series shown in Figure 6.7. We will not let this moderate autocorrelation trouble us, since we cannot get rid of it by differencing. Furthermore, since we are testing the significance of autocorrelations at the 0.05 level of significance, we could expect to find at least one significant

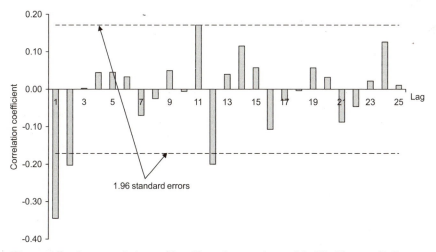

Figure 6.7 Autocorrelations of hotel/motel room demand in Washington, D.C., twelve-span differences of one-span differences
Source: author

autocorrelation in twenty consecutive lagged values even of a truly random series (Makridakis, Wheelwright and Hyndman, 1998: 326). That is, in one case out of twenty, an autocorrelation may appear to be significant when it is really not significant.

Consequently, we will use the series represented in Figure 6.7 to identify the most appropriate form of our ARMA model.

Identification phase

In this stage, the combination of two forecasting processes producing the best simulation of the historical series is tentatively identified. The two methods are autoregression, as discussed in Chapter 5, and a moving average process which is completely different from the concept of moving averages we discussed at the outset of Chapter 4.

Autoregressive models

Recall the form of the autoregression equation discussed in Chapter 5:

$$A_t = a + b_1 A_{t-1} + b_2 A_{t-2} + \cdots + b_n A_{t-n} \qquad (6.3)$$

where A = actual value in the time series
        a = a constant identified through computational iteration
        b = coefficient identified through computational iteration, called the 'autocorrelation'
        t = some time period
        n = number of past values included.

'Computational iteration' indicates that, from a set initial value of the constant or a coefficient, a computer program tries different values to improve the ability of the equation to simulate the time series, that is, reduce the squared error (or some other measure of error) of the forecast series compared to the actual time series.

The number of past values included on the right side of the autoregressive equation (that is, the value of n) identifies the model's *order*. If, for example, we include only one past value (A_{t-1}), then it is a first order autoregressive model. If we include three past values (A_{t-1}, A_{t-2}, and A_{t-3}), then we have a third order autoregressive model. Of course, the number of autocorrelations equals the number of terms on the right-hand side and the order of the model.

Moving average models

Unfortunately, the term, 'moving average,' has been adopted in this context to refer to a type of model that has no relationship to the moving average models discussed in Chapter 4. Here, 'moving average' refers to a relationship between actual values in our time series and successive error terms (the actual values minus the forecast values). The general form of the moving average model is:

$$A_t = a + e_t - c_1 e_{t-1} - c_2 e_{t-2} - \cdots - c_m e_{t-m} \qquad (6.4)$$

where   A = actual value
$\quad\quad\quad a$ = a constant identified through computational iteration
$\quad\quad\quad c$ = coefficient identified through computational iteration
$\quad\quad\quad e$ = error term
$\quad\quad\quad t$ = some time period
$\quad\quad\quad m$ = number of past error values included.

As for the autoregressive model, the order of the moving average model is indicated by the number of error terms included in the equation (that is, the value of m).

The Box–Jenkins approach combines these two models (called an autoregressive moving average, or ARMA, model) in order to produce the best simulation of the time series. The general equation of such a combined model is:

$$A_t = a + b_1 A_{t-1} + \cdots + b_n A_{t-n} + e_t - c_1 e_{t-1} - \cdots - c_m e_{t-m} \qquad (6.5)$$

where   A = actual value
$\quad\quad\quad a$ = a constant identified through computational iteration
$\quad\quad\quad b_i$ = coefficient identified through computational iteration
$\quad\quad\quad c_i$ = coefficient identified through computational iteration
$\quad\quad\quad e$ = error term
$\quad\quad\quad t$ = some time period
$\quad\quad\quad n$ = number of past actual values included
$\quad\quad\quad m$ = number of past error values included.

Procedures for identifying the appropriate model

There are a large number of autoregressive models we might use to best represent our time series for forecasting purposes. There is also a large number of moving average models we might use as well. And there are an even larger number of ARMA models available to us. One of the distinctive features of the Box–Jenkins strategy is the process of examining certain data in order to provisionally identify the appropriate ARMA model in advance for forecasting.

The data examined are the autocorrelations and the partial autocorrelations. The autocorrelations are the same correlation coefficients we discussed with regard to identifying trend or seasonality in our time series. We compute these coefficients for a number of past values individually and chart them similarly to Figure 6.5.

It is helpful to examine twenty or so autocorrelations for certain patterns that suggest the appropriate model. Computing twenty equations similar to Equations 6.3, 6.4 or 6.5 is tedious and prone to error in a spreadsheet program. Rather, you should use a statistical package, such as Statistica™ that performs the relevant analyses for you to examine.

Partial autocorrelations represent the degree of association between A_t and any A_{t-n} after the effects of intervening lagged values have been removed or 'partialled out'. Recall autoregression Equation 6.3 above. This form is used to compute the partial autocorrelation coefficients for our series:

$$A_t = a + d_1 A_{t-1} + d_2 A_{t-2} + \cdots + d_n A_{t-n} \tag{6.6}$$

where   A = actual values
      t = some time period
      a = constant term
      d = partial autocorrelation coefficient
      n = number of past values included.

Equation 6.6 is an autoregression equation, that is, the correlation coefficients are estimated by least squares regression (see Chapter 7 for more on this). The d values estimate the partial autocorrelation coefficients of the length of the lag. For example in Equation 6.6, the second partial autocorrelation coefficient is d_2 because the lag is two periods.

It is customary to examine twenty or so partial autocorrelation coefficients to discern certain patterns. If, for example, you wanted to compute twenty partial autocorrelation coefficients, you would have to compute twenty equations similar to Equation 6.6. This is tedious to say the least, and underlines the importance of using a statistical package to conduct the Box–Jenkins analysis.

Table 6.3 is a decision matrix for identifying the appropriate form of the ARMA model. The order of the autoregressive or moving average model is suggested by the pattern of the autocorrelations and partial autocorrelations.

Table 6.3   ARMA models suggested by a time series' autocorrelations and partial autocorrelations

Model (order)	Autocorrelations	Partial autocorrelations
Autoregressive (p)	Tail off	Cut off after lag p
Moving average (q)	Cut off after lag q	Tail off
ARMA (p,q)	Tail off	Tail off

Source: Vandaele (1983: 94).

To 'cut off' means to drop immediately to statistical insignificance, while to 'tail off' is to decline over time into insignificance.

Figures 6.8–6.12 present examples that illustrate the decision matrix. Figure 6.8 shows autocorrelations and partial autocorrelations for the autroregressive models of order 1: that is, models containing one past value on the right-hand side of Equation 6.6. The dashed horizontal lines indicate the 1.96 standard error threshold for significance at a 95 per cent confidence level. In both cases, the first autocorrelations are substantial, but they tail off in an exponential fashion to zero. The bottom two examples in Figure 6.8 demonstrate a decaying sine wave (see Figure 7.2 in Chapter 7). It is the

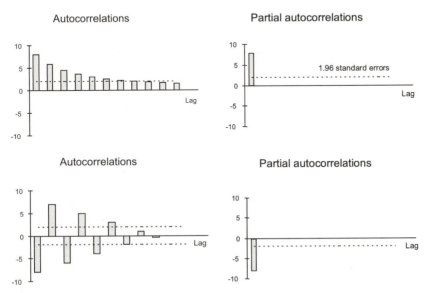

Figure 6.8   Autoregressive models of order 1
Source: author

pattern of the partial autocorrelations that indicates whether the autocorrelation model should include one past value, or two. This is indicated by the number of significant partial autocorrelations. For an autoregressive model of order 1, there should be only one partial autocorrelation significant at the 95 per cent confidence level.

Figure 6.9 indicates that the autocorrelation model of order 2 also shows autocorrelations tailing off to zero rather quickly. However, two partial autocorrelations are significantly different from zero, rather than only one as in the order 1 model. Note the middle two examples in this figure indicate decaying sine waves.

Figures 6.10 and 6.11 display the salient characteristics of moving average models of orders 1 and 2, respectively. Moving average models show partial autocorrelations declining to zero rapidly. It is the number of significant partial autocorrelations that determine whether the moving average model is of order 1 or 2.

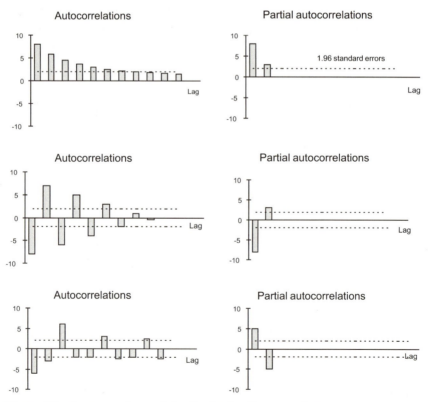

Figure 6.9   Autoregressive models of order 2.   *Source*: author

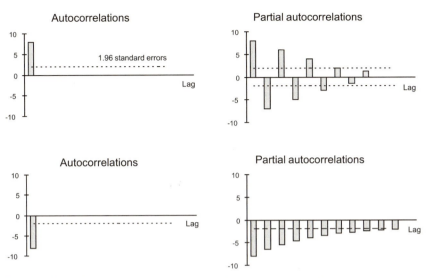

Figure 6.10 Moving average models of order 1. *Source*: author

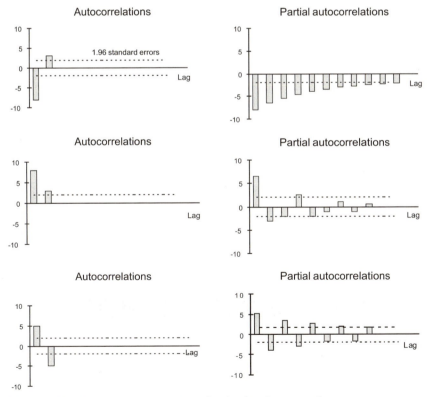

Figure 6.11 Moving average models of order 2. *Source*: author

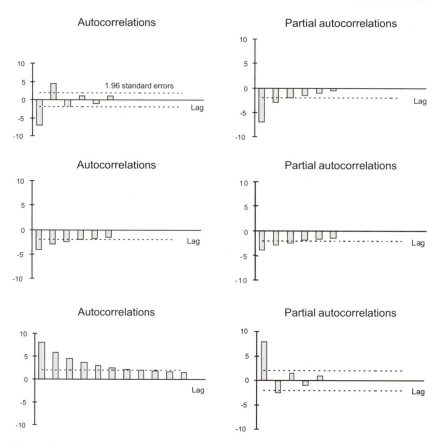

Figure 6.12 Autoregressive moving average models order 1,1
Source: author

Finally, Figure 6.12 shows the patterns suggesting an autoregressive moving average model of order 1,1: that is, including one lagged variable and one error term. Patterns of more complex ARMA models are beyond the scope of this text.

Identifying the appropriate room-demand ARMA model

Figure 6.13 shows the autocorrelations and partial autocorrelations for hotel/motel room demand in Washington, D.C. (the autocorrelations chart is a repeat of Figure 6.7). The autocorrelations (disregarding the outlier value at twelve months lag) cut off into insignificance after two months, suggesting a moving average model of two lags, or MA(2). The partial autocorrelations tail off to

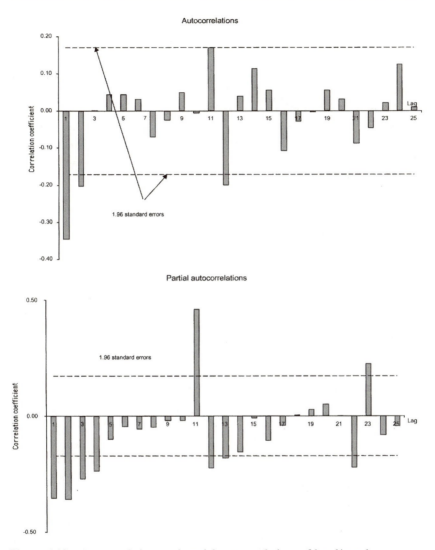

Figure 6.13 Autocorrelations and partial autocorrelations of hotel/motel room demand in Washington, D.C., twelve-span differences of one-span differences
Source: author

insignificance, also suggesting a moving average model. Consequently, a moving average model of order MA(2) is our first choice.

We will test the validity of this model. It is important to have backup models we can turn to if this first choice model proves invalid through diagnostic checking. Upon review of Figure 6.12, it seems appropriate to include ARMA models incorporating autoregressive processes of orders 1 and

2 along with the order 2 moving average process. This is usually represented by ARMA(1,2) and ARMA(2,2). These will be tested if our MA(2) model fails its diagnostic checking.

Identification phase summary

In the identification phase of the Box–Jenkins approach, we examine the autocorrelations and the partial autocorrelations to determine which of three methods to test for developing a good forecasting model: the autoregressive method, the moving average method or the autoregressive moving average method.

- If the autocorrelations decay exponentially and there is one significant partial autocorrelation, than the autoregressive model of order 1 – AR(1) – is suggested.
- If the partial autocorrelations decay exponentially and there is one significant autocorrelation, then the moving average model of order 1 – MA(1) – is suggested.
- If both the autocorrelations and the partial autocorrelations decay exponentially to zero at lags p and 8, respectively, then the ARMA model is suggested – AR(p,q).
- If the autocorrelations show a decaying sine wave pattern, and there are two significant partial autocorrelations then an AR(2) model is indicated.
- If the partial autocorrelations indicate a decaying sine wave pattern, then an MA(2) model is suggested.

It is seldom useful to proceed beyond these models into higher order ones.

Estimation phase

We have identified the most appropriate model and two backup models. However, before we estimate the parameters of the preferred model, we need to make one additional choice: whether to include a constant in the model or not. Recall that we are forecasting a series that has been differenced once by a span of one period and again by a span of twelve periods. Theory does indicate whether a constant is appropriate for such a series or not. Consequently, we can estimate the model twice: once with a constant and second without a constant.

The least squares regression method is seldom appropriate for estimating the parameters (coefficients) of an ARMA model. Rather, a maximum likelihood estimation is used in most computer programs. The process is iterative and finds the values of a set of parameters that maximizes the likelihood of having

Table 6.4 Parameters of a moving average (2) model of Washington, D.C., hotel/motel room demand twice-differenced series

Model/parameter	Estimated value	t-Statistic	t-Statistic significance level
Constant included:			
Constant	0.047	0.059	0.953
$q(1)$	−0.669	−7.947	0.000
$q(2)$	−0.131	−1.554	0.122
No constant:			
$q(1)$	−0.669	−7.975	0.000
$q(2)$	−0.131	−1.561	0.121

generated our actual sample of observations. The program selects starting values for the parameters and tries different values until it finds the combination that minimizes the sum of the squared errors. Occasionally, the parameter estimates in a program may not converge after fifty iterations or so. This is a signal to try different starting values for the parameters.

Table 6.4 shows the results of this process for the second order moving average model of our twice-differenced series.

The constant turned out to be not significantly different from zero (note the t-statistic is significant only at the 0.953 level), so we drop it and focus on the moving average model without a constant. The order 2 moving average model has one significant parameter, $q(1)$, or the first error term. The second error term is significantly different from zero at the 0.122 level of confidence, rather high. This does not appear to be a good model for forecasting the differenced series of hotel/motel room demand.

Instead, we investigate whether one of the alternative ARMA models may prove more successful in achieving significant coefficients. Indeed, the ARMA(1,2) and ARMA(2,2) models produce parameters all significantly different from zero at the 0.05 level of significance or lower. We decide to drop the MA(2) model and submit these alternatives to the next phase: diagnostic checking.

Diagnostic-checking phase

We have identified two ARMA models that appear to be valid for forecasting hotel/motel room demand in Washington, D.C., In this phase, we examine these models to see if they provide sound estimates of parameters that fit the

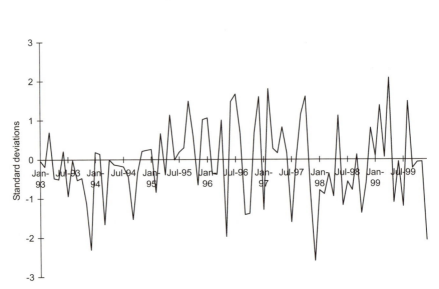

Figure 6.14 Errors from the ARMA(1,2) model of the differenced series of hotel/motel room demand standardized to variance of 1, monthly, 1993–99
Source: author

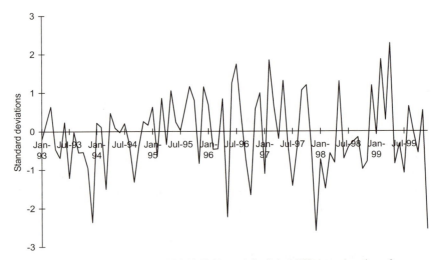

Figure 6.15 Errors from the ARMA(2,2) model of the differenced series of hotel/motel room demand standardized to variance of 1, monthly, 1993–99
Source: author

time series well. Four tests are available for checking the validity of the model (Vandaele, 1983: 123):

1 Stationarity analysis.
2 Residual analyses.
3 Fitting extra parameters.
4 Omitting parameters.

We will focus here on one of the most important diagnostic checks: residual analyses.

If a model accurately represents the ARMA process governing our time series, the errors of the model should have a mean of zero, a constant variance, and be uncorrelated with each other over time. We can examine the first two assumptions by viewing plots of the errors of our ARMA(1,2) and ARMA(2,2) models in Figures 6.14 and 6.15. The errors have been standardized to a variance of one, so that the values are ratios at each month of the error to the standard deviation for the series. This aids inspection of the errors: there are no absolute values greater than 3 that should be investigated for measurement error or some other explanation for being an outlier.

These charts indicate that both models have means near zero but variances that are somewhat larger for later values than for earlier ones. This is troublesome but not fatal for either model. This, coupled with the lack of alternative models, encourages us to move onto the next test.

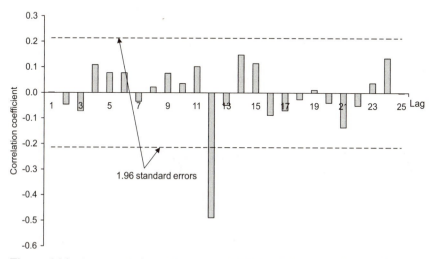

Figure 6.16 Autocorrelations of errors for ARMA(1,2) hotel/motel room demand model
Source: author

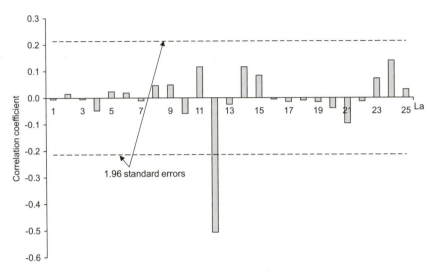

Figure 6.17 Autocorrelations of errors for ARMA(2,2) hotel/motel demand model
Source: author

An important assumption of the ARMA model is that the errors are not correlated with one another. We can investigate this assumption by reviewing the autocorrelations of the errors. If there are a number of significant autocorrelations, then the model has not been specified properly, and an alternative should be tried.

Figures 6.16 and 6.17 present the autocorrelations of the errors for the ARMA(1,2) and ARMA(2,2) models. The horizontal dashed lines indicate the thresholds at the 0.05 level of significance (1.96 standard errors): any autocorrelations greater than this threshold are significant at this level. In both models, only one correlation is greater than the 0.05 level of significance: the span of twelve periods. This single autocorrelation is not enough to cause us to reject either of these models.

Portmanteau tests for autocorrelation

An alternative test is available to identify significant autocorrelations: the Ljung–Box test (Makridakis, Wheelwright and Hyndman, 1998: 319). In contrast to the previous method of checking for significant autocorrelations one autocorrelation at a time, this test is part of a class called 'portmanteau tests' because, like a portmanteau or suitcase, it checks the set of autocorrelation coefficients all at the same time, as a portmanteau or suitcase holds a variety of clothing all at once.

The Ljung–Box Q* statistic is computed as follows:

$$Q^* = n(n + 2) \sum_{k=1}^{h} \frac{r_k^2}{n - k} \qquad (6.7)$$

where Q* = Ljung–Box Q* statistic
   n = number of data points or observations
   k = a lag
   h = maximum lag considered.
   r = autocorrelation coefficients for different lags

The resulting Q* is compared to the chi-square distribution with ($h - m$, m = number of parameters in the fitted model) degrees of freedom to determine if the collection of autocorrelation coefficients is significantly different from zero.

Applying the Ljung–Box test to our ARMA(1,2) and ARMA(2,2) models finds the Q* statistic for each between the 0.05 and 0.10 levels of significance for 81 degrees of freedom by the chi-square test. Consequently, we reject the hypothesis that the errors for either model are correlated with one another.

The older Box–Pierce test is another portmanteau test that has often been applied here, the distribution of its 'Q statistic' is not as close to the chi-square distribution as is the Ljung–Box Q* statistic (Makridakis, Wheelwright and Hyndman, 1998: 319).

In summary, we selected two alternative models to the one suggested by the identification phase, because the ARMA(0,2) failed to produce significant parameters. We then submitted the alternative ARMA(1,2) and ARMA(2,2) models to diagnostic checking. This revealed that the error terms show variances that grow somewhat over time. The terms show significant autocorrelations only at the span of twelve months. We would expect that at the 0.05 level of significance that one out of twenty autocorrelations would appear to be significant when it is not. The Ljung–Box test for autocorrelation similarly suggests the errors are not correlated with one another.

We would prefer models that have constant variances and no autocorrelation of the error terms. But given the lack of viable alternative ARMA models, the ARMA(1,2) and ARMA(2,2) models are employed to forecast our hotel/model room demand time series to see how well they perform over the past.

Forecasting phase

The final phase of the Box–Jenkins approach is to use the best model or models that pass diagnostic checking to forecast future values of the time series. We begin by forecasting the next period from the model, and then

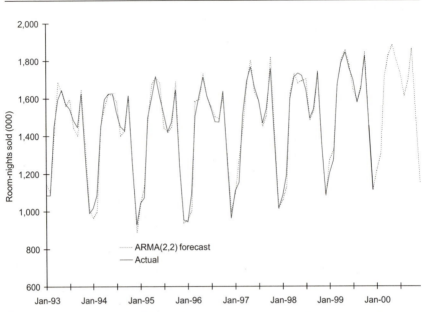

Figure 6.18 Actual and ARMA(2,2) forecasts of hotel/motel room demand in Washington, D.C., monthly, 1993–2000
Source: author

successive periods as far out as we wish. At some point, we will be using forecast values rather than know past values for the A_{t-n}. When we run out of past values of the error term, we assume it to equal zero for all future values. The further ahead we forecast with the model, the greater the chances of substantial forecast error, however.

Once we have obtained our forecasts, we need transform them back into the terms of our original series. If we transformed the original series into logarithms, we need to produce the anti-logarithms of the forecasts. If we differenced the series to achieve stationarity or remove seasonality, we achieve a forecast series of these differences. The forecast differences should then be added to the original series to produce the series of forecast values.

In our case, the ARMA(1,2) produces a MAPE of 4.3 per cent, while the ARMA(2,2) achieves 2.2 per cent. This gives the edge to the ARMA(2,2) model and it is chosen as the best ARMA model for forecasting hotel/motel room demand in the Washington, D.C., area by the Box-Jenkins approach. The Theil's U-statistic for this model over the 1993–9 period is 0.108, indicating it is considerably more accurate than the naive model.

Figure 6.18 shows the actual hotel/model room demand series for the Washington, D.C., area, along with the series forecast by the ARMA(2,2) model of the differenced series. As the MAPE indicates, the forecast model follows the actual series quite closely, certainly more closely than the seasonal naive model with its 4.0 per cent MAPE.

Applications

Di Benedetto and Bojanic (1993) used the Box–Jenkins approach to model visits to Cypress Gardens, Florida, to test the tourism area life cycle hypothesis. This hypothesis states that tourism areas go through an evolution over time, described by an S-shaped pattern. Their visitor volume rises rapidly after opening, then continues to grow for a time but at slower rates. Finally, visitor volume reaches a peak (stagnation) and will decline if efforts are not made to rejuvenate demand, such as targeting new markets or adding new attractions. Their best ARIMA model of 139 quarters of visitor volume produced accurate forecasts over periods not characterized by rejuvenation efforts. It was not quite as good as a regression model tested against it.

Witt, Witt and Wilson (1994) found a Box–Jenkins ARIMA model outperformed five other methods in forecasting quarterly visitor flows from the U.K. to four countries. However, it was not much more accurate than the Naive 1, no-change model. They also found that the international terrorist activity occasioned by the U.S. bombing of Libya in 1986 depressed U.K. travel to Greece and Spain.

Turner, Kulendran and Pergat (1995) compared the accuracy of ARIMA models to an exponential smoothing method for forecasting quarterly visitor arrivals in New Zealand from five countries and five multinational regions. They concluded that where the series showed a regular trend and highly variable seasonality, then the exponential smoothing method performed better. But when trend and seasonality were not marked, then the ARIMA model produced the more accurate forecasts. However, the MAPEs for their best origin models ranged from 6 per cent to 38 per cent. This suggests that testing other methods would prove fruitful.

Dharmaratne (1995) tested a number of Box–Jenkins ARIMA models on simulating long-stay visitor arrivals in Barbados over 1956–92 and for producing ex post forecasts of one to five years in length. He found that an ARIMA(2,1,1) produced 'excellent' forecasts for one to two years out, but that no method was very accurate for longer forecast periods.

In an extension of Dharmaratne (1995), Dalrymple and Greenidge (1999) report on quarterly forecasts of arrivals in Barbados from the U.S., Canada and the U.K. They reported that U.S. arrivals were 'not very predictable in behaviour', and discrepancies between forecast and actual visitors from

Canada were significant, as well. Overall, the ARIMA models chosen produce ex post forecasting errors of up to 9.5 per cent, but no comparisons against the naive model were reported.

Turner, Kulendran and Fernando (1997a) compared six different methods for forecasting quarterly tourism flows to each of Japan, Australia and New Zealand from seven originating countries over the 1978–95 period. They grouped the quarters into four 'periodic series' for each origin-destination pair and applied Holt's exponential smoothing method and the autoregressive method to the series to develop ex post forecasts. They tested these against Winters's exponential smoothing method and the Box–Jenkins ARIMA for the straight seasonalized series. They found that the ARIMA models applied to the seasonalized series generally proved more accurate than any of these others.

Testing the results of Chan (1993), Chu (1998b) compared the forecasting accuracy of a Box–Jenkins ARIMA model dealing with seasonal and annual differences and a sine wave model for forecasting visitor arrivals in Singapore. The models were built with monthly arrivals data over July 1977 to December 1988 and tested over the ex post period of the ensuing nineteen months. The ARIMA model produced only two turning-point errors out of a possible sixteen, but its MAPE was only marginally better than the sine wave model.

Chu (1998c) tested six forecasting methods in forecasting monthly visitor arrivals in ten Asian-Pacific nations over the 1975–94 period: Naive 1, Naive 2, time trend regression, sine wave regression, ARIMA and Holt-Winters. Using the MAPE as his measure in eighteen-month ex post forecasts, he found ARIMA models produced superior forecasts for nine of the ten countries. The ARIMA models also reproduced most of the turning points in the base time series, as well. The Holt-Winters method was the second most accurate in this forecasting.

Chan, Hui and Yuen (1999) compared different models in capturing the effect of the Gulf War on arrivals in Singapore from five long-haul origins. Developing ARIMA, exponential trend, quadratic trend, and Naive 1 and 2 models on seasonally adjusted monthly series covering August 1984 to July 1990, and August 1985 to July 1991 periods, the authors compared these in capturing the effects of the Gulf War of August 1990 to February 1991. Comparing MAPEs of the models over the two periods, the Naive 2 model proved best at forecasting the effects of the Gulf War (the first period tested), while it vied for first place with an ARIMA model over the second period. The authors surmised that the Naive 2 performed best in the earlier period because it quickly incorporated the most recent data while the other models included outmoded data in producing their forecasts.

1. Check for stationarity in the mean and variance of the historical time series, and resolve any nonstationarity by transforming the original series, first for variance and then for means.

2. Check for seasonality and resolve by seasonal differencing.

3. Compute the autocorrelations and the partial autocorrelations in the transformed series.

4. Examine these to rank the most likely forms of the forecasting model.

5. Compute the coefficients of this model and inspect its parameters for significance; if one or more are not significant, choose the next model suggested.

6. Use the model that produces significant parameters to forecast your transformed series.

7. Examine the residuals for stationarity of mean and variance and test for autocorrelations; if any are found, try the next best model in step 4.

8. Once you have found a satisfactory model, use it to forecast the transformed series.

9. Transform the forecast series back into the terms of the original time series and compute its MAPE and Theil's U-statistic for acceptability.

Figure 6.19   Steps in applying the Box–Jenkins approach

Conclusion

The Box–Jenkins approach is a powerful if complex approach to building a forecasting model for time series. (Figure 6.19 summarizes the process.) Examination of certain correlations of a series suggests the best model to forecast it. This is then diagnosed for validity and, if it passes the tests, is used for forecasting.

While the ARMA variations are nearly endless, in most cases a first or second order model will produce reliable forecast values. Going beyond this does not appear to provide significant advances in reliability or validity (Makridakis, Wheelwright and Hyndman, 1998: 345).

The Box–Jenkins approach is not well suited for the computer spreadsheet. Rather, the forecaster should make use of one of the statistical packages currently available for the personal computer. These programs usually have the additional advantage of identifying parsimonious models, which usually are the best. Some forecasting packages determine the best model 'behind the scenes' and only present it to you at the end. The forecaster then accepts this model on blind faith. Others present results at each step and allow the forecaster to choose the next procedure. These 'manual' packages allow the forecaster to exercise informed judgement and avoid outrageous errors.

Notes

1 Published by StatSoft™, Inc., 1994.
2 In this context, the F-test determines whether the variances of two samples are statistically equal, that is their difference is not due to chance. Formally, the F-statistic is the ratio of the variances of the two samples. If this ratio exceeds a certain threshold value, then the differences are not due to chance. The threshold value is derived from the distribution of the F-statistic, and depends on the sizes of the samples.

For further information

Jarrett, J. (1991). *Business Forecasting Methods*. 2nd edition, ch. 9. Blackwell.

Makridakis, S., Wheelwright, S. C. and Hyndman, R. J. (1998), *Forecasting: Methods and Applications*. 3rd edition, ch. 7. Wiley.

Moore, T. W. (1989). *Handbook of Business Forecasting*, pp. 87–94. Harper & Row.

Shim, J. K., Siegel, J. G. and Liew, C. J. (1994). *Strategic Business Forecasting*, ch. 8 Probus.

Vandaele, W. (1983). *Applied Time Series and Box–Jenkins Models*, chs 2–6, Academic Press.

7

Causal methods: regression analysis

We now move into the realm of causation, where we are interested in how one or more variables affect the one we are trying to forecast. Instead of trying to model a relationship between the current and past values of a time series, we now look for the best model that explains *why* our variable changes as it does over time.

> causal methods . . . develop projections based on the mathematical relationship between the series being examined and variables which influence that series. (Moore, 1989: 109)

There are two major approaches to causal modelling popular in tourism forecasting. One is the *linear regression method*, where our forecast variable is dependent on, or explained by, one or more independent variables. We attempt to quantify this relationship in a single equation through statistical analysis.

The other approach is to develop a set of regression equations linked together by certain variables that are both dependent and independent variables. These are often called *structural models*.[1] This approach to tourism demand forecasting is discussed in Chapter 8.

This chapter explores the advantages and limitations of the *linear regression method* and its logic. The simplest application in forecasting is presented, followed by more complex models. Then we discuss the procedures for developing a linear regression model of tourism demand, with special attention to variables that can help explain tourism demand, and how to evaluate the model's validity. Finally, applications of this method in tourism forecasting are briefly presented, followed by resources for learning more about linear regression analysis in forecasting tourism demand.

Linear regression analysis

The general form of a *linear regression model* is:

$$Y = a + b_1X_1 + b_2X_2 + \ldots + b_nX_n + e \tag{7.1}$$

where Y = the dependent, or forecast, variable (for example, tourism demand)

a = the intercept constant

b = slope coefficients

X = independent, or explanatory, variables

n = number of explanatory variables

e = residual.

The objective in forecasting is to derive sound estimates of the coefficients or parameters (a, b_1, b_2, etc.) so that we can estimate the forecast variable based on the values of the explanatory variables.

Advantages of regression analysis

The linear regression method has a number of advantages over extrapolative methods:

- *It explicitly addresses causal relationships that are evident in the real world*. These include the effects of prices, income changes, marketing programmes and competitors' actions on tourism demand.
- *It aids assessment of alternative business plans*. Managers can simulate the effects of various marketing plans or government policies (for example, taxes, expenditures, regulation and subsidies) on tourism demand.

- *It provides several statistical measures of accuracy.* Regression models provide a great deal of information that can be used to assess their validity and improve them.
- *Regression models accommodate a wide range of relationships.* These include linear and non-linear associations, as well as lagged effects of explanatory variables over several periods.

Limitations of regression analysis

There are disadvantages to using the linear regression method for general applications:

- *The time and money costs of operating regression models can be large.* Except for simple models, regression analysis requires special computer programs to handle the data. Moreover, the time needed to gather, analyse and prepare the data for regression modelling is substantial. Finally, identifying a valid and statistically significant model can be quite time consuming.
- *Developing the correct relationships requires substantial skill.* Theory gives some guidance, but many important relationships must be 'teased' out of the data. The more you work with regression analysis, the better you become at discovering important connections among data series.
- *Often explanatory variables must be forecast in order to obtain forecasts of the variable of interest.* This adds additional time and money costs. Moreover, forecasting the explanatory variables increases the chances of forecasting error.
- *It assumes the explanatory variables are not affected by the dependent variable.* In many cases this assumption causes no problem. However, there may be occasions where there is a feedback of the dependent variable, say tourism expenditures abroad, on one of the explanatory variables, such as exchange rates. Another potential case is where rising visitor volumes push up prices at a destination, which is often a variable used to 'explain' visitor volume to that destination.

Despite these limitations, regression analysis remains the most widely used approach in tourism forecasting.

There are two domains where one can profitably conduct regression analysis: cross-sectional analysis and time series analysis. In cross-sectional analysis, we analyse relationships among variables across space with time usually held constant. For example, we could regress the number of visitors to twenty countries in 1999 against expenditures on visitor promotional programmes, price structures, exchange rates and visitor capacities of these countries. This could be helpful in suggesting the factors that affect visitor flows among countries during a year.

In time series regression analysis it is time that varies, not space. We look for patterns among variables over time, to determine how to quantitatively relate variables that help explain movements in our dependent variable.

We are limiting our discussion here to the use of regression analysis across time, with space held constant. We are interested in the shape of the future for a given destination or other tourism product or market.

The logic of regression analysis

Consider Figure 7.1, which presents the annual series on hotel/motel room demand in the Washington, D.C., metropolitan area. One forecasting approach is to summarize these data in a straight line that we can then extend out into the future, in this case, 2000. There are at least three different extrapolations that might provide this summary.

The *mean line* in Figure 7.1 is the mean of the time series over the 1987–99 period. While it is a summary of these data, it is not a very accurate forecasting model for 2000, because it does not capture the rising trend of the data. The *end-point line* simply connects the 1987 value to the 1999 value and extends this straight line to 2000. It, too, summarizes the data and has the

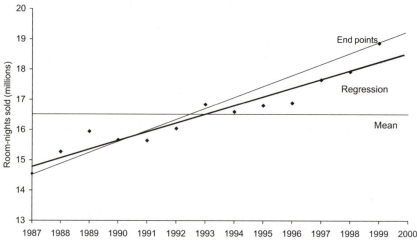

Figure 7.1   Simple models of Washington, D.C., hotel/motel room demand, annually, 1987–99
Source: Smith Travel Research and author

advantage of actually incorporating two values from the series. However, it can be highly volatile over time, varying in slope with the first and last values in the series.

The *regression line* is a linear time trend regression of the room-demand values on the years they relate to. It has the advantage of providing the best 'fit' of the data. That is, it is designed to minimize the sum of the distances between the regression line and each actual value, called the *residuals*. It actually minimizes the sum of the squared vertical departures (that is, residuals) of the data from the regression line; as a result, the technique is called 'least squares regression' or, sometimes, 'ordinary least squares regression' (OLS). It is much less sensitive to the beginning and final values in the time series than is the end-point line.

Simple regression: linear time trend

We begin with simple or univariate regression, where there is only one explanatory variable. One of the easiest and most popular forecasting methods is to regress a time series such as a measure of tourism demand on the periods to which it relates. In other words, it uses changes in time, such as the year or month, to 'explain' variations in the series to be forecast. In its simplest form, the *linear time trend* regression indicates the number of units the dependent variable (for example, room-nights sold) changes for each one unit change in time (for example, a month). If this is successful over the past values, that is, the regression equation is statistically significant and valid over our time series, then we can have confidence that it can simulate future values, as well.

A discussion of time trend regression will illustrate the major features of simple least squares regression models, that is, regression models that have only one equation and one explanatory variable affecting the variable of interest to us.

The form of the *simple regression model* is:

$$Y_t = a + bX_t + e_t \tag{7.2}$$

where Y = the dependent or forecast variable, such as tourism demand
   t = a time period
   a = intercept constant estimated by least squares regression
   b = slope coefficient estimated by least squares regression
   X = explanatory (independent) variable
   e = residual.

In the regression line in Figure 7.1, the number of hotel/motel room-nights sold annually in the Washington, D.C., metropolitan area is the dependent variable, and the year is the explanatory variable. The intercept constant (also called the 'constant term') a is the value of the dependent variable when the explanatory variable equals zero.[2] Since it is customary to chart the dependent variable Y on the vertical axis, or Y-axis, and the explanatory variable X on the horizontal axis, or X-axis, the intercept constant marks where the regression line crosses the Y-axis when the X-axis value is zero.

The slope coefficient b indicates at what rate the regression line rises as the explanatory value increases. Formally, it is the ratio of the increase in Y to the increase in X. The intercept constant and the slope coefficient make up the *parameters* of the regression equation. Most of the effort in applying regression analysis is devoted to estimating these parameters, because they represent our best estimate of what the true values are of these characteristics over the population of all time periods.

A comment about sample and population in the context of time series is appropriate here. Our *sample* is the actual time series of data we have. In this case, our sample is hotel/motel room demand for the years 1987–94. We can think of this as drawn from the *population* of all years, from the distant past to the distant future.

As a practical matter, we are seldom interested in 'forecasting' months prior to our time series (sometimes called 'backcasting') as an end in itself. But we are inherently interested in months, quarters or years to come, at least over some reasonable future. Consequently, in building forecasting models by linear regression, we are trying to infer something about the *population* of all periods from our recorded past into our future from our *sample* of only some past periods included in our time series.

Finally, the residual term reminds us that we are producing *estimates* of the dependent variable and that these will not necessarily equal the actual values for every period. For most periods, there will be a difference between the OLS estimate and the actual value, that is, a residual. Least squares regression is designed to make the sum of the squared residuals as small as possible.

There are a number of forms of the equation for computing the intercept, a, and the slope coefficient, b. One of the easiest approaches to use is:

$$b = \frac{n \sum XY - (\sum X)(\sum Y)}{n \sum X^2 - (\sum X)^2} \qquad (7.3)$$

$$a = \overline{Y} - b\overline{X} \qquad (7.4)$$

where b = slope coefficient
        n = number of observations or data points
        X = explanatory (independent) variable
        Y = dependent (forecast) variable
        a = intercept constant
        $\overline{Y}$ = mean of the dependent variable series
        $\overline{X}$ = mean of the explanatory variable series.

We will deal here only with least squares regression models that are *linear in their coefficients*, that is, they take the form of Equation 7.1. These need not be linear in their data, however. By transforming, or redefining, the original data series, we can employ least squares regression to produce non-linear trend lines, as we will see later.

Continuing with our example, we are attempting here to develop a regression model of annual hotel/motel room demand in Washington, D.C., that is:

$$H_t = a + bT_t + e_t \tag{7.5}$$

where H = room-nights sold annually
        t = a unit of time
        a = intercept constant
        b = slope coefficient
        T = a year
        e = residual.

Table 7.1 presents the Washington, D.C., hotel/motel room demand data and the computation of the time trend regression equation for this annual series.

The resulting forecast equation is thus:

$$H_t = -557.8 + 0.2882 * T_t \tag{7.6}$$

To obtain a forecast for any future year n years from now $(t + n)$, simply substitute the year into Equation 7.6. For example, the forecast for 2000 is:

$$H_{2000} = -557.8 + 0.2882 * 2000 = 18.60 \tag{7.7}$$

Non-linear time trends

The ordinary least squares regression methods used in tourism forecasting must be linear in their coefficients. However, this does not mean we are stuck with modelling only straight-line time trends. We can attempt to fit non-linear

Table 7.1 Computation of hotel/motel room demand regression coefficients

1. Period (t)	2. Time (T)	3. Room-nights sold in millions (H)	4. T * H	5. T²
1	1987	14.55	28 914	3 948 169
2	1988	15.27	30 362	3 952 144
3	1989	15.95	31 718	3 956 121
4	1990	15.67	31 174	3 960 100
5	1991	15.64	31 149	3 964 081
6	1992	16.04	31 956	3 968 064
7	1993	16.84	33 557	3 972 049
8	1994	16.59	33 088	3 976 036
9	1995	16.80	33 519	3 980 025
10	1996	16.88	33 694	3 984 016
11	1997	17.65	35 251	3 988 009
12	1998	17.92	35 807	3 992 004
13	1999	18.86	37 708	3 996 001
Sum	25 909	214.7	427 897	51 636 819
Mean	1993	16.51		

$$b = \frac{n\sum (T * H) - (\sum T)(\sum H)}{n\sum T^2 - (\sum T)^2}$$

$$b = \frac{(13 * 427\,897) - (25\,909 - 214.7)}{(13 * 51\,636\,819) - 25\,909 * 25\,909} = 0.2882$$

$$a = \overline{H} - b * \overline{T}$$

$$a = 16.51 - (0.2882 * 1993) = -557.8$$

trends to our data through models that are *non-linear in their data* but still linear in their coefficients. That is, linear regression models that incorporate transformed or redefined data.

Figure 7.2 shows four non-linear time trend models that are linear in their coefficients. The equations for these curves indicate the logarithmic, parabolic and sine transformations that underlie these curves. They can handle a variety of time trend patterns.

Nolan (1994) provides a strategy for achieving linearity in a time series by transforming data according to set rules and order, and this is summarized in Figure 7.3.

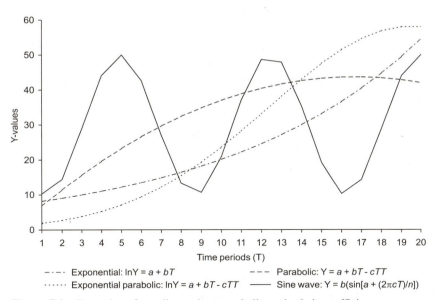

Figure 7.2 Examples of non-linear time trends linear in their coefficients
Source: author

A. Type of time series curve	B. Shape of time series curve	C. Possible transformations of Y values	D. Possible transformations of X values
Type 1		$Y \rightarrow Y^2 \rightarrow Y^3 \rightarrow Y^4$	$X \rightarrow \sqrt{X} \rightarrow \log X \rightarrow -1/\sqrt{X} \rightarrow -1/X$
Type 2		$Y \rightarrow \sqrt{Y} \rightarrow \log Y \rightarrow -1/\sqrt{Y} \rightarrow -1/Y$	$X \rightarrow \sqrt{X} \rightarrow \log X \rightarrow -1/\sqrt{X} \rightarrow -1/X$
Type 3		$Y \rightarrow \sqrt{Y} \rightarrow \log Y \rightarrow -1/\sqrt{Y} \rightarrow -1/Y$	$X \rightarrow X^2 \rightarrow X^3 \rightarrow X^4$
Type 4		$Y \rightarrow Y^2 \rightarrow Y^3 \rightarrow Y^4$	$X \rightarrow X^2 \rightarrow X^3 \rightarrow X^4$

Figure 7.3 Suggested transformations to achieve linearity in time series data
Source: Nolan (1994: 227).

To apply the transformations suggested in Figure 7.3, first look at the shape of the time series curve. For example, chart A in Figure 7.4 reproduces the non-linear series of short-haul international visitors from Israel shown in Figure 4.5 in Chapter 4. This series looks like a Type 3 curve in Figure 7.3. Consequently, we can apply the transformations suggested in column D of Figure 7.3, in the order suggested, beginning with the square root of the visitor volume. Chart B of Figure 7.4 indicates this transformation does not remove all of the non-linearity, so we proceed to the next transformation suggested, the logarithm of the series.

As presented in chart C of Figure 7.4, this produces a linear series. Consequently, we redefine the regression model for forecasting short-haul visitors from Israel to be:

$$bg\ Y_t = a + bX_t \tag{7.8}$$

We can then apply the ordinary least squares regression method to Equation 7.8.

Note that the third transformation Nolan suggests, the negative reciprocal of the square root of visitor volume as shown in chart D of Figure 7.4, does not achieve additional linearity, but instead introduces further concavity compared to chart C. We follow the transformations suggested in Figure 7.4 and stop when we achieve linearity.

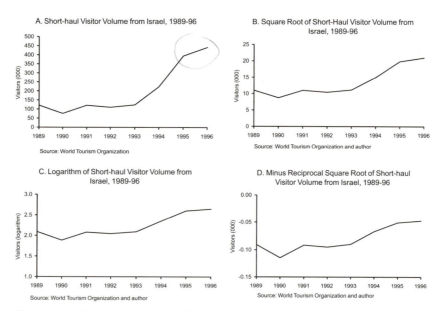

Figure 7.4 Transformations of a Type 3 time series curve to achieve linearity

If none of the transformations of the *Y*-variable in our time series achieves linearity, then we should try transforming the *X*-variable, as suggested in chart C of Figure 7.4. One of these transformations may be the only way to achieve linearity, but then we lose the simplicity of associating a visitor volume figure with a given year. But this may be a small price to pay to achieve linearity.

Misspecification

Before we move on to the multivariate regression method, we need to understand an important point. The simple regression method has limited application beyond the time trend. Tourism demand in its many aspects (airline traffic, hotel room demand, attraction attendance, etc.) is affected by more than one major variable. Consequently, when we try to model demand for a tourism product using one explanatory variable, we will necessarily misspecify the model and ensure the estimated relationship is statistically unreliable and invalid.

Misspecification, or specification error, occurs when the following assumption of linear regression analysis is violated: 'the conditional expectation of the dependent variable is an unchanging linear function of known independent variables' (Kennedy, 1992: 91).

Thus there are three sources of misspecification:

- when the set of independent variables omits relevant explanatory variables or includes irrelevant ones
- when the actual relationships are non-linear in the parameters
- when the parameters do not remain constant.

Tourism demand is generated by a complex of factors relating to the traveller, the destination, characteristics of the trip and other elements. A number of these are presented in Figure 7.6. Since the simple regression model includes only one independent variable to explain the future course of tourism demand, it is misspecified by definition. No amount of transformation of variables or change in model structure can redress this failure.

The linear time trend model is helpful in demonstrating the long-term trend of our forecast variable, which may be helpful in identifying the appropriate explanatory variables at work. This model may be useful in suggesting the general magnitude of our forecast variable in the long-term future. However, aside from these explanatory uses, simple regression models should be avoided by the forecaster who seeks an accurate, valid explanatory model of future tourism demand.

One other clarifying point. If you are working with monthly or quarterly data, then there is no inherent numerical value to represent each observation as there is when you use annual data. Consequently, you should number each observation consecutively from the first data point (number one) to the last data point. This time series of observation identifiers then serves as your explanatory variable in the simple time trend regression.

Multiple regression

As noted above, a regression model is misspecified when one or more relevant explanatory variables are excluded from the equation. The way we deal with this misspecification is to include other variables that significantly affect the one of interest to us. This is done by expanding the simple linear regression model into a multiple (or 'multivariate') regression model by including two or more explanatory variables in our regression equation. Please note that while simple regression analysis can be accomplished in a computer spreadsheet as shown in Table 7.1, multiple regression requires statistical programs to deal with the complex calculations. Some computer spreadsheet programs, such as Microsoft® Excel, include regression analysis modules that can perform multivariate regression analysis. There are also statistical programs that do so as well, such as Statistica™.

The general form of the multiple regression equation was presented as Equation 7.1. It is presented here specifically as a forecasting model:

$$Y_t = a + b_1 X_{1,t} + b_2 X_{2,t} + \cdots + b_n X_{n,t} + e_t \tag{7.9}$$

where Y = dependent (forecast) variable
a = intercept constant
b = slope coefficients
X = explanatory (independent) variables
t = a time period
n = number of explanatory variables
e = residual.

If there are two explanatory variables, then the equation describes a plane in three-dimensional space, with the slope coefficients indicating its tilt. If more than two explanatory variables are present, we are in 'hyperspace' of more than three dimensions. It is difficult to imagine this and impossible to display on a two-dimensional page.

We employ the same least squares regression technique discussed with regard to simple regression analysis to minimize the sum of the squared

1. *Draft your theory* of factors that affect the variable you wish to forecast, identifying the forecast (dependent) variable and important explanatory variables.

2. *Obtain time series of the dependent and explanatory variables you have identified.*

3. *Examine the correlations among these explanatory variables to identify any multicollinearity,* and remove this from your model.

4. *Specify expected relationships* of your explanatory variables to the dependent variable in mathematical form indicated by your theory:
   a. signs of the slope coefficients
   b. presence of lagged variables
   c. presence of dummy variables
   d. functional form, e.g., linear or non-linear.

5. *Identify initial models* as to form of the equation, explanatory variables included, and estimated parameters.

6. *Evaluate the model's validity* in light of your expectations in (4) and revise the model to deal with any aberrations.

7. *Assess the model's significance* and revise the model to rectify any problems.

8. *Use the model to forecast* future values when you are satisfied that it is theoretically correct and valid.

Figure 7.5   The regression model estimation process

residuals in multiple regression. That is, ordinary least squares minimizes the difference between the actual data in hyperspace and the hyperplane designated by our regression coefficients across all combinations of the values of the explanatory variables.

Figure 7.5 outlines the steps in developing and using a regression forecasting model.

Since multivariate regression forecast modelling is a complex activity and difficult to do well, we will walk through these steps using the annual Washington, D.C., hotel/motel room demand series as our example.

1 Draft your theory

Figure 7.6 lists a number of variables that should be considered for inclusion in a tourism demand forecasting model. In reviewing these, our emphasis in forecasting time series by regression analysis should be on variables that have changed significantly over the period of our historical series (here, 1987–99, inclusive). If a variable has not changed or changed only negligibly, it will not usually add much explanatory power to our forecasting model.

Push factors, sometimes called 'emissive' factors, are those characteristics of a population in an origin market that encourage travel away from home. For

1. Push factors (of origin)
   a. population size
   b. GDP and income trends
   c. income distribution
   d. education distribution
   e. age distribution
   f. leisure time
   g. family structure
   h. momentum

2. Pull factors (of destination)
   a. friends/relatives
   b. climate/weather
   c. commercial ties
   d. social/cultural ties
   e. destination marketing programmes
   f. distribution channels
   g. destination attractiveness
   h. special events
   i. complementary destinations
   j. habit

3. Resistance factors
   a. prices
      i. product price(s)
      ii. prices of substitutes
      iii. prices of complements
      iv. prices of necessities
      v. exchange rates
      vi. taxes and fees
   b. competitors' actions
   c. supply capacities
   d. distance
   e. travel time
   f. origin country exchange controls
   g. border control, customs and other frontier formalities
   h. arrival/departure taxes and terminal fees
   i. war/terrorism/crime/civil unrest
   j. natural and human-made disasters
   k. physical barriers

Figure 7.6 Potential explanatory variables in a regression model to forecast tourism demand

example, all else being equal, a larger *population* of an origin region will generate more trips than a smaller one. This is sometimes accounted for by placing the number of trips or travel expenditures on a per capita basis from the generating region in the regression model.

Gross domestic product and income trends acknowledge that a growing economy generates more sales, jobs and personal income than a stagnant one, and can be expected to originate more business and leisure travel than a sluggish one. Indeed, measures of overall personal income appear to be the most popular explanatory variables in tourism demand regression models. Often a measure of personal *disposable* income is used, by removing income-related taxes from gross personal income. In most developed countries, however, GDP, personal income and disposable personal income are highly correlated with one another, so there is often no clear advantage of one over the other.

Certain *income*, *age* and *educational* groups travel more than others do. If these groups are growing in an origin market, this can accelerate travel away from home. It is thought that *leisure time*, measured by number of days of paid vacation available or days in a year less workdays, is positively correlated with vacation travel, although it may be inversely correlated with business travel. *Certain family structures* (for example, husband-wife-no children, single adults) may travel more than others, such as those with school-aged children. If these are growing relative to the overall population of an area, additional travel may be generated.

Momentum refers to the effects of habit, friends' or relatives' recommendations, institutional relationships and other factors that may impel a future period's demand. This is often represented by including the value of the dependent variable lagged one or two periods as an explanatory variable. Some forecasters include time (for example, year, quarter, month) as an explanatory variable along with others. You should avoid this as it obscures interpretation of the other explanatory variables, since time will often capture some of the effects of these on the dependent variable. However, a time trend alone can be a useful explanatory variable for certain tourism demand series, as discussed below.

Pull factors are those which attract visitors to a certain destination. *Visiting friends and relatives* is a major motivation for leisure visits, and cities with major ethnic populations may especially benefit from this travel. *Commercial ties* include the presence of head offices of major corporations at a destination, or having a concentration of financial or manufacturing firms. *Social/cultural ties* can include special ethnic neighbourhoods or institutions, such as cultural centres, religious sites, museums and monuments. Religious similarities between two countries may also be a strong influence on travel between them. Other such factors include similarity of language and the presence in one country of a large population of natives of the other.

It would seem that *destination marketing programmes*, as measured by national tourism office (NTO) expenditures, should be a useful explanatory variable for forecasting visitation to a country. However, results have been mixed (for a discussion, see Crouch, 1994b: 15). The fact that NTO budgets are frequently dwarfed by promotional spending by airlines, cruise lines, resorts and city destination marketing agencies, and that data seldom exist on these expenditures by target market, makes teasing out the relationships quite problematic. There is some evidence, however, that the effectiveness of destination advertising appears to decrease as the distance away from the target market is increased. Moreover, this spending may affect demand with a sizeable lag, as markets, particularly distant ones, respond slowly to the promotional programmes.

Distribution channels include travel agents, tour operators, meeting and convention planners, travel clubs and other media which can help a traveller become aware of a destination, gather information about it and make reservations for transportation, lodging and other tourism services. It is common for an emerging destination to depend upon tour operators and their packages for a substantial proportion of its leisure visitors.

Destination attractiveness includes all other factors of a permanent nature that attracts visitors, such as architecture, participant and spectator sport complexes, arts and entertainment centres, topography, natural and scenic attractions, zoos and gardens. This can be increased for a city that, for example, revitalizes downtown areas and adds parks and other amenities. *Special events* pull visitors for short periods at certain times of the year and include festivals and fairs, conventions and trade shows, major sporting events and concerts. Note that the special event need not occur in the destination country in order to boost travel to it. For example, Turner, Kulendran and Pergat (1995) maintain that the 1988 Expo and Bicentenary events in Australia boosted U.S. visitor arrivals in New Zealand that year.

A destination may enjoy a *complementary* relationship with another, nearby one, such as Australia and New Zealand do. This effect may well operate to the extent that one destination is included with another in package tours, and to the attractiveness of both and the ease of movement between the two.

Habit in this context is similar to momentum among the push factors. Travellers may follow the pattern of visiting the same destination on their holiday trips. This is often incorporated in the causal model by a lagged value of the forecast variable.

Resistance factors comprise those variables that constrain travel between an origin and a destination. Most of these in Figure 7.6 are self-explanatory, although the price factors need some explanation.

Price is a resistance variable because most potential travellers have limited incomes, especially in relation to their day-to-day and long-term needs. The higher prices are, the fewer items this income can finance. This has been the second most popular explanatory variable in tourism demand regression models over the past three decades (Crouch, 1994a: 48). However, tourism forecasters do not agree on the appropriate measure of price, and there is a number of choices.

Product price refers to the cost to the consumer of the item for which demand is being estimated. If a destination is the product for which demand is being modelled, than this is a complex of prices for lodging, food, entertainment and recreation, and local transportation. There is evidence that a country's consumer price index is a 'reasonable proxy for the cost of tourism', but that exchange rates are not (Witt and Witt, 1992a: 46). Research suggests the effort of constructing a special visitors' price index is not adequately compensated in terms of improved forecasting accuracy.

Prices of substitutes represent what it costs to purchase competing alternatives to the product under study. For example, substitutes for air fares include bus fares, train fares, and automobile operating expenses. Substitutes for Jamaica include the Bahamas, Aruba, Barbados and other destinations in the Caribbean as well as south Florida. When the price of a substitute goes up relative to your destination, then your visitor demand should rise, as well. A common method of incorporating the substitute process in tourism forecasting models is to include the ratio of the consumer price index in the destination country to the index in the origin country. However, this assumes that the only competitor destination for the foreign one is in the visitors' own country.

If you are trying to estimate demand for a product, such as auto rentals, for which there is another product that normally is purchased jointly, such as air transportation, then the cost of that product is a *complement price* that may affect your demand. For example, when air fares are cut, this generates more air travel as well as a larger demand for rental cars. Indeed, transport costs are the most important complement prices because virtually all tourism requires some transportation purchase, even if it is only fuel. There is evidence that the 50 per cent cut in published airline fares available for U.S. domestic travel in the summer of 1992 substantially increased demand for hotel/motel rooms in many major cities during that period.

Changes in the cost of consumer *necessities* can affect travel demand. For example, rapid inflation in heating oil, petrol and other fuel oils during the energy crises of 1973–4 and 1979–80 dissuaded some Americans from travelling during and immediately after those periods because their household budgets were so constricted by higher energy costs. So, when the price of necessities rises, the demand for tourism may well fall.

Forecasters have found that currency *exchange rates* affect travel between countries. However, they have sometimes found it difficult to separate these effects from changes in national price levels. Some believe that potential visitors are well informed on exchange rates but relatively ignorant about price levels in destination countries. Tourism demand may be more sensitive to exchange rates in the short-run than to price level changes, but research has indicated that the exchange rate is not a good representative of tourism costs (Witt and Witt, 1995: 454, 458). In general, as the cost of your country's currency rises in terms of the currency of an origin market, then tourism demand from that origin is expected to fall, all else being equal.

Escalating *taxes and fees* can dissuade travel as well. Here taxes include all that reduce consumer income or constrain business resources, such as income taxes, sales taxes, property taxes, value-added taxes and special business assessments. Arrival and departure taxes, including airport 'passenger facility charges', and other user fees are also an increasingly popular way for governments to attempt to increase revenues at the expense of visitors, who do not vote for elected officials of the destination. Fees include special licence charges for visitor-related activities (for example, hunting, fishing and diving), admissions fees levied by parks, museums and similar facilities, and fines levied on visitors when they transgress traffic or foreign exchange laws. In the extreme, this latter category includes bribes forced from tourists by corrupt officials.

Effective marketing programmes and other *competitors' actions* can reduce travel to a given destination, as can inadequate transport, lodging, and entertainment/recreation *supply capacities* to or in that destination. Some countries still impose *exchange controls* on the amount of the national currency residents can take out of their country when they travel abroad. This is a deterrent to outbound travel.

Natural disasters (earthquakes, hurricanes, etc.) are well-known deterrents to visitation, but *human-made* ones are a major problem in some areas as well. The latter includes fires, plagues, illness caused by improper food handling and sanitation, and failing electrical systems.

Finally, *physical barriers* include those that prevent certain groups of potential travellers from visiting a destination. This includes access barriers to the handicapped, and asthma sufferers' aversion to high altitudes and damp places. This category may also include topographical barriers to travel between places, such as mountains or deserts.

Given the plethora of potential explanatory variables in tourism demand regression models, it would be good if there was some guidance on which to employ. Witt and Witt (1992a: 28) built log-linear models for twenty-four country pairs and tested the following explanatory variables:

1 Personal disposable income.
2 Cost of living.
3 Exchange rate.
4 Cost of travel by air.
5 Cost of travel by surface.
6 1973 and 1979 oil crises.
7 U.K. currency restrictions.

Unfortunately, they concluded: 'The set of explanatory variables which appears to influence the demand for international tourism varies considerably from one origin-destination pair to another, and according to transport mode, where the data are disaggregated' (Witt and Witt, 1992a: 61). This supports the assumption that each tourism demand time series tends to have a personality of its own, and there is no standard way to model it for forecasting.

Forecasting Washington, D.C., tourism demand

For our model of Washington, D.C., hotel/motel room demand, the origin area is primarily the U.S.A. and secondarily the rest of the world. We can incorporate measures of U.S. economic trends, income and population size because the annual data are readily available. Information on other push factors cannot be obtained so easily.

The preferable alternative is to develop a regression equation for each origin market. However, we do not have access to the monthly distribution of room-nights sold by origin.

Turning to the pull factors, one that changes over time and can thus be related to changes in the dependent variable in a regression equation is the budget for the Washington Area Convention and Visitors Association, which is spent on attracting convention and other visitors to the region. The most significant recurring special event is the presidential inauguration festivities once every four years. This can be included in the model through one or more *dummy variables*.

Dummy variables

Normally, we view a time series we are attempting to forecast as being continuous and operating under the same conditions throughout the period. Every observation is affected by the explanatory variables in the same way during the period under study. However, there are situations when we should consider relaxing this constraint.

In Washington, D.C., the presidential inauguration occurs in January of each year after a presidential election (years even divisible by four). This super-annual event boosts hotel/motel occupancy towards saturation for a week or so during a month when occupancy rates are usually near their lowest. Thus, years of presidential inaugurations can be considered as falling under a different set of conditions than other years.

We can attempt to capture the effect of these different conditions on our dependent variable by including a 'dummy' explanatory variable. Such a dummy variable is dichotomous; that is, unlike other explanatory variables, this one can only take one of two values: zero or one. In this case, if the year is an inaugural one (for example, 1989, 1993, 1997 and 2001), then our dummy takes on the value of one. For other years, it takes on the value of zero.

Dummy variables are used extensively in forecast modelling by regression. They can distinguish between two or more continuous periods, such as the years of Second World War, and the postwar period, or the years a country was under a communist government versus a period under democracy. They can distinguish periods of disaster, such as terrorist attacks or hurricanes, from normal periods. They have been used in tourism demand forecasting models to represent travel restrictions, world fairs and other special events, and oil crises.

Dummy variables can also be used to handle seasonality in a regression. Here, each of eleven months is assigned its own dummy variable. The special effects of the twelfth month are captured by the equation with all of the dummy variables equal to zero. Finally, they are sometimes used to account for measurement discontinuities, such as the use of different data sources in a time series or changes in definitions.

This is an important principle of dummy variable analysis. The number of dummies included in an equation should always be one less than the number of different periods you are trying to distinguish. (For a lucid discussion of the use of dummy variables in other ways, see Rao and Miller, 1971: 88–93.) Consequently, the coefficient of a dummy variable, such as the one for presidential inauguration years in our hotel/motel demand equation, represents the average difference between the collection of such years in our time series and the years not represented by a dummy variable.

Resistance factors

Turning back to Figure 7.6, we can include the price of a hotel/motel room in Washington, D.C., as a resistance factor. Among complementary prices, airline fares should certainly have some effect. Optimally, we need a composite fare representing air ticket prices to and from Washington, D.C., from its main origin markets. We do not have such a series, but the U.S. Bureau of Labor Statistics gathers data on representative airline fares throughout the country and prepares an index of these as a component of the Consumer Price Index. In addition, the Air Transport Association of America publishes the annual cost per revenue passenger mile for U.S. air carriers in domestic services. We will test these two series as representing fares to Washington, D.C., and return.

The foreign country supplying the most visitors to Washington in a year is Canada. Therefore, the exchange rate between the U.S.A. and Canada may be a good measure of changing resistance on the price side for Canadian visitors.

A review of the other possible resistance factors in Figure 7.6 does not reveal any others that have changed markedly over the 1987–99 period for which we have relevant and accurate data. This is often the case in tourism demand modelling. We can conceive of many more explanatory variables than we can collect sound, relevant data on.

To summarize, Figure 7.7 lists the explanatory variables we will test in our regression models for Washington, D.C., hotel/motel demand. Some of these are available only an annual basis, so we will build an annual forecasting model.

2 Obtain relevant time series

At this point, we need to collect the data we plan to use to represent our dependent and independent variables. As discussed in Chapter 2, we should check to satisfy ourselves that each data series appears reasonable. Then we ensure the data are entered properly in whatever electronic medium we plan

---

A. Push factors
  1. Real disposable personal income, from the U.S. Department of Commerce

B. Pull factors
  1. Promotional budget of Washington, D.C., Convention and Visitors Association, from the association
  2. Presidential inaugurations

C. Resistance factors
  1. Room rates, from Smith Travel Research
  2. Airline fares Index, from U.S. Department of Labor
  3. Canadian dollar cost of $U.S., from Federal Reserve System

---

Figure 7.7 Explanatory variables to be considered for inclusion in the regression model for Washington, D.C., hotel/motel demand

to conduct our analysis in. Figure 7.7 lists the sources of the data to be tested in our regression forecasting model for hotel/motel room-nights sold in the Washington, D.C., metropolitan area (from Smith Travel Research).

3 Identify any multicollinearity

Sometimes two or more time series being considered as explanatory variables move together over time. The most common cases are where these series show upward or downward linear trends together.

This correlation among explanatory variables is called *multicollinearity*. If two explanatory variables are highly correlated, then the least squares regression procedure has difficulty in assigning coefficients to each. The result is that the two slope coefficients will show high standard errors and thus are highly unstable. Forecasters have noted that this can reach the point where different computer programs using the same data and functional form will produce different estimates of the slope coefficients. Moreover, to the extent that one coefficient is estimated as being too high, the other will be underestimated. Finally, a forecasting equation may produce a high R^2, but have few if any significant coefficients. Crouch (1994a: 43) calls multi-collinearity 'the most common methodological problem encountered' in the eighty-five tourism demand forecasting models he reviewed.

There are a number of approaches to identifying multicollinearity (for example, Gujarati, 1992: 298–303), but two relatively simple standards have been suggested to identify highly correlated explanatory variables. One is to compute the correlations among all potential explanatory variables and to avoid including two variables with correlations above a certain threshold, such as 0.8. This rule may persuade you to exclude variables that in reality differ from one another and have important explanatory powers. An alternative, less stringent rule is to see if the simple correlation between the two variables is larger than the correlation of either or both with the dependent variable. If so, then you have a multicollinearity problem and should not include both as explanatory variables. If this does not hold, than you can assume you do not have this problem.

The simple solution to multicollinearity is to exclude one of the two correlated explanatory variables. This is clearly warranted if you believe the two variables are measuring the same activity. But if these variables are measuring different factors affecting tourism demand, then you are not warranted in excluding one. Indeed, this leads to misspecification. Instead, you should seek to transform the variables to remove the multicollinearity.

Table 7.2 shows the correlations among a number of U.S. examples of variables often considered for inclusion in a tourism demand forecasting model. Those with correlations coefficients of greater than 0.8 are highlighted in bold.

Most of these time series have grown continually over the last fifteen years and thus show high correlations. In some cases, we could reasonably exclude one or more variables that appear to be measuring the same activity.

A '1' appears in each diagonal cell because each variable is perfectly correlated with itself. The top triangle is empty because the correlations are already given in the bottom triangle: the correlation between GDP and real disposable personal income is the same as the correlation between real disposable personal income and GDP.

Note that real GDP, real disposable personal income and personal consumption expenditures are highly correlated. It is likely that they are all measuring the same factor, which might be termed overall purchasing power in the economy. If we want to incorporate a measure of consumer buying power in our equation, we could exclude GDP and personal consumption expenditures in favour of including only disposable personal income as an explanatory variable.

However, population, non-agricultural employment, consumer prices, travel prices and airline capacity (available seat-miles) are also highly correlated with disposable personal income. This is probably because they are all following a secular trend upward rather than because they are directly related to consumer buying power. Indeed, this correlation does not extend to these series' first differences for the most part, confirming a lack of relationship among these series. We are not justified in excluding them just because they are following an upward trend: each may be measuring different forces that could affect hotel/motel room demand.

Table 7.3 shows the correlations of the first-differences of the same variables as in Table 7.2. Note that only four sets of series show correlations of 0.8 or higher: real disposable personal income and GDP, real personal consumption and GDP, real personal consumption and real disposable personal income, and the Consumer Price Index (CPI) and the Travel Price Index (TPI). We can decide against including either personal consumption or GDP in our regression model, since we can employ disposable personal income to represent the same force that is represented by these variables: overall economic activity and income.

By the same reasoning, we might wish to include both overall consumer prices and travel prices even though they are highly correlated over the long run: the CPI measures the costs of all items American purchase while the TPI measures the costs of travel, which may compete with the other consumer items. Indeed, there have been times in the past when these two series have diverged, such as during petroleum crises and prolonged droughts.

If you have reason to believe that both variables are important in explaining your dependent variable, then, instead of eliminating one, you can transform

Table 7.2 Intercorrelations among potential explanatory variables in a tourism demand forecasting model, U.S. annual, 1985–99

1. Variable	2. Real gross domestic product	3. Real disposable personal income	4. Real personal consumption	5. Population	6. Non-agricultural employment	7. U.S. domestic ASM*	8. Consumer price index	9. Travel price index	10. Domestic airline yield**	11. Canadian dollar/$U.S.
2. Real gross domestic product	1									
3. Real disposable income	0.998	1								
4. Real personal consumption	0.999	0.998	1							
5. Population	0.983	0.989	0.983	1						
6. Non-agricultural employment	0.996	0.993	0.995	0.978	1					
7. U.S. domestic ASM*	0.978	0.977	0.979	0.972	0.980	1				
8. Consumer price index	0.969	0.978	0.967	0.994	0.965	0.949	1			
9. Travel price index	0.969	0.978	0.967	0.992	0.962	0.946	0.999	1		
10. Domestic airline yield**	0.830	0.843	0.822	0.846	0.843	0.786	0.882	0.882	1	
11. Canadian dollar/$U.S.	0.553	0.522	0.562	0.485	0.519	0.483	0.441	0.443	0.150	1

Notes:
*ASM is available seat-miles, a measure of airline supply of passenger travel
**Airline yield is average airline revenue per passenger-mile of paying passengers
Source: U.S. Department of Commerce, U.S. Department of Labor, Air Transport Association of America, Travel Industry Association of America, Federal Reserve Board

Table 7.3 Intercorrelations among potential explanatory variables in a tourism demand forecasting model, U.S. annual differences, 1985–99

1. Variable	2. Real gross domestic product	3. Real disposable personal income	4. Real personal consumption	5. Population	6. Non-agricultural employment	7. U.S. domestic ASM*	8. Consumer price index	9. Travel price index	10. Domestic airline yield**	11. Canadian dollar/$U.S.
2. Real gross domestic product	1									
3. Real disposable personal income	**0.869**	1								
4. Real personal consumption	**0.901**	**0.858**	1							
5. Population	-0.144	-0.063	-0.008	1						
6. Non-agricultural employment	0.790	0.596	0.732	-0.194	1					
7. U.S. domestic ASM*	0.313	0.278	0.463	0.515	0.325	1				
8. Consumer price index	-0.565	-0.504	-0.626	-0.512	-0.364	-0.408	1			
9. Travel price index	-0.454	-0.364	-0.433	-0.536	-0.388	-0.298	**0.858**	1		
10. Domestic airline yield**	-0.015	-0.056	-0.050	-0.678	0.240	-0.372	0.525	0.420	1	
11. Canadian dollar/$U.S.	0.248	0.134	0.337	0.237	0.015	0.038	-0.507	-0.409	-0.392	1

Notes:

*ASM is available seat-miles, a measure of airline supply of passenger travel

**Airline yield is average airline revenue per passenger-mile of paying passengers

Source: U.S. Department of Commerce, U.S. Department of Labor, Air Transport Association of America, Travel Industry Association of America, Federal Reserve Board

your explanatory variables to remove the multicollinearity. The most common transformation is to take the first differences of one of the variables and include this in the equation, along with the original values of the other variable. Another choice is to transform the series into logarithms and include this redefined series as an explanatory variable. Still another is to compute ratios of the offending explanatory variable(s) to base series to remove multicollinearity. For example, use the ratio of retired persons in a country to the country's total population, or the ratio of travel prices to overall consumer prices.

Table 7.4 shows correlations between each explanatory variable considered for estimating hotel/motel room demand in Washington, D.C., and between each explanatory variable and all other such variables. Correlations of 0.8 or greater are marked in bold.

Examining Table 7.4, we find the correlation of real disposable personal income and room-nights sold in the second column, row 5: 0.976. This indicates that real disposable personal income is a prime candidate for an explanatory variable in our model.

However, this variable is also highly correlated with the following potential explanatory variables: average room rate, airline fare price index, domestic airline yield and Canadian dollar cost of $U.S. Table 7.5 summarizes all of the correlations among potential explanatory variables higher than 0.8. By our first criterion, we should not allow both of any pair in this table to appear as explanatory variables in our regression equation.

Our second criterion compared the correlation of two potential explanatory variables to the correlation of each with the independent variables, and is applied in column 4 of Table 7.5. If 'Yes' applies in any row of this column, then both of these variables should not be included as explanatory variables in our regression equation because of multicollinearity. For example, average room rate and the airline fare price index are correlated at 0.941. Now, average room rate shows a greater correlation with room-nights sold than with the airline fare price index. But the airline fare index shows a greater correlation with average room rate than with the dependent variable. Consequently, both average room rate and the airline fare price index should not be included under our second criterion.

Six cases violate our second criterion and indicate pairs of variables that should not both be included as explanatory variables in our regression equation.

In only one set of variables is it likely that both are measuring the same underlying magnitude or activity: airline fare price index and domestic airline yield, as indicated in column 6 of Table 7.5. We should pick one or the other of these to represent air fares to Washington, D.C. This leaves five pairs of

Table 7.4 Intercorrelations among potential explanatory variables in a hotel/motel room demand regression model for Washington, D.C., annual, 1987–99

1. Variable	2. Room-nights sold	3. Average room rate	4. Airline fare price index	5. Domestic airline yield	6. Real disposable personal income	7. Canadian dollar cost of $U.S.	8. Promotional budget	9. Presidential inauguration
2. Room-nights sold	1							
3. Average room rate	**0.973**	1						
4. Airline fare price index	**0.939**	**0.941**	1					
5. Domestic airline yield	**0.845**	**0.801**	0.833	1				
6. Real disposable personal income	**0.976**	**0.995**	0.963	**0.813**	1			
7. Canadian dollar cost of $U.S.	0.763	**0.818**	0.788	0.407	**0.807**	1		
8. Promotional budget	0.748	0.722	**0.819**	0.787	0.768	0.381	1	
9. Presidential inauguration	0.145	0.017	0.002	0.253	0.019	0.109	0.007	1

Source: U.S. Department of Commerce, Air Transport Association of America, U.S. Department of Labor, Washington Area Convention & Visitors Association, Federal Reserve Board

Table 7.5 Unacceptable correlations found among potential explanatory variables in a hotel/motel room demand regression model for Washington, D.C.

1. Explanatory variable 1	2. Explanatory variable 2	3. Correlation coefficient	4. Correlation greater than with dependent variable (room-nights sold)?	5. Likely to be measuring the same activity?
A. Average room rate	Airline fare price index	0.941	No, **Yes**	No
	Domestic airline yield	0.801	No, No	No
	Real disposable personal income	0.995	**Yes, Yes**	No
	Canadian dollar cost of $U.S.	0.818	**Yes**, No	No
B. Airline fare price index	Domestic airline yield	0.833	No, No	Yes
	Real disposable personal income	0.963	**Yes**, No	No
	Promotional budget	0.819	No, **Yes**	No
C. Domestic airline yield	Real disposable personal income	0.813	No, No	No
D. Real disposable personal income	Canadian dollar cost of $U.S.	0.807	No, **Yes**	No

Source: Table 7.4.

variables that violate our second multicollinearity criterion, down from eight that violated our first criterion and measured distinct magnitudes. Allowing for duplication in the pairings, we are forced to reduce potential explanatory variables from the seven we started with to three to avoid multicollinearity in our hotel/motel demand equation expressed in terms of levels.

This reduces our options substantially and opens us to the threat of misspecification, of excluding an explanatory variable that truly belongs in the regression model. Our simplest alternative is to transform the variables to eliminate multicollinearity.

Transforming them into logarithms retained high correlations among several. However, taking the annual first differences of each reduced all intercorrelations to below 0.8, as indicated in Table 7.6. Consequently, the multivariate regression model for forecasting hotel/motel room demand in Washington, D.C., is stated in terms of annual differences.

4 Specify expected relationships

Based upon our theory of how hotel/motel room demand is determined in an area, we can outline how we expect our model to look once it is complete. This procedure helps us to assess the validity of our model, that is, that it indeed incorporates relationships that hold in the real world.

Table 7.7 lists the explanatory variables we have selected for our forecasting model, and what we expect their relationship will be to hotel/motel room demand.

Economic theory posits that demand is inversely related to price, so we expect the coefficient of average room rate (expressed in rate of change) to be negative. Airline fares are considered to be the price of a complementary product, so we expect that as they rise, travel is retarded and hotel/motel demand slows: a negative relationship as well. The TPI summarizes movements in all costs of travel away from home. As this measure rises, overall travel costs regardless of transport mode are growing, possibly discouraging trips to Washington, D.C. Finally, the Canadian dollar cost of purchasing U.S. dollars is a price to potential Canadian visitors of travelling in the U.S.A., so as this price rises, it is also expected to have a negative impact on hotel/motel demand.

Rising real disposable income should stimulate travel away from home, so this is expected to show a positive relationship to hotel/motel demand. Similarly, the quadrennial presidential inauguration boosts room demand in the years in which it occurs.

Looking at the third column in Table 7.7, only one of these variables, the presence of the inauguration, is represented by a dummy variable. In the years

Table 7.6 Intercorrelations among potential explanatory variables in a hotel/motel room demand regression model for Washington, D.C., annual differences, 1988–99

1. Variable	2. Room-nights sold	3. Average room rate	4. Airline fare price index	5. Domestic airline yield	6. Real disposable personal income	7. Canadian dollar cost of $U.S.	8. Promotional budget
2. Room-nights sold	1						
3. Average room rate	0.660	1					
4. Airline fare price index	0.147	0.083	1				
5. Domestic airline yield	0.472	0.318	0.312	1			
6. Real disposable personal income	0.416	0.744	-0.311	-0.082	1		
7. Canadian dollar cost of $U.S.	-0.132	0.036	0.235	-0.450	0.065	1	
8. Promotional budget	-0.137	-0.349	0.093	-0.033	-0.361	-0.496	1

Note: excludes the Presidential inauguration dummy variable since its annual differences are not meaningful
Source: U.S. Department of Commerce, Air Transport Association of America, U.S. Department of Labor, Washington Area Convention & Visitors Association, Federal Reserve Board

Table 7.7 Theoretical characteristics of potential explanatory variables in a regression model of hotel/motel room demand

1. Explanatory variable	2. Coefficient sign	3. Dummy variable?	4. Lagged variable?
1. Average room rate	Negative	No	Possibly
2. Domestic airline fares	Negative	No	Possibly
3. Travel price index	Negative	No	Possibly
4. Real disposable personal income	Positive	No	Possibly
5. Canadian dollar cost of $U.S.	Negative	No	Possibly
6. Promotional budget	Positive	No	Possibly
7. Presidential inauguration	Positive	Yes	No

of this event (1989, 1993 and 1997 in our time series), it will be represented by a dummy with a value of one. For other years, the value is set at zero.

Finally, we need to consider whether the impact of any of our explanatory variables is a lagged one. In other words, is the value one or two years earlier expected to be more highly correlated with current room demand than the current value? It seems clear that the presence of a presidential inauguration will affect room demand in the current period, rather than a year or two later. But our other explanatory variables might work with a lag. For example, a rise in airline fares this year may not affect hotel/motel visitors until next year, when businesses and consumers have time to adjust their plans.

Indeed, it is possible that last year's values of each our other explanatory variables may affect this year's decision to travel. So lagged values of these should be considered in building our model. We do not have enough advance information, however, to specify that these variables must be lagged in our model. We can test both current and lagged effects during the model-building process.

One final phase of this step is to specify the mathematical, or functional, form of these relationships. The simplest form is to assume the levels of the explanatory variables are associated with the levels of the dependent variables. Another simple form is to relate changes in the dependent variable from period to period to the explanatory variables. Under this form, the series are all transformed into new series of the first differences, with one less data point than the original series. This is the form of the variables we will use, to avoid the multicollinearity problem identified earlier.

A popular functional form in tourism forecasting is the log-linear equation, where the logarithm of the dependent variable is regressed on the logarithms of the explanatory variables. This is an elasticity model, where the relationship of the logarithmic terms indicates that percentage changes in the explanatory variables produce a certain percentage change in the dependent variable. There is evidence that this is the preferred form for forecasting tourism flows among places because it usually yields significant coefficients with expected signs. Crouch (1994a: 42) found it was by far the most popular form for models forecasting tourism demand among countries. One deficiency of such models is that they assume the demand elasticity is constant which 'can produce absurd results when explanatory variables extend well beyond their original range' (ibid.). Song and Witt (2000: 124–34) suggest an advanced econometric method to allow elasticities to vary over time.

Other forms that could be used in a tourism demand regression forecasting model correspond to those depicted in Figure 7.2 and discussed earlier. These all produce non-linear relationships of the variables yet the regression equations remain linear in their parameters, a basic requirement for valid least squares regression analysis. Figure 7.8 plots the first differences of hotel/motel room-nights sold and suggests linearity in the independent variable values. (Figure 7.7 suggests that the levels of room-nights sold in Washington are linear, too.)

Once we have thoughtfully outlined how we expect our explanatory variables to affect hotel/motel room demand, the next step is to identify an initial model.

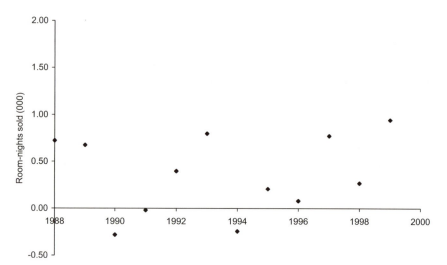

Figure 7.8 Hotel/motel demand in Washington, D.C., annual differences, 1988–99
Source: Smith Travel Research

5 Identify initial model

At this stage, we take the expected form of our equation and enter various combinations of explanatory variables into it to find combinations of variables that produce the best fits of the dependent variables historical data series. One of the most popular methods of arriving at an initial model is called *stepwise regression*. This procedure for identifying a regression model tries different combinations of explanatory variables to identify one or more combinations that fit the data well and produce slope coefficients significantly different from zero.

Several procedures have been suggested for stepwise regression. The one detailed in Figure 7.9, sometimes called 'forward stepwise regression', is based on the recommendations of Makridakis, Wheelwright and McGee (1983: 279–81).

---

1. Compute the simple correlations of the explanatory variables with the dependent variable and array these in a table.

2. Regress the dependent variable on the explanatory variable with the highest correlation and correct sign and record the $\overline{R}^2$ or F-statistic (both are measures of the goodness of fit and are discussed below), and the *t*-statistic for the slope coefficient (a measure of the significance of the slope coefficient, also discussed below).

3. Add the potential explanatory variable with the next best correlation with the dependent variable and correct sign and run the regression again. If the $\overline{R}^2$ increases and the slope coefficient for both explanatory variables are significant at some specified confidence interval (e.g., 90 or 95 per cent), record the *t*-statistics and the $\overline{R}^2$ and move to the next step. If $\overline{R}^2$ declines, drop this explanatory variable. If the slope coefficient for a variable becomes insignificant or takes on the wrong sign, reject this variable and move to the next step.

4. Add the potential variable with the next highest correlation with the dependent variable. If the $\overline{R}^2$ increases and all *t*-statistics remain significant, move on to step 5. If the $\overline{R}^2$ decreases or the *t*-statistic of the new variable is not significant, delete the latest variable and move on to the next step. If the $\overline{R}^2$ increases, but the *t*-statistic for the coefficient of one of the earlier variables becomes insignificant or takes on the wrong sign, drop this variable and run a regression again. If the new regression produces a higher $\overline{R}^2$ than the original and *t*-statistics of all slope coefficients are significant, move on to the next step.

5. Continue this process until no additional variable increases the $\overline{R}^2$. Now you have a table of candidate regression models to examine for use.

Figure 7.9 The stepwise regression estimation process

The objective is to derive two or three equations that produce high $\overline{R}^2$ or F-statistics and significant parameters. Then, these models should be tested against our theoretical expectations of the parameters, and those that do not pass this test can be discarded. Finally, we will examine a number of tests of the validity of your models to select the best one.

This stepwise regression process can be tedious in a spreadsheet even with an efficient regression application, and you may prefer to use a statistical program with this capacity. In a number of such programs, the computer actually tests all combinations of explanatory variables and indicates the most successful. However, it is wise to examine the results of each step yourself rather than to accept the program's choice of explanatory variables, because some programs ignore the significance of the coefficients and focus exclusively on achieving the highest $\overline{R}^2$. You may end up with several irrelevant explanatory variables in your model, a clear case of misspecification.

In our collection of explanatory variables for annual differences in hotel/ motel room demand, the one with the highest correlation with annual changes in room demand and the correct sign is the dummy variable for the presidential inauguration years (Table 7.8). Consequently, the stepwise regression procedure begins with this explanatory variable and added and subtracted additional variables in order to maximize the F-statistic. Several equations were identified that produced good fits with the room demand time series, and these are detailed in the next section.

Table 7.8 Correlations of potential explanatory variables with hotel/motel room-nights sold in Washington, D.C., annual differences, 1988–99

	Correlation	
A. Variable	B. Coincident	C. Lagged one period
1. Average room rate	0.660	0.150
2. Airline fare price index	0.147	−0.685
3. Domestic airline yield	0.472	−0.365
4. Real disposable personal income	0.416	0.593
5. Canadian dollar cost of $U.S.	−0.132	0.107
6. Promotional budget	−0.137	−0.094
7. Presidential inauguration	0.554	NA

Note: NA = not applicable.

Note that a *lagged* series of real disposable personal income (RDPI) changes was included as a potential explanatory variable (Table 7.8). This is because several equations in the stepwise process included RDPI but with a negative coefficient, indicating that as consumer income rose, room demand in Washington, D.C., declined, and vice versa. This did not appear reasonable, so the lagged variable was incorporated to test the hypothesis that income affected room demand with a one-year lag. The promotional budget series was lagged as well, for the same reasons.

Table 7.8 reveals some surprises, given our theoretical expectations of the signs of the explanatory variable coefficients in Table 7.7. Annual changes in average room rate are positively correlated with room-night sales increments, suggesting raising rates is the way to increase occupancy. If this were true, then we would expect occupancies to be nearly 100 per cent for each year, since hoteliers would have no reason to restrain rates. On the contrary, the monthly data indicate that room rates appear to 'chase' demand: hoteliers try to increase demand during months with traditionally low occupancies by offering lower room rates than they do during high occupancy months. The same may be true for the annual series as well. But in a multivariate regression equation, we should expect price changes to be negatively correlated with changes in room demand.

The Washington, D.C., promotional budget is also negatively correlated with room demand. Again, this contradicts theory and suggests that this budget is either chasing demand as well or has no measurable effect on our measure of tourism demand. This is supported by the fact that even lagged changes in the series are negatively correlated with room demand increments.

6 Evaluate model validity

At this step in our regression modelling, we should now have a small number of equations, say two or three, differing in the explanatory variables included and/or the units of measurement (for example, levels versus annual differences). In the case of annual Washington, D.C., hotel/motel lodging demand over the 1987–99 period, the author first examined all of the likely combinations of the annual differences in the explanatory variables and annual differences in room-night demand according to the stepwise procedures in Figure 7.9. Unfortunately, only one model resulted with a significant F-statistic and all coefficients significant at the 0.10 level (often the threshold for difference models). The explanatory variables were the presidential inauguration and coincident change in real disposable personal income in this model.

This led the author to look again at levels of the dependent and explanatory variables, being careful to avoid including two explanatory variables with high correlations. Here he found two equations with extraordinarily high F-statistics and $\overline{R}^2$s, with the coefficients of the explanatory variables all significant at the 0.05 level. This provided a set of three 'best' equations for further consideration.

We can order these best equations by their measures of goodness of fit and coefficient significance, such as below for our hotel/motel demand problem:

$$RNS \ = 4.89 + 0.00215*RDPI + 0.439*PID \qquad (7.10)$$
$$\ \ \ (8.93) \qquad (21.2) \qquad \quad (3.55)$$

$$\overline{R}^2 = 0.974 \quad F = 229 \ (p = 0.0000)$$

$$RNS \ = 4.45 + 0.00230*LRDPI + 0.387*PID \qquad (7.11)$$
$$\ \ \ (6.32) \qquad (17.1) \qquad \quad (2.54)$$

$$\overline{R}^2 = 0.961 \quad F = 150 \ (p = 0.0000)$$

$$\Delta RNS \ = -0.342 + .00340*\Delta RDPI + 0.659*PID \qquad (7.12)$$
$$\ \ \ (-1.41) \qquad (2.31) \qquad \quad (3.35)$$

$$\overline{R}^2 = 0.551 \quad F = 7.14 \ (p = 0.0166)$$

where
RNS   = hotel/motel room-nights sold (millions)
RPDI = real disposable personal income in 1996 chained dollars ($\$10^9$)
PID   = dummy variable for presidential inauguration years
LRPDI = real disposable personal income in 1966 chained dollars, lagged one year ($\$10^9$)
ΔRNS = annual change in hotel/motel room-nights sold (millions)
ΔRDPI = annual change in real disposable personal income ($\$10^9$).

The number shown in parentheses below each coefficient is the *t*-statistic for that coefficient. All are significant at the 0.05 level, except the intercept term in Equation 7.12. This is not a fatal weakness but it does position this equation as somewhat less preferable to the other models with significant intercept terms.

The selection process included discarding equations with coefficients contrary to those listed in Table 7.7. All three models or equations (7.10 to 7.12) include coefficients of acceptable sign, indicating each are valid representations of expected relationships.

7 Assess the model's significance

Once we have developed one or more valid causal models, we must then examine them for significance. That is, we try to determine whether the estimated relationships embodied in our regression model truly depict associations among the variables, or are an artefact of the estimation process. If a model's relationships accurately reflect the data describing the present world, than we can be much more confident they can be used to describe the future. If the quantified relationships instead reflect features of the way we have organized and processed the data, then we cannot expect them to be good descriptions of how the world works now and how it will in the future.

To determine whether we have indeed achieved a valid least squares regression model for forecasting tourism demand, there are five basic questions we should ask about it:

1 Does it accurately simulate the historical time series?
2 Is our test for simulation accuracy valid?
3 Have we included any irrelevant explanatory variables?
4 Have we excluded any important explanatory variables?
5 How stable is the model?

Each of these questions will be discussed in turn, with appropriate tests presented and remedies suggested.

(A) Accurate simulation of the historical time series
We can have much more confidence that our model can predict the future course of a data series if it successfully simulates its past course. We employed a test for the extrapolative models discussed in Chapter 4 based on the average percentage error, the MAPE.

For regression analysis, we have a useful analogue in the coefficient of determination adjusted for degrees of freedom, or $\overline{R}^2$. This statistic indicates the per cent of the variation of the dependent variable around its mean that is explained by our explanatory variables. As such, it varies between zero and one, with zero indicating the explanatory variables have no power to explain the variation in the dependent variable and one indicating they explain all of this variation. Formally, $\overline{R}^2$ is computed by the following formula:

$$\overline{R}^2 = 1 - \left[\left(1 - \frac{\sum(\hat{Y}_t - \overline{Y})^2}{\sum(Y_t - \overline{Y})} \right) \left(\frac{n-1}{n-k-1} \right) \right] \qquad (7.13)$$

where $\overline{R}^2$ = coefficient of determination adjusted for degrees of freedom

$\hat{Y}$ = dependent variable as estimated by the regression equation

t = a time period

$\overline{Y}$ = the mean of the dependent variable data series

Y = actual dependent variables in the data series

n = number of observations in the dependent variable data series

k = number of parameters (explanatory variables plus one).

Note that this statistic is an altered version of the simple coefficient of correlation, or R^2. As you add explanatory variables to a regression equation, the R^2 naturally rises, since each added variable usually can explain some of the variance in the dependent variable. $\overline{R}^2$ adjusts for the number of explanatory variables, so that we can truly determine whether a model with five explanatory variables is more significant than one with only two.

We should, of course, prefer models with high values of $\overline{R}^2$, but there is no standard as to what 'high' means. The $\overline{R}^2$ value can depend very much on what we are trying to forecast. For a tourism demand series affected by many factors, such as the number of Mexican visitors to the U.S.A., an $\overline{R}^2$ of 0.7 might be considered high. Models forecasting first differences of a tourism demand series are also considered reliable if they achieve with $\overline{R}^2$ of 0.7 or more, because first differences tend to be more volatile than their underlying time series.

However, for a series showing stable trends over time, such as hotel/motel room demand in the Washington, D.C., metropolitan area, an $\overline{R}^2$ of 0.7 may well be considered too low. There is no definitive guide to the significance of this statistic. Fortunately, we have a related statistic that is accompanied by a guide to its significance: the F-statistic.

In our use of it in regression analysis, the F-statistic is the ratio of an equation's explained variance in the dependent variable to its unexplained variance. The equation is:

$$F = \frac{\sum(\hat{Y} - \overline{Y})^2 / k}{\sum(Y - \hat{Y})^2 / (n - k - 1)} \qquad (7.14)$$

where   F = F-statistic

$\hat{Y}$ = dependent variable estimated by the regression equation

$\overline{Y}$ = the mean of the data series

Y = actual dependent variables in the data series

n = number of observations in the dependent variable data series

k = number of parameters (explanatory variables plus one).

In essence, the F-statistic can tell us whether movements in the explanatory variables do indeed 'explain' changes in the dependent variable, or, alternatively, that the apparent correlation is just random. You can look up the value of your F-statistic in tables found in most statistical textbooks and determine whether it is significant or not according to some level of confidence (usually set at 0.1 or 0.05). As a rule of thumb, if you have two explanatory variables or more, and the number of observations less the number of explanatory variables equals six or more, then an F-statistic of 5 or above indicates your regression model is significant at the 0.05 level. Since the $\overline{R}^2$ and the F-statistic are linearly related, this indicates your coefficient of determination is 'high enough' as well.[3] In short, your forecast equation provides a good fit with the historical data series.

As suggested by the equations, computation of $\overline{R}^2$ and the F-statistic can be tedious on a spreadsheet. Fortunately, statistical packages for personal computers that conduct regression analysis print out these two statistics as a matter of course. In the case of the F-statistic, its level of significance is indicated as well.

Note that $\overline{R}^2$ is not available for time series analysis models, so you need to compute MAPEs when comparing these to regression models. Indeed, it is always wise to compare the MAPEs of alternative regression models among themselves, for a high $\overline{R}^2$ is no guarantee of a low MAPE.

There is a tendency among forecasters to focus on the $\overline{R}^2$ value to indicate the most accurate forecasting model. However, this is to confuse explanatory power of a regression model with its ability to correctly forecast future values. Witt and Witt (1992a) have clearly documented the two are not the same in tourism demand forecasting. They found in a comparison of a number of regression models for international travel flows among countries that in fewer than one-fifth of the cases did the regression model with the highest $\overline{R}^2$ produce the most accurate forecast of future levels of tourism demand. Other forecasters agree that a 'high $\overline{R}^2$ alone is not a convincing reason for accepting a forecasting model' (for example, Calantone, di Benedetto and Bojanic, 1987: 37).

(B) Validity of the test for simulation accuracy

One of the critical assumptions of least squares regression analysis is that the residuals, or errors of fit, are random, that is, independent of one another. The alternative is that they show a pattern. This pattern indicates that the model is not taking account of all the important information on relationships to the dependent variable. In particular, this signals that at least one important explanatory variable has been left out of the equation, that is, that the model is misspecified. (The ramifications of this are discussed below.)

In addition, this pattern, called 'serial correlation' or 'autocorrelation of the residuals', will bias the estimates of our equation's goodness of fit, $\overline{R}^2$ and the F-statistic. The most common case in time series data is positive serial correlation, where residuals in one time period are positively correlated with residuals in the previous time period. If this is present in a regression model, then the goodness of fit measures as estimated appear higher than they actually are, giving an overly optimistic picture of the success of the regression.

In addition, this may lead to our recognizing some explanatory variables as significant and worthy of inclusion in our model, when in fact they are not significant. This has been called 'spurious regression' (Makridakis, Wheelwright and Hyndman, 1998: 391).

The most popular way to identify serial correlation of the residuals is the Durbin–Watson (DW) statistic:

$$\text{DW} = \frac{\sum (e_t - e_{t-1})^2}{\sum e_t^2} \tag{7.15}$$

where DW = the Durbin–Watson statistic
e = residual
t = a time period.

The numerator computes the squared differences between successive residuals for each time period in the data series and adds them up. Then the sum of the squared residuals are added up in the denominator and divided into the numerator. If the residuals show a slow-moving course, that is, are close to one another, the DW statistic will be small. If there is a distinct, fast-moving pattern, then the successive residual differences will be large and the DW statistic will be large. These are the two cases of serial correlation that will bias our measures of a regression model's goodness of fit to the historical data.

The DW statistic ranges from zero to four. If the DW statistic is 2.0, the residuals are completely independent and there is no serial correlation. Most statistical textbooks contain tables of the critical values of this statistic to suggest whether there is serial correlation, there is no serial correlation or we are in an indeterminate region where we do not know whether serial correlation is present or not. These regions vary substantially by number of observations and number of explanatory variables in the equation. As a rule of thumb, if the DW statistic falls between 1.5 and 2.5, we can be reasonably sure that no serial correlation exists among the residuals in most cases.

If your DW statistic falls outside of this region, there is a good chance you have serial correlation of your residuals. The best remedy is to look for missing explanatory variables and include them in your model. Another remedy is to transform some of your explanatory variables by differencing or taking their logarithms. There are methods that directly correct any serial correlation in the residuals, but these ignore the problem of omitted variables: even though you may remove the serial correlation, you will still have a misspecified model.

(C) Heteroscedasticity

A second assumption of the linear regression model is that any set of the residuals all have the same variance. If this is assumption is violated, we are said to have *heteroscedasticity*, the name given to the condition where the residuals do not maintain constant variance across the entire time series.

This condition is frequently found over long time series showing a marked trend, such as many tourism demand series. In some long tourism demand series, such as U.S. air passenger travel in Figure 6.2 in Chapter 6, the order of magnitude changes over the course of the series. In the complete series, the value for 1994 is forty-nine times the value for 1950. In some series of this kind, as the variable becomes larger in magnitude, its variance tends to become larger, too. This is heteroscedasticity. (The opposite and preferred condition, where the variance of the residual terms does not change over the series, is called *homoscedasticity*.)

When heteroscedasticity occurs, the major practical implication is that the variance of the estimated parameters is biased and our t-test of their significance may give false signals of significance. That is, we may accept an explanatory variable as being significantly related to our dependent variable when we should not. Moreover, heteroscedasticity also biases the F-test, and we may accept an overall equation as our best model when we should not.

One way to identify heteroscedasticity is to chart the residuals and examine them to see if their variance changes over time. Figure 7.10 charts the residual terms from the linear time trend shown in Figure 7.1. It does not appear that they are larger in the latter half of the series than they are in the first half, the sign of heteroscedasticity. However, we will apply the test for hetero-scedasticity for confirmation.

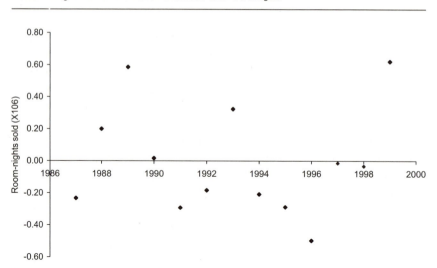

Figure 7.10   Residuals from the time trend regression of hotel/motel room demand in Washington, D.C., annually, 1987–99
Source: author

Pindyck and Rubinfeld (1981: 148–9) suggest a five-step test for the presence of heteroscedasticity in a regression equation, as shown in Figure 7.11.

In the Figure 7.10 example, the ratio is 0.62 by excluding only the one central value since the series is so short. The degrees of freedom are $6 - 2 = 4$ and $6 - 2 = 4$, or 4,4. The F-statistic for these degrees of freedom at the 0.05 level of significance is 6.4. Since the F-statistic for our ratio falls short of this, then we

---

1. Order the observations by size of the independent variable, in this case, year.

2. Omit one-fifth of observations in the centre of the series.

3. Fit separate linear time tend regressions to the observations in the first part of the remaining time series and the second part.

4. Compute the sum of the squared residuals, and divide the sum for the second part by the first part.

5. Apply the F-test to this ratio; the degrees of freedom are the number of observations in the first part of the series less two, and the number of observations in the second part of the series less two. If the resulting ratio is smaller than the F-statistic for these degrees of freedom, then the variances can be considered to be equal and we have homoscedasticity and thus no problem.

Figure 7.11   A test for heteroscedasticity in a time series

accept the hypothesis that the variances of the two parts of our time series are equal. In short, we have found no heteroscedasticity in this series.

If you find heteroscedasticity in your time series, try to remove it by transforming the dependent variable into first differences, logarithms or square roots as discussed in Chapter 6. Then use the transformation that removes it in your forecast variable.

(D) Irrelevant explanatory variables

Relying on theory or intuition, the forecaster may include a number of explanatory variables that are not statistically related to the dependent variable. This violates the principle of parsimony and may contribute to higher forecast errors in the future. Fortunately, there is a simple test for the significance of the relationship between an explanatory variable and its dependent: the t-test.

The t-statistic is computed as follows:

$$t_s = \frac{b_i}{se_{b_i}} \tag{7.16}$$

where t_s = the t-statistic
        b = slope coefficient
        i = one of the explanatory variables
       se = standard error of the slope coefficient.

The standard error of the slope coefficient is computed as follows:

$$se_{b_i} = \frac{\sum (Y_t - \hat{Y})^2 / (n - k)}{\sum (X_{i,t} - \overline{X})^2} \tag{7.17}$$

where se = standard error of the slope coefficient
       b = a slope coefficient
       i = one of the explanatory variables
      Y = dependent variable
      $\hat{Y}$ = dependent variable estimated by the regression equation
      n = number of observations
      k = number of parameters (i.e., explanatory variables plus one)
      X = an explanatory variable
      $\overline{X}$ = mean of the explanatory variable data series.

Since the t-statistic is obtained from the least squares regression, it has a statistical distribution. Based on the degrees of freedom (number of data points less the number of explanatory variables plus one) and the degree of confidence you seek, you can look up the critical value in tables in most statistical textbooks. Assuming a 95 per cent confidence interval[4] and six or more degrees of freedom, a *t*-statistic of 2.0 or more indicates the coefficient is significantly different from zero, and thus its explanatory variables should be retained in the forecasting model.

Note that since the coefficient can be negative, the *t*-statistic can be negative, too. Consequently, look for a *t*-statistic with an *absolute* value of greater than 2.0.

If a coefficient fails to pass this test, you should exclude the related explanatory variable from your equation. Its coefficient has a value only due to sampling error and this value is as likely to be zero as to be any other number. In other words, there is no evidence that this explanatory variable explains any of the variation in the dependent variable and should be omitted from the model as irrelevant. To include it is to misspecify the model.

(E) Omitted explanatory variables

A forecasting model is designed to be a simplified representation of a complex reality. By its very nature, the model cannot include all factors that affect tourism demand in reality. However, we should take pains to ensure the most important explanatory variables are included.

If we exclude an important explanatory variable, we obtain biased estimates of the slope coefficients for the variables we do include. This means they are not accurate representations of past relationships between the explanatory variable and the dependent variable. We can assume they will fail to be so in the future, as well.

One way to guard against omitting relevant variables is to carefully develop a theory of what affects tourism demand and how. This will suggest variables that can explain the course of your dependent variable over time. Variables that offer the potential for explaining tourism demand are listed in Figure 7.6.

One way to explore whether relevant explanatory variables have been left out of the equation is to examine the residuals of your model. If these show a non-random pattern (that is, serial correlation), this indicates one or more important variables related to your dependent variable have been left out. A popular test for such patterns is the DW statistic explained in Section B, above.

(F) Stability of the forecasting model

Throughout this discussion of causal forecast modelling, we have been focusing on estimating the intercept constant and slope coefficients through least squares regression. Once we have assured ourselves (and our clients or supervisors) that we have accurately estimated these according to statistical tests of significance and validity, we need to have confidence that they are stable. That is, that we do not stretch reason too far in assuming these coefficients will apply in the future we are forecasting.

While we can never be certain that what pertains now will operate in the future, we can test our model for stability, that is, that the coefficients have remained fairly constant over our time series. One test for this stability is the Chow predictive failure test described by Song and Witt (2000: 39).

This test checks for a significant difference between the values of our dependent variable predicted by our model over a latter part of the time series and the actual values over that period. If a statistically significant difference is found, then we must reject the hypothesis that there has been no change in the estimated coefficients, and assume that our model is too unstable to predict the future of our dependent variable.

To apply the Chow predictive failure test, follow the procedures in Figure 7.12.

Table 7.9 summarizes the various validity tests applied to our three candidate forecast equations for hotel/motel room demand in the Washington, D.C., area. The results of the earlier examination of the signs of the coefficients are included, as well, in the last row. Those characteristics in bold are the best for a given test.

---

1. Designate some number, n (say three or four), of the final observations of your time series, TS, as comprising its second sub-sample.

2. Using your regression model, compute the residuals for the entire time series, and for the first sub-sample (i.e., TS − n), square them, and calculate sums for each of the two sets of squared residuals, SSR.

3. Enter the values in the following equation:

$$F_c = \frac{(SSR_{ts} - SSR_1)(n_1 - k)}{SSR_1 \, {}^*n_2} \qquad (7.18)$$

where

F_c = estimated F-statistic
SSR = sum of squared residuals from one part of the time series
ts = total sample
n = number of values in one of the two sub-samples of the time series
k = number of parameters estimated (i.e., number of coefficients plus one)

4. Compare this Chow statistic to the F-statistic for n_2, n_1-k degrees of freedom. If the Chow statistic exceeds the F-statistic, then the structure of the data between the two sub-samples has changed and the model fails to accurately predict during the final period. This is a good reason to reject the model and test an alternative.

Figure 7.12 Steps in applying the Chow test for predictive failure

Table 7.9   Comparisons of three hotel/motel demand forecasting models on tests of validity

Characteristic		Model (7.10)	Model (7.11)	Model (7.12)
1.	$\bar{R}^2$	**0.974**	0.961	0.551
2.	F-statistic (significance level)	229	150	6.96
		(0.0000)	**(0.0000)**	(0.015)
3.	MAPE	**0.8%**	1.0%	1.3%
4.	DW statistic	1.22*	1.38*	**2.03**
	Parameters' significance			
5.	Intercept constant	**0.0000**	0.0001	0.17
6.	Coefficients not significant at 0.05	**0**	**0**	**0**
7.	Coefficients not significant at 0.10	**0**	**0**	**0**
8.	Stability (last 3 values at 0.05)	**No change**	**No change**	**No change**
9.	Theil's U-statistic	**0.295**	0.407	0.507
10.	Coefficients with questionable signs	**0**	**0**	**0**

Note: *The Durbin–Watson test for serial correlation is inconclusive here.

Model (7.10) shows the most superior characteristics (that is, nine out of ten are in bold). Model (7.11) is a close second on six of the validity tests, and equal to (7.10) on four of them. Equation (7.12) holds third place in these tests, and deals with annual differences rather than levels. This is the only equation with a conclusive DW statistic indicating clearly there is no serial correlation among the residuals.

It is clear that model (7.10) is our best bet for forecasting the future of annual hotel/motel room sales in the Washington, D.C. metropolitan area. It is considerably better than the naive model, as indicated by the low Theil's U-statistic. However, it may be useful to use all three models and compare annual forecasts. If their forecast values converge, then we can be more confident that we have accurate forecasts than if we used only one model.

8 Use the model to forecast

Once we have settled on our best regression model for forecasting tourism demand, we should employ it to develop forecasts of our future. At its most basic, this involves substituting values for the explanatory variables that will produce the forecast for the period we are interested in.

If lagged explanatory variables appear in the regression model, then we can often use the actual values for these since they are known. More often, however, we must resort to forecast values for our explanatory variables to forecast our dependent variable. This requirement necessarily increases our forecast errors. The less reliable the forecast explanatory variables available to us, the less reliable will be our forecast of the dependent variable.

In many cases, you can obtain forecasts of important economic variables for reputable forecasting firms. Sometimes you will need to contact tourism industry sources for predictions of tourism-related variables. In any case, try to evaluate the quality of these forecasts just as carefully as you evaluate your own forecasting model. The tests for such evaluation have been discussed above, and are summarized in the next section.

The three satisfactory models are reproduced here with values entered for 2000. The forecast of real disposable personal income for 2000 is derived from the consensus forecast of *Blue Chip Economic Indicators* (Panel Publishers, 2000).

$$RNS = 4.89 + 0.00215*6553 + 0.439*0 = 18.99 \text{ million} \qquad (7.18)$$

$$RNS = 4.45 + 0.00230*6349 + 0.387*0 = 19.04 \text{ million} \qquad (7.19)$$

$$\Delta RNS = -0.342 + .00340*203.2 + 0.659*0 = 0.410 \text{ million} \qquad (7.20)$$

Table 7.10 summarizes various ways of looking at the forecasts for 2000 for the three models and shows a comparison with the mean over the prior five years for actual hotel/motel room-nights sold in the Washington, D.C., metropolitan area. It seems clear that the annual differences and per cent changes (rows B and C in Table 7.10) are reasonable forecasts given the experience over the previous five years. However, the volumes or levels of room-nights sold vary significantly, with model (7.10) showing very little growth over the actual value for 1999 (18.86 million).

Figure 7.13 shows why this is so. The 1999 value produced by model (7.10) is 18.55 million room nights, while the actual value was 18.86 million. And

Table 7.10   Summary of forecasts for 2000 of the three acceptable models of hotel/motel room night sales in Washington, D.C.

1. Measure	2. Model (7.10)	3. Model (7.11)	4. Model (7.12)	5. Actual 1995–9
A. Volume (millions)	18.99	19.04	19.27	NA
B. Annual difference (millions)	0.437	0.557	0.410	0.454
C. Annual per cent change	2.4%	3.0%	2.2%	2.6%

Note: NA = not applicable

the forecast for 2000 comes off this low base for this model. Consequently, we obtain what appears to be an unacceptably low volume for 2000 from model (7.10), a problem that the other two models do not have.

Unless your regression equation fits your time series perfectly, or by chance the last value in your historic time series is correctly forecast by your model, your forecast will be inconsistent with your actual time series. As a result, the change from your last historic value to your first forecast value will be exaggerated. Appendix 3 discusses this problem and the solutions for it.

But here we would be justified in concluding that hotel/motel room-nights sold in Washington, D.C., in 2000 will increase by 2.2 per cent to 3.0 per cent over 1999, and grow by 410 000 to 560 000 over 1999.

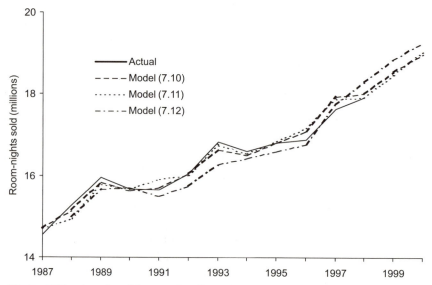

Figure 7.13   Actual and forecast hotel/motel room demand by three models, annual, 1987–2000
Source: author

Applications

The Austrian Institute for Economic Research carried out a lengthy econometric investigation of tourism demand for Austria by Austrians (domestic tourism) and other country's residents (inbound tourism), and by Austrians for other country destinations (outbound tourism) over the 1961–77 period (Schulmeister, 1979). The institute was particularly interested in developing models to forecast the long-term demand for tourism, short-term demand as affected by the general business cycle and before and after the

1973–4 worldwide petroleum crisis to determine if changes in the structure of tourism demand had taken place.

This study found that Austrian residents' rising demand for tourism, both domestic and international, over the long run was mainly due to increases in income, which short-term fluctuations were primarily influenced by changes in school vacations (duration and timing), weather conditions and fluctuations in private consumption. This last variable showed an inverse relationship to overall tourism demand, explained by the reasoning that rapid domestic price inflation accelerated consumption expenditures for necessities and tourism demand suffered as a result.

The petroleum crisis depressed Austrian outbound tourism through high rates of inflation, and demand was shifted to domestic destinations. However, there was no evidence that the structure of tourism demand changed as a result of the crisis: the list of explanatory variables remained the same and their coefficients changed little (Schulmeister, 1979: 65–6). However, the institute found that during political and economic crises, 'sudden fluctuations in the expectations of private households have a very strong short-term effects on the demand for tourism' (ibid.: 76). Fluctuations in indexes of 'consumer sentiment' (that is, personal evaluations of current or future general economic conditions) may be important explanatory variables in regression models during such crisis periods.

Choy (1984) used a linear time trend method to develop models of visitor arrivals in the Asian/Pacific region, and Hong Kong from individual origin areas. He found it to be considerably more accurate than the naive model as measured by MAPE over the 1974–82 period. He also found that low MAPEs did not necessarily accompany high $\overline{R}^2$ or vice versa, and that models for several of the origin area series produced unacceptably high MAPEs. Choy (1985) extended the usefulness of this model by relating it to demand for hotel room-nights in Hong Kong.

Witt and Martin (1987) report on a study of the impact of destination advertising on international arrivals in Greece from eight generating countries over the 1972–82 period. Per capita personal income in the origin countries, cost of travel between the origin and Greece, the ratio of the consumer price index in Greece to the origin country's index, Greece's promotional expenditures in the origin country and a dummy variable for the threat of war with Turkey in 1974 were included as explanatory variables. While they achieved high $\overline{R}^2$ values for most of the origin country models, in only five of eight equations did they obtain a significant coefficient for advertising expenditure. They note that determining the effect of such advertising on arrivals is complicated by the fact that the impact may be spread over several years and may vary by media purchased.

Brady and Widdows (1988) developed regression models of U.S. travel to three European countries during the summer months in order to quantify the effects of the Chernobyl nuclear disaster, the *Achille Lauro* attack, and terrorism directed against the U.S.A. as a result of raids on Libya on this tourism in the summer of 1986. They used airfares, disposable personal income, exchange rates, dummy variables for months and hotel/motel room rates in the U.S.A. as explanatory variables. They concluded this travel declined from one-quarter to two-thirds during the summer of 1986, with Greece suffering the greatest loss.

Smeral (1988) suggested a 'two-stage decision process, separable for each country' as a forecasting model of international tourism. In the first stage, the total amount of real expenditures on individual consumer products by the residents of a country are each forecast, including domestic tourism and international tourism specifically. In the second stage, the country of destination and expenditures in that country are determined by the size of the foreign tourism promotion budget for the country and the U.S. dollar prices of tourism goods and services in all countries. He provides the theoretical foundation in Smeral (1994), along with forecasts of average rates of tourism demand growth for eighteen countries.

Using three forms of the regression model estimated for travel among nine West European countries, Smeral investigated the effects of different income growth rates and price changes. He found that the distribution of travel expenditures differed significantly depending on the model used and the rate of income growth or price change. He also found that reductions in tourism prices in one country can increase tourism demand for that country as well as others. Smeral noted his models failed to take into account variables other than price and income, such as age structure, leisure time, tastes and supply constraints.

Smeral, Witt and Witt (1992) extended this model to project the impact of post-1992 European Union integration and political changes in Eastern Europe on national tourism imports and exports to 2000. They estimated a tourism import equation and a tourism export equation for each of the eighteen countries by ordinary least squares regression, employing annual data for 1975 through 1988. Explanatory variables for tourism imports (associated with outbound tourism) in terms of $U.S. adjusted for inflation included GDP of the generating country, the ratio of tourism import prices to consumer prices in the generating country and a dummy variable representing trend influences. On the export side (associated with inbound tourism), the explanatory variables were total tourism imports (representing the 'foreign travel budget'), the ratio of country consumer prices to other countries' prices, and a dummy trend variable. They also added dummy variables for the petroleum crises of 1974 and 1979, and for national recessions as well.

They achieved high R^2 for most equations. The income coefficient was significant at the 5 per cent level and had the correct sign in all cases. The relative price coefficients were significant at the 5 per cent level with the correct signs for most equations. One result is that the European Union travel deficit with the rest of the world is expected to increase at a greater rate than before integration. Another report on this study concluded that Canada is likely to enjoy an increase in its tourism balance with the European Union as a result of integration.

Smeral and Witt (1996) improved their original models and produced forecasts to 2005 based on 1975–92 annual data. The two-stage forecasting process forecasts demand for all foreign tourism goods and services for each of eighteen major industrial countries (first stage), and then allocates each country's demand among the eighteen countries and rest of the world (second stage). The first stage demand is modelled as a function of disposable personal income and relative consumer prices, while the second stage distribution of the origin country's foreign tourism demand is modelled as a function of relative consumer price levels, special events (for example, the 1974 and 1979 oil crises, the Eastern European market economies in the early 1990s). Slow economic growth and fast growth scenarios were employed, as well.

Darnell, Johnson and Thomas (1990) used a log-linear regression equation to model quarterly visitor volume to the North of England Open Air Museum at Beamish. Their explanatory variables included visitor volume lagged one period, admission price, real disposable personal income, the retail price index, and dummy variables for new attractions, Easter Sunday falling in the first quarter or second quarter, and exceptionally good weather. They reported nearly all tests of regression model accuracy and validity, except the MAPE. They found admission prices and income to be the most significant explanatory variables.

Crouch, Schultz and Valerio (1992) developed a regression model of annual inbound visitors, 1970–89, from five origin countries specifically to investigate the power of the marketing expenditures of the Australian Tourist Commission (ATC) to increase arrivals. Explanatory variables included personal income in the origin country, consumer prices in Australia relative to those in the origin country, the cost of travel to Australia, ATC marketing expenditures, a trend term to allow for changing 'tastes', and dummy variables for special events and disturbances, both positive and negative. They reported $\overline{R}^2$, the DW statistic, significance of the coefficients, the sign of the coefficients, and a measure of multicollinearity of the explanatory variables.

Crouch, Schultz and Valerio concluded marketing expenditures were significantly related to inbound tourism, and produced benefit-cost ratios of between 9 and 220: that is, the ratio of increased international visitor receipts to the increase in marketing expenditures was 9 for the U.S.A. and 220 for New Zealand. They also found that marketing expenditures appear to work with a lag of up to one year.

Witt and Witt (1992a) examined the relationship between validity and forecasting accuracy in thirty-five regression models of tourism flows between country origins and destinations. Their validity criteria comprised:

- coefficient of determination adjusted for degrees of freedom ($\overline{R}^2$)
- coefficient of determination (R^2)
- DW statistic
- relative number of significant coefficients at the 5 per cent level.

Their conclusion is not encouraging:

> The assessment of the likely forecasting ability of econometric models of tourism demand on the basis of common criteria such as goodness of fit, statistical significance of the coefficients, and the like may well be misleading. Conditions such as high goodness of fit and large proportion of statistically significant coefficients do not appear to be sufficient to ensure a high level of forecasting accuracy (Witt and Witt, 1992a: 66).

In other words, these four criteria do not ensure an accurate model for forecasting tourism flows among countries.

This conclusion may be due to:

1 Employing the wrong validity criteria for regression models (for example, they did not deal with possible multicollinearity, heteroscedasticity or stability in their time series).
2 Idiosyncrasies in the time series used (however, there is no evidence presented that data irregularities characterized the series used).
3 The failure of validity criteria to indicate the most accurate regression model.

Of these, the third reason is the most disturbing. If we accept this conclusion, then we are left without an *a priori* method of determining the best regression forecasting model. Moreover, the ultimate implication is that regression methods are useless for building accurate tourism forecasting models because their tests of validity do not ensure accurate forecasts.

These authors' conclusion is that the tests of regression model validity are necessary but not sufficient conditions for selecting the most accurate model for forecasting the future. They should all be applied, including the test for stability. The model or models that best satisfy these criteria are then those most likely to produce accurate forecasts. (The forecasts may even be averaged as Witt and Witt suggest – 1992a: 66). This is the best insurance against accepting an inaccurate model, but will not guarantee accuracy.

These two authors have also investigated the explanatory variables that influence international tourism through the use of regression analysis (Witt and Witt, 1994). They found that the set of such variables varies from one origin-destination pair to another, and that their relative influences do as well. This confirms the potential for error in assuming that one regression model can suffice for several pairs of destinations.

Smeral and Weber (2000) modified Smeral and Witt's 1996 study by weighting the destination tourism prices faced by each of twenty origin countries' travellers by the distribution of visitor nights among these destinations. And the relative tourism price of a destination country compared to all other destinations in the study set was computed by weighting the price indices by the visitor nights of each competitor destination and combining them into a single price index compared to the given destination country's price index. The dependent variables of tourism imports (that is, resident expenditures abroad) and tourism exports (that is, visitor expenditures in a country), real GDP and all price indices were expressed in U.S. dollars indexed to 1985 and the models of export and import levels were developed over the 1975–96 annual period. Results include visitor expenditures in the U.S.A., Portugal, Ireland and France growing at the fastest rates to 2010. In terms of generating visitor expenditures (that is, imports), Sweden, Spain, Greece and Portugal will grow the most rapidly.

Di Benedetto and Bojanic (1993) investigated the tourism area life cycle hypothesis at Cypress Gardens, Florida, over 139 quarters through regression analysis. This hypothesis states that demand for a tourism area goes through six stages over time, marking out an S-shaped curve. They used a 'step-logarithmic' form of the regression equation, which incorporated a trend variable from the series' beginning and another trend variable when Walt Disney World opened in 1971, boosting visitor volume to the entire area. They employed dummy variables to handle seasonality, the addition of new attractions on site, and external events such as the world oil crises of 1973–4 and 1979.

These authors employed nearly all of the tests of a valid, reliable regression forecasting model and concluded theirs did follow the life-cycle curve traced out by the actual series. They tested it against a Box–Jenkins ARIMA model and found they performed equally as well as measured by MAPE.

Jørgensen and Solvoll (1996) developed log-linear regression equations to forecast Norwegian residents' demand for inclusive tour charters in each of three seasons of the year over the 1969–93 period. Their explanatory variables comprised real disposable personal income, consumer expectations of future prosperity (measured by the national government's forecast of changes in personal consumption), indexes of tour prices and an index of the summer weather. The last was included to account for the fact that nearly 40 per cent of annual tours are taken in the June–August period and appear to be related to previous summer's weather conditions: the cooler and wetter the summer, the more Norwegians tend to buy inclusive tours during the subsequent summer.

Their reported R^2s were relatively low, but each of their three equations were significant by the F-test. They had difficulty with serial correlation however. They found that tour demand in the winter is least sensitive to income in the winter and most sensitive in the summer. Prices had the most adverse effects in the winter and least in the summer. They found that the poorer the summer weather in a year, the higher the demand for tours during the following twelve months. Finally, contrary to intuition, they found that their measure of consumer expectations was inversely related to tour demand: the more optimistic consumers became, the fewer tours they bought.

Chan (1993) fitted a linear trend and a sine wave to monthly seasonally adjusted tourist arrivals in Singapore over a twelve-year period, and found a complete cycle lasted 170 months. This model achieved a MAPE of 2.6 per cent, far lower than those produced by Naive 1, Naive 2, simple linear regression or ARIMA models.

Testing the results of Chan (1993), Chu (1998b) compared the forecasting accuracy of a Box–Jenkins ARIMA model dealing with seasonal and annual differences and a sine wave model for forecasting visitor arrivals in Singapore. The models were built with monthly arrivals data from July 1977 to December 1988 and tested over the ex post period of the ensuing nineteen months. The ARIMA model produced only two turning-point errors out of a possible sixteen, but its MAPE was only marginally better than the sine wave model.

Carraro and Manente (1994) describe a set of regression equations representing tourism flows from twenty-one countries to Italy and from Italy to these twenty-one countries, using a three-stage process. The first step is to estimate the amount of national income in a country in a year and the allocation between savings and consumption. The second stage is to forecast how much of the consumption total in a country will be allocated for outbound travel for the year. The third stage is to estimate how much of this will be allocated to travel to Italy, or from Italy to an individual destination country in the year. Given the paucity of data on expenditures, the third stage generated estimates of visitors rather than visitor expenditures. Measures of income, absolute and relative prices, leisure time, climatic conditions, exceptional events including terrorism were tested in log-linear regression equations over the 1976–91 period. Among conclusions are that travel to Italy from the U.S.A. and Japan are *more* sensitive to economic conditions in the origin countries than the other nineteen, and visitors from Central Europe are the least affected *by* economic variations.

Smith (1995: 131–40) suggests a gravity model be estimated for significant destinations in a country and then used to forecast future visitor volume to individual destinations. For ten provinces of Canada, he assumed travel from origin i to destination j was directly related to the product of the population of origin i, the attractiveness of destination j (represented by the population of j), and a constant representing the intercept factor in the usual regression model. This product was then divided by the distance between origin i and destination j taken to some power estimated by regression. He found a high R^2 for the given year of estimation, but found the model overpredicted short trips and underpredicted long ones. He also noted this model is unconstrained, placing no limit on the number of trips estimated from an origin.

Qiu and Zhang (1995) examined seven determinants and two functional forms (linear and log-linear) of annual visitors to Canada from the U.S.A., the U.K., the former West Germany, France and Japan. Employing visitor data for 1975–90 and expenditure data for 1979–89, they found they could produce accurate (as measured by $\overline{R}^2$) simulations of the visitor time series for all countries but the U.S.A. and of expenditures for all countries but Japan. Generating country gross national product (GNP) per capita and Canadian travel prices were the most powerful explanatory variables for the visitor volume models, while GNP per capita and exchange rates were most influential in the expenditure models. They also concluded that the linear and log-linear forms of their equations were 'empirically equivalent' in accuracy.

González and Moral (1995) applied structural time series modelling to monthly tourism receipts and visitor arrivals in Spain over the 1979–93 period. Such models combine explanatory variables used in regression models with trend and seasonal variables as handled in ARIMA models. These authors tested the explanatory variables of real national income (represented by monthly series of industrial production), an index of the ratio of tourism prices in Spain relative to those in a set of origin countries (that is, consumer price indexes adjusted by exchange rates) and an index of the ratio of tourism prices in Spain to those in a set of competing destinations (that is, consumer price indexes adjusted by exchange rates). Taking annual differences and seasonal differences, they found that the income variable was not significant in explaining tourism expenditures, but that it was for explaining arrivals. They also concluded that large price increases in Spain since it joined the European Economic Community in the mid-1980s depressed visitor expenditures in Spain.

Qu and Zhang (1996), using 1970 to 1982 annual international visitor data, combined a linear time trend model with an autoregressive model to forecast visitor volumes for twelve countries in the East Asia and Pacific region for 1982–92. The approach first fitted the linear time trend regression to the actual data and then applied autoregression to the residuals, discarding lags not significant at the 0.05 level of significance. Unfortunately, they only reported MAPEs for these models, which varied from 3.3 per cent to 20 per cent over the ex post forecast period. They concluded that arrivals in these twelve countries would rise from 41 million in 1992 to 155 million in 2005, an average annual growth rate of 10.8 per cent.

Qu and Lam (1997) applied stepwise regression analysis to forecast annual visitor arrivals in Hong Kong from mainland China using the 1984–95 time series. Among seven explanatory variables tested, only disposable income per capita and a dummy variable representing relaxation of visa requirements in 1994 proved significant at the 0.10 level of significance, producing an $\overline{R}^2$ of 0.99. Exchange rates, relative consumer price levels, and dummy variables for the Tiananmen Square incident (1989) and the Gulf War (1990) did not prove significant.

Lim (1997) found that 83 of 100 published papers she reviewed on international tourism demand forecasting models reported using ordinary least squares regression models. The DW statistic was reported in 55 of these 100 studies making it by far the most popular diagnostic test applied to these models.

Turner, Kulendran and Fernando (1997b: 311) used the following dummy variables (which they called 'intervention variables') in modelling quarterly arrivals in Australia from the U.S.A., Japan, the U.K. and New Zealand: the *Crocodile Dundee* movie, America's Cup yacht race, Japan's policy to boost travel abroad beginning in the third quarter of 1987, the World Exposition in Brisbane, Australia, and Australia's airline pilot's strike.

Wong (1997a), in an investigation of annual international arrivals series for six regions of the world and seventeen countries over the 1964–92 period found that most of them were not stationary in their variances and that this could be removed by taking first differences.

Wong (1997b) tried modelling quarterly visitor arrivals in Hong Kong over the 1975–91 period in order to capture the cyclical behaviour evident in the series. Ex post forecasting tests of various models indicated that single and double sine wave regression models, along with the log quadratic trend (ln Visitors $= a + bT + cT^2$) produced the lowest MAPEs at about 4 per cent. The best ARIMA model produced a MAPE of nearly 12 per cent.

Akis (1998) found that a simple set of regression equations relating the logarithm of visitor arrivals in Turkey to the logarithm of national incomes in eighteen generating countries and relative prices in Turkey compared to the generating countries over the 1980–93 period produced R^2s of 0.80 or above for twelve of them. Seven of the generating countries showed negative relative price coefficients significant at the 5 per cent level of significance, while another three showed negative coefficients significant at the 10 per cent level.

Chu (1998a) examined the impact on the accuracy of forecasting international visitor arrivals in Singapore of combining the results of two models. Fitting an ARIMA model developed by Box–Jenkins procedures to July 1977–December 1987 de-seasonalized monthly data, and a sine wave time series regression model to the same period, Chu combined forecasts for an ensuing nineteenth-month period by weighting each by their relative error terms. He found the resulting combined forecast model produced forecasts with a MAPE somewhat lower than the ARIMA model alone, and significantly lower than the sine wave model.

Frechtling (2000) investigated the explanatory power of national income and the population age structure of 20 countries in generating international trips. Time series for each country on outbound long-haul and short-haul international visitor volumes, population trends by age group, and real Gross Domestic Product (GDP) were analyzed through single-equation regression models over the 1989–98 period to discern major relationships among these variables. Projections of population by age group and real GDP for these countries were then used to project outbound international long-haul and short-haul travel for these countries to 2010.

He found that long-haul travel generated by the Republic of Korea, Taiwan, Germany, Brazil, and Spain will be especially robust in the next decade, but that the U.S. will remain by far the largest source of such travel. On the other hand, Germany and the U.K. will be by far the largest sources of short-haul visitors in 2010. Moreover, the retired age cohort is a major force for generating short-haul and long-haul travel gains over the next decade for most of the countries studied. However, forecasting short-haul travel proved much more difficult than the long-haul activity, suggesting the former is more sensitive to inflation, exchange rates, and other variables not examined in this forecasting exercise.

Conclusion

This chapter presents the linear regression model, a powerful and popular model for estimating the quantitative relationship between tourism demand and one or more variables associated with that demand. It is important to recognize the limitations of this very popular method. Above all is the limitation that regression analysis does not prove that a cause-and-effect relationship exists between a dependent variable and its explanatory variables. Rather, it indicates variations in the former are associated with certain variations in the latter variables. Cause and effect can only be proved by experimentally manipulating changes in an explanatory variable and measuring the resulting changes in the dependent variable while holding all other contributing factors constant. As one group has observed, 'regression analysis results should therefore be treated as *prima facie* evidence of a cause-effect relationship and not as conclusive proof' (Crouch, Schultz and Valerio, 1992: 206).

Since tourism demand is generally the product of a complex set of factors, simple linear regression models employing one explanatory variable are rarely successful and never valid for simulating the time series. Rather, the forecaster needs to carefully consider a range of variables that stimulate tourists to travel away from home, that attract visitors, and that act as barriers to tourism flows between origins and destinations.

As the discussion of building a multiple regression model of hotel/motel room demand in the Washington, D.C., showed, it is sometimes difficult to derive a valid, significant, accurate forecasting model by this technique. Even a model that passes the myriad of tests with flying colours can fail to make reasonable forecasts. Considerable experience with such models will aid you in knowing when you have a model that 'works' or not.

In some cases, you may need to review a model someone else has developed and its products. If so, you should look for the characteristics of sound regression models presented above to aid your assessment. These are summarized in Table 7.11.

In a thorough comparative study of various international tourism forecasting methods, Witt and Witt (1992a) found that regression models (which they call 'econometrics') were less accurate than the naive method of assuming the next period's value equals the last period's in forecasting the level of tourism demand. They were, however, the most accurate among seven methods

Table 7.11 Characteristics of a sound forecasting model and their indicators

Characteristic	Test indicators
Is the model valid?	Expected signs of coefficients, lagged variables, dummy variables
Are explanatory variables uncorrelated with one another?	Examine intercorrelations for multicollinearity
Does the model accurately simulate its time series?	$\overline{R}^2$, F-statistic, MAPE
Are the $\overline{R}^2$ and F-statistic tests valid?	DW statistic; test for heteroscedasticity
Are any irrelevant variables included?	*t*-test
Are any relevant explanatory variables omitted?	DW statistic
Is the model stable?	Chow predictive failure test

examined in forecasting changes in the direction of a series, that is, whether next year's value would be higher or lower than this year's.

It appears the considerable time and expense required to build a valid regression model for forecasting tourism demand may not be justified on the basis of its accuracy in forecasting next year's values. However, such a model is indispensable if we want to understand what factors affect tourism demand and how. Indeed, Witt and Witt (1992a: 166) conclude: 'the main use of econometric [i.e., regression] models to a practitioner is with respect to the identification of the size of the effects that changes in the explanatory variables are likely to have upon tourism demand, and not as a direct forecasting tool'.

In short, we may not expect a great deal of accuracy in forecasting levels from such models, but we should demand they perform well in predicting whether next year's value will be greater or less than this year's.

Notes

1 'Econometric model' is also used by some to include both one equation models as well as multiple equation models (see Witt and Witt, 1992a: 13–15). To avoid confusion, the term 'structural econometric model' will be used in this book to describe systems of regression equations that are linked together and attempt to represent salient causal relationships at work.

2 Some statisticians object to this interpretation of the constant term in a regression equation. They argue that it represents the mean effect on the dependent variable of all of the excluded variables (Rao and Miller, 1971: 6).

3 For multiple regression equations, the relationship is

$$F = \frac{R^2/k}{(1 - R^2)/(n - k - 1)},$$

where n is the number of observations and k is the number of parameters, i.e., number of explanatory variables plus one (Makridakis, Wheelwright, and Hyndman, 1998: 253).

4 This appears to be the most popular confidence interval in tourism demand forecasting models. It means that over a large number of samples, 95 per cent of them would contain the population mean within the confidence interval. This statement is the same as postulating a '5 per cent level of significance'. These statements are used interchangeably in this book (Pindyck and Rubinfeld, 1981: 36–7). When investigating models with annual differences, 90 per cent confidence intervals are often used because these magnitudes tend to vary much more than levels or logarithms of levels.

For further information

Calantone, R. J., di Benedetto, C. A. and Bojanic, D. (1987). A comprehensive review of the tourism forecasting literature. *Journal of Travel Research*, **26** (2), Fall, 28–39.

Clifton, P., Nguyen, H. and Nutt, S. (1992). *Market Research: Using Forecasting in Business*, pp. 127–51. Butterworth-Heinemann.

Cunningham, S. (1991). *Data Analysis in Hotel and Catering Management*, ch. 12. Butterworth-Heinemann.

Gujarati, D. (1992). *Essentials of Econometrics*, chs 5–13. McGraw-Hill.

Kennedy, P. (1992). *Guide to Econometrics*, 3rd edition. MIT Press.

Levenbach, H. and Cleary, J. P. (1981). *The Beginning Forecaster: The Forecasting Process through Data Analysis*, chs 12–17. Lifetime Learning.

Makridakis, S., Wheelwright, S. C. and Hyndman, R. J. (1998), *Forecasting: Methods and Applications*. 3rd edition, chs 5 and 6. Wiley.

Mentzner, J. T. and Bienstock, C. C. (1998). *Sales Forecasting Management*, ch. 4. Sage.

Pindyck, R. S. and Rubinfeld, D. L. (1981). *Econometric Models and Economic Forecasts*. 2nd edition, chs 1–10. McGraw-Hill.

Rao, P. and Miller, R. L. (1971). *Applied Econometrics*, chs 1–3. Wadsworth.

Saunders, J. A., Sharp, J. A. and Witt, S. F. (1987). *Practical Business Forecasting*, chs 5 and 6. Gower.

Shim, J. K., Siegel, J. G. and Liew, C. J. (1994). *Strategic Business Forecasting*, chs 4 and 5. Probus.

Smeral, E. (1994). Economic models. In *Tourism Marketing and Management Handbook* (S. F. Witt and L. Moutinho, eds) 2nd edition, pp. 497–503. Prentice-Hall.

Smith, S. L. J. (1995). *Tourism Analysis: A Handbook*. 2nd edition, ch. 6. Longman Scientific and Technical.

Witt, S. F. (1994). Econometric demand forecasting. In *Tourism Marketing and Management Handbook* (S. F. Witt and L. Moutinho, eds) 2nd edition, pp. 516–520. Prentice-Hall.

Witt, S. F. and Witt, C. A. (1992). *Modeling and Forecasting Demand in Tourism*. Academic Press.

Witt, S. F. and Witt, C. A. (1995). Forecasting tourism demand: a review of empirical research. *International Journal of Forecasting*, **11** (3), September, 447–75.

8

Causal methods: structural econometric models

Recall the discussion in Chapter 7 that economic theory suggested that the following model might explain most of the variance in hotel/motel room nights sold in Washington, D.C.:

$$HRS = a + b_1 RDPI - b_2 ARR - b_3 AF - b_4 CAN + b_5 PB + b_6 PI \qquad (8.1)$$

where HRS = hotel/motel room-nights sold
RDPI = real disposable personal income
ARR = average hotel/motel room rate
AF   = airline fares
CAN = Canadian dollar cost of the $U.S.
PB   = promotional budget for Washington, D.C.
PI   = a presidential inauguration year
a = intercept constant
b = slope coefficients.

A multivariate regression was run to estimate the parameters (the intercept, a, and the slope coefficients, b_n). The parameters, then, quantify the relationship between the explanatory variable and the dependent variable. The nature of regression analysis assumes the relationship is all one way, that is, from the explanatory variables to the dependent variable. Moreover, it assumes minimum relationships among the explanatory variables. If we found high correlations among potential explanatory variables, we either transformed them or dropped them from consideration to guard against the deleterious effects of multicollinearity.

In short, the single multivariate regression equation assumes the only causality operating in the world is from each explanatory variable to the forecast variable. A little reflection suggests this may well do violence to reality.

For example, there may be a feedback mechanism operating from hotel/motel room-nights sold to average room rate. If demand for rooms is pushing against capacity thus raising occupancy rates, this may well encourage hoteliers to raise room rates more rapidly than when occupancy rates are low, so that we might envision:

$$\text{ARR} = a_2 + b_7\text{HRS} \qquad (8.2)$$

Moreover, the budget available for promoting Washington, D.C., is partially financed by hotels and motels in the area. A year's budget may be based on some proportion of the past year's hotel sales, so we could well have:

$$\text{PB}_t = a_3 + b_8\text{HRS}_{t-1} \qquad (8.3)$$

There may also be relationships at work among the explanatory variables. Some have found the demand for air travel from U.S. carriers (AD) is closely related to the growth in the U.S. economy, as measured, say, by real disposable personal income (RDPI). And as air travel demand pushes against airline capacity, air fares (AF) rise more rapidly. This suggests:

$$\text{AD} = a_4 + b_9\text{RDPI} \qquad (8.4)$$

$$\text{AF} = a_5 + b_{10}\text{AD} \qquad (8.5)$$

Finally, years of presidential inaugurations (PI) may be associated with higher hotel/motel room rates, as follows:

$$\text{HRS} = a_6 + b_{11}\text{PI} \qquad (8.6)$$

$$\text{ARR} = a_7 + b_{12}\text{HRS} \qquad (8.7)$$

These feedback and cross-dependencies cannot be captured in a single equation multivariate regression model. Rather, economic forecasters have developed systems of interdependent equations to more faithfully represent the important relationships in the real world, and these are called *structural econometric models*[1] because they attempt to replicate the important structures of the economy and other elements of the real world. '[Structural] econometric models can include any number of simultaneous multiple regression equations [and] denote systems of linear equations involving several *interdependent variables*' (Makridakis, Wheelwright and Hyndman, 1998: 299; italics added).

In reviewing Equations 8.2–8.7, it is clear that the terms 'dependent variable' and 'explanatory variable' have lost their distinctions. In some equations (8.1 and 8.6) hotel room-nights sold is the dependent variable, but in others (8.2, 8.3 and 8.7) they are explanatory variables. Instead, forecasters make use of the terms *endogenous variable* and *exogenous variable* in a structural econometric model.

Endogenous variables are all those determined within the structure. That is, they appear at least once on the left-hand side of an equation in a structural econometric model, such as hotel room-night sales in Equation 8.6 and average room rate in Equation 8.7. *Exogenous variables* are determined outside the structure, by forces that do not appear within the structure. In this model, these include presidential inaugural years and the exchange rate between the Canadian dollar and the U.S. dollar. These never appear on the left-hand side of an equation as affected by another variable in the mode.

How many endogenous variables and exogenous variables to include is up to the structural model builder. You will base this decision and that concerning the number of equations to include on theory and on the availability of valid data.

Structural econometric models are composed of *simultaneous equation systems*. The distinctive characteristic of these systems is that all of the relationships involved are needed for determining the value of at least one of the endogenous variables. Correctly solving these systems to estimate valid parameters is at the heart of structural model estimation.

A tourism demand structural econometric model

The following is an example of a structural econometric model for forecasting hotel/motel room sales.

$$\text{HRS}_t = a_1 + b_1\text{GDP}_t - b_2\text{ARR}_t - b_3\text{AF}_t + e_{1,t} \tag{8.8}$$

$$\text{GDP}_t = a_2 + c_1\text{C}_t + c_2\text{I}_t + c_3\text{G}_t + e_{2,t} \tag{8.9}$$

$$\text{C}_t = a_3 + d_1\text{GDP}_{t-1} + e_{3,t} \tag{8.10}$$

$$AF_t = a_4 + f\frac{RPM_{t-1}}{ASM_{t-1}} + e_{4,t} \tag{8.11}$$

$$RPM_t = a_5 + gGDP_t + e_{5,t} \tag{8.12}$$

$$ARR_t = a_6 = h\frac{TC_{t-1}}{HRS_{t-1}} + e_{6,t} \tag{8.13}$$

where

HRS	=	hotel/motel room-nights sold
GDP	=	gross domestic product
ARR	=	average hotel room rate
AF	=	average airline fare
C	=	personal consumption expenditures
I	=	capital investment
G	=	net government purchases of goods and services
RPM	=	airline revenue passenger-miles
ASM	=	airline available seat-miles
TC	=	total hotel operating costs
e	=	residual
t	=	some time period
a	=	intercept constant
b,c,d,f,g,h	=	slope coefficients.

There are three types of equations that can appear in such models. First, are those that describe the *behaviour* of consumers and other actors: Equations 8.8, 8.10 and 8.12. Second are equations that describe *technical relationships*, such as production functions and price functions: Equations 8.11 and 8.13. Finally are *identity* equations, which are true by definition: Equation 8.9 defines gross domestic product. It is not necessary to include all three types in a structural econometric model, but you should consider what might productively be included from each category.

Advantages and disadvantages

Structural econometric models offer a number of advantages over single-equation models:

- They more fully represent the interdependencies of variables in the real world.
- They allow detailed simulations, that is, forecasting the results of changes in certain exogenous variables for policy analyses.
- The process of building a structural model improves our understanding of how the portion of the world we are interested in works.

There are, of course, limitations of structural econometric models that the forecaster should understand:

■ They are far more complex and costly to build than single regression equation models.
■ They require a great deal of input data.
■ Multicollinearity is an even more serious problem than in multiple regression models.
■ Omission of an important explanatory variable will result in large forecast errors (called the 'specification problem').
■ The ordinary least squares estimation procedures lead to biased and inconsistent estimates of parameters in these models and cannot be used.
■ Random errors can become magnified by the structural relationships.
■ There are no standard sets of rules for building these models.
■ They must be continually monitored and adjusted.

Since ordinary least squares regression produces biased estimates of parameters in structural econometric models, it is not used for such estimation. Rather, one or a combination of the following methods is employed:

■ two stage least squares, the most popular method
■ indirect least squares
■ full information maximum likelihood
■ limited information maximum likelihood.

Discussion of these is beyond the practical orientation of this book, but the interested reader is directed to the sources of further information at the end of this chapter.

Given the challenges of constructing, operating and maintaining such models, it is not surprising that there are so few such models available for forecasting tourism demand. More often, there are sets of independent equations for forecasting tourism demand from an origin for a number of different destinations, or for projecting visitor flows among countries. These employ a large number of multivariate regression equations, where the explanatory variables for each equation are drawn from a large set of possible variables.

The inherent complexity of developing structural econometric models ensures they are not likely to appeal to any but large business organizations, government and the occasional university. There are several consulting firms that have specialized in building large structural econometric models of national economies. These can be queried should a manager seek to have a structural model of tourism demand developed.

The estimation process

Figure 8.1 outlines the steps in building and using a structural econometric model.

There are two special problems associated with structural equation models that must be resolved in order to achieve valid models and reduce forecast error. The *specification problem* arises when one or more important variables are omitted from the model. This produces biased parameters in single equation regression models as well, but the error is magnified in a structural econometric model because a number of equations are affected.

There is a requirement in structural models that there be one, and only one, equation for explaining each endogenous variable. If an endogenous variable does not have an equation explaining it, then it should be treated as exogenous. If there are more endogenous equations than endogenous variables, errors of estimation and reduced significance of the parameters estimated result.

The *identification problem* is a mathematical question associated with simultaneous equation systems. It is concerned with the possibility of

---

1. Detail your theory of what variables are important to explaining the course of your tourism demand variable and how they are related.

2. Designate the exogenous and endogenous variables.

3. Specify the expected relationships in mathematical form, including:
   a. parameter signs
   b. parameter approximate magnitudes
   c. functional form, e.g. linear, log-linear
   d. leads and lags.

4. Choose the estimation procedures, *e.g.,* indirect least squares, two stage least squares, etc.

5. Assemble relevant data.

6. Estimate the coefficients, which show the relationships between individual explanatory variables and the forecast variable.

7. Conduct statistical tests of the model to evaluate validity.

8. If satisfactory, use the model to forecast future values.

9. Monitor the residuals and make appropriate changes to improve the model's accuracy.

Figure 8.1   Structural model estimation process

obtaining meaningful estimates of the model's parameters, so it is an issue of validity.

One way to view this problem is to consider the forecasting of hotel room demand. The actual values we have in our time series reflect actual demand behaviour. However, they also reflect the realities of supply: the number of rooms purchased on a given day is the intersection of the demand curve and the supply curve. Unfortunately, we do not know which is dominating the outcomes we observe: hotel/motel room-nights sold and room rates. To resolve this, we must transform the structural equations so that no single equation can be mimicked by a linear combination all of the equations. For example, we might add a measure of consumer income to the demand equation but exclude it from the supply equation.

Applications

Jenkins and Frechtling (1991) experimented with an existing large-scale global structural econometric model (the Fair World Model) to indicate how terrorist attacks against tourism targets, such as occurred in 1985–6, and rapid increases in the cost of petroleum would affect the travel of West German residents to ten major destination countries. The Fair World Model indicated the linkages between the consumer, government, business and financial sectors of West Germany and the ten other countries. These and the airline distances, along with dummy variables for the petroleum price inflation in 1973–4 and 1979–80, were correlated with the outbound tourism that West Germany generated to these countries. The estimation method was unusual in that it allowed elasticities to vary over time rather than remain constant as is assumed in most tourism demand regression models.

The authors generated baseline forecasts for West Germany travel to each of the ten countries, assuming no terrorist attacks and petroleum remaining at $20 per barrel in 1989 prices. The 1985–6 terrorism was found to produce no measurable impact on German travel to Australia, Austria, France, Italy and Japan. With the price of oil doubling, and the presence of terrorism, West German travel to the U.K. was projected to drop by one-third and to the U.S.A. to three-quarters. Travel to Canada, Greece and Iceland dropped by percentages between these extremes.

Coopers and Lybrand (1997) (now PriceWaterhouseCoopers) have developed a structural econometric forecasting model of U.S. hotel/motel room-nights sales, average daily room rates and room supply. Room-night sales are captured in a regression model as a function of real GDP in a four-quarter first-degree polynomial (that is, 36 per cent of the impact of GDP on room-night sales occurs in the current quarter, 29 per cent in the following quarter,

21 per cent in the quarter after that and 14 per cent in the succeeding quarter) and real average daily room rates. Elasticity of room-nights sold to real GDP is 1.4 and to the average daily rate is –0.26. Percentage change over the year earlier in average daily room rate is a function of change in the Consumer Price Index (positive relationship), lagged occupancy rates (positive) and lagged room supply (negative). Hotel/motel room supply is driven by new starts as a negative function of real user cost of capital, positive function of real average daily room rates, real commercial/ industrial loan volume and lagged room supply. From this forecast is subtracted the number of rooms closed each quarter to get net rooms supplied.

Turner, Reisinger and Witt (1998) built a structural model to examine quarterly tourism flows from the U.K. to seven European destinations over the 1978–95 period. They broke these flows down into three endogenous variables by purpose: holidays, business and visit friends and relatives (VFR), and investigated the influence of one on another. Exogenous variables tested were classified as nine economic (measures of income, prices and international trade) and four social variables (measuring population, immigration/ emigration and confidence). Differencing was used to minimize serial correlations, and logarithms were taken to approximate normal distributions, and the maximum likelihood method was employed to estimate the coefficients.

Among the endogenous variables, the authors found only two significant interactions: business flows influenced holiday flows from the U.K. to France, and business and VFR flows influenced U.K. holiday flows to Germany. Several economic variables played the dominant role in explaining business travel flows, while the social variables were more important in determining holiday flows. Surprisingly, social variables played a lesser role in explaining VFR tourism to the seven countries than the economic variables. The authors concluded, 'as different explanatory variables are relevant for different types of tourism (holiday, business, VFR), it appears that the widely accepted practice in existing literature of estimating tourism demand functions aggregated by purpose of visit may not be valid' (Turner, Reisinger and Witt, 1998: 322–3).

Conclusion

Structural econometric models have the advantage of explicitly reflecting the interdependencies among variables that exist in the real world. However, they are costly to build and difficult to build well. There appear to be few such models for estimating tourism demand today, and the above discussion suggests why. They require a great deal of resources in terms of time, money, expertise and input data. There appears to be little interest among forecasters in building econometric structural models today, primarily because their demonstrated forecasting accuracy has not justified their costs (see Kennedy, 1998: 168–9; Makridakis, Wheelwright and Hyndman, 1998: 301–2). However, they do have value 'for increasing the understanding of the way an economic system works and for testing and evaluating alternative policies' (Makridakis, Wheelwright and Hyndman, 1998: 301).

Note

1 This rather clumsy term is designed to distinguish this approach to forecasting from the single equation forecasting models discussed in Chapter 7 and from structural econometric time series models (Kennedy, 1998: 265–6).

For further information

Almon, C. (1989). *The Craft of Economic Modeling*. 2nd edition. Ginn Press.

Granger, C. W. J. (1989). *Forecasting in Business and Economics*. 2nd edition, ch. 5. Academic Press.

Holden, K., Peel, D. A. and Thompson, J. L. (1990). *Economic Forecasting: An Introduction*, ch. 5. Cambridge University Press.

Jarrett, J. (1991). *Business Forecasting Methods*. 2nd edition, ch. 6. Blackwell.

Kennedy, P. (1998). *A Guide to Econometrics*. 4th edition, ch. 10. MIT Press.

Kmenta, J. (1971). *Elements of Econometrics*, ch. 13. Macmillan.

Makridakis, S., Wheelwright, S. C. and McGee, V. (1983). *Forecasting: Methods and Applications*. 2nd edition, ch. 7. Wiley.

Pindyck, R. S. and Rubinfeld, D. L. (1981). *Econometric Models and Economic Forecasts*. 2nd edition, ch. 11. McGraw-Hill.

9

Qualitative forecasting methods

Chapters 4 through 8 have presented various *quantitative* techniques for forecasting tourism demand. These seek to state the relationship of the forecast value to its earlier values or to explanatory variables in numerical terms. We now turn to *qualitative* forecasting methods, also called 'judgemental methods' or 'subjective forecasting'.

Qualitative forecasting methods rely on the experience and the judgement of individuals assumed to be experts in the field under study. The expert, or 'judge', rather than the computer, is the processor of information. Moreover, the qualitative forecaster is usually not trying to estimate a value for a given variable but to suggest the boundaries within which the future value will lie.

Specifically, we will look at four qualitative forecasting techniques in the context of tourism demand in this chapter:

1 Jury of executive opinion.
2 Subjective probability assessment.
3 Delphi method.
4 Consumer intentions survey.

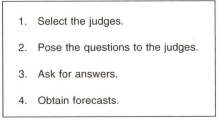

1. Select the judges.

2. Pose the questions to the judges.

3. Ask for answers.

4. Obtain forecasts.

Figure 9.1   Steps common to qualitative forecasting models

All of the qualitative forecasting methods discussed here follow a simple four-step process, as shown in Figure 9.1. The methods differ in how the judges are selected, what information is provided along with the questions, the degree of interaction among judges and how the judges' reports are processed to obtain the final forecasts. The four methods follow the biblical admonition that 'plans fail for lack of counsel, but with many advisers they succeed' (Proverbs 15:22, New International Version).

Occasions for qualitative methods

Qualitative forecasting methods are normally applied under one or more of the following conditions.

There are insufficient historical data. In some cases, we do not have enough past data for use in a quantitative model to produce valid forecasts. This is especially true in the case of a new product, such as a supersonic aircraft, a new luxury resort in a country that has none, or a new reservations technology for consumer use.

The time series available is not reliable or valid. We may have a long time series of data that are suspect as to quality and relevance to what we wish to measure. Measuring same-day visitors, or day-trippers, is difficult for a number of countries and the series they publish may not be accurate. Many countries, including the U.S.A., do not publish estimates of same-day visitors. Some countries, such as Australia, report no counts of total overnight visitors.

The macroenvironment is changing rapidly. The *macroenvironment* comprises external factors that are beyond the control of the tourism marketer but which affect demand. These include the economies of major source markets, exchange rates, political changes, weather, labour unrest and the spread of digital technologies, to name a few. It is difficult, for example, to imagine accurate quantitative model forecasts of visitor volume to the Czech Republic, Yugoslavia and Russia for the post-1989 period, or tourism generated from these countries. Similarly, quantitative models would prove ineffective in forecasting travel to and from Hong Kong after reversion to the People's Republic of China, and from a united Germany after reunification.

Major disturbances are expected. Whereas macroenvironmental changes may be slow to develop and can last for years, *disturbances* are essentially unanticipated, short-term major changes in factors affecting tourism. These include wars, terrorism, political upheavals, and floods and other natural disasters. This condition appears to characterize tourism to and from most Middle Eastern countries at the current time, and several African ones.

Long-term forecasts are desired. Reliable forecasts for periods of three to five years or more in the future are difficult to generate from quantitative models. This is primarily due to the greater number of factors that may then affect visitor flows and to their greater variability in the long run. Yet sometimes tourism managers, planners and others need to understand the possible shapes of a distant future which qualitative techniques can provide.

Questions often asked about the long-term future of tourism demand include:

■ What events may occur in the next ten years that could critically affect our product or markets?
■ By what year will a new technology be widely used?
■ What will our visitor volume be in ten years?

Advantages and disadvantages

Advantages of qualitative techniques is that they are usually inexpensive, they do not require a high level of statistical skill, and they often comprise the only methods of dealing with certain forecasting problems, as indicated above.

However, errors can arise due to the lack of expertise or bias of chosen judges, the human tendency to confuse desires for the future with forecasts of it and judges' predisposition to be anchored in the present and underestimate future changes. Moreover, there is less restraint on the forecaster from asserting his or her own views in a qualitative forecast than for a quantitative one.

Jury of executive opinion

One of the simplest and most widely used forecasting approaches is the jury of executive opinion. In its most basic form, the method comprises corporate executives or government officials meeting together and reaching consensus estimates of key variables in the future. The output is specific values or a range of values expected at specific points in the future.

An advantage of this technique is its simplicity. Very little skill or training is required to participate, and only knowledge about the variables to be forecast is required. It does not require much historical data, although describing the recent past may be helpful in establishing a common foundation for the discussion. The method serves to pool the experience and judgement of those most familiar with the variables to be forecast. Finally, it is eminently feasible without long historical series.

The disadvantages are several. Perhaps the most damaging is that often the most forceful or most senior executive's opinion carries the most weight in this group discussion. Yet these may not have the best ability to describe the most likely future. Related to this is the fact that this method disperses responsibility for developing accurate forecasts, with the result that the judges may not devote serious effort to the task. When a group is responsible, no one person can be held accountable for forecasting errors.

Another disadvantage is that the jury of executive opinion requires costly executive time. This cost may be hidden, but a careful accounting may well show that other forecasting methods are cheaper and more accurate. Finally, this method does not necessarily produce detailed forecasts that are consistent with one another. For example, using this group consensus method to forecast arrivals in a hotel generated by various market segments (for example, meeting and conventions, individual business travellers, group leisure travel and individual leisure travellers) may produce expected arrival volumes for certain months that are larger than the hotel's capacity.

Figure 9.2 summarizes the four-step process for the jury of executive opinion.

---

1. Select the judges: people familiar with the variables you are forecasting, their recent history, and what affects them.

2. Pose the questions to the judges: in a group setting where discussion is encouraged; include background material.

3. Ask for answers: record the various forecasts of point estimates from the group where all can see them.

4. Obtain forecasts: discuss the various forecasts until a consensus on point forecasts of the variables is reached.

Figure 9.2 The jury of executive opinion process

Makridakis, Wheelwright and Hyndman (1998: 505–8) suggest that providing appropriate background information on the activities being forecast can considerably improve this process. Specifically, they recommend presenting the group with time series of the variables to be forecast, along with linear time trend forecasts of annual percentage changes for the future periods before the group meets. Each participant is asked to consider macroenvironmental factors (especially economic and technological ones), competitive developments, industry-wide factors and any others they think will work to increase or decrease this trend, and by how much.

For example, hotel sales executives might be presented with a 3 per cent trend growth rate for recent years and a form to record their expectations for the coming year. In considering the economic outlook (say, a recession that will cut one percentage point off of this growth), technological prospects (larger planes flying into the local airport adding 1 per cent), competitive developments (new hotel opens cutting 0.5 per cent), and the industry trend toward higher energy costs forcing rates up (reducing trend growth by 0.2 per cent), one participant may conclude the appropriate growth rate will be $3 - 1 + 1 - 0.5 - 0.2 = 2.3$ per cent.

Gathering all of these forms and summarizing them, the meeting facilitator presents the consensus growth rate and opinions on the major factors affecting this for discussion. The meeting concludes with a consensus growth rate or set of forecasts by exploiting the advantage of a statistical method plus the executive opinions affecting that rate.

Despite its limitations, the jury of executive opinion will remain a popular method for forecasting tourism demand for individual facilities, attractions and destinations due to its celerity and simplicity.

Applications of the jury of executive opinion

In 1998, the WTO developed forecasts of visitor flows between forty-four pairs of subregional country groupings to 2020. The research team first developed the time series of these flows and then surveyed the views of WTO's 211 member countries and territories, and fifty international industry leaders and academic researchers. Additional interviews were conducted in Asia in 1997–8 to assess the impact of the financial crises there. The team added extensive study of economic, social and industry trend research and developed growth rates for the subregion pairs to 2020. These were presented and discussed at regional seminars around the world in order to reach a consensus on visitor flow growth rates expected among the subregions.

Moutinho and Witt (1995) chose the jury of executive opinion over the Delphi method to rank the importance and impact of twenty-five possible future developments in science and technology affecting tourism, the probability of the occurrence of each and the most likely year of occurrence up to 2030. They felt it was important to permit discussion among the twenty-five experts to facilitate the exchange of ideas and allow for clarification of reasoning before the forecasts were made due 'to the rather innovative/radical nature' of these developments. They found among other things that mean probability of occurrence was inversely correlated with the mean year of expected occurrence.

Subjective probability assessment

The jury of executive opinion forecasting method usually produces point estimates of future variables as the most likely forecast, with perhaps a range on either side of possible values, as well. In the subjective probability assessment method, the members of a group are each asked to suggest a probability distribution for the forecast variable. This is often easier for a judge to deal with than trying to specify a single future value.

To begin, we select the judges. These may be corporate executives, government officials, outside experts or some combination of these. In posing the questions, it is useful to include background information that helps to bring all judges up to the same level of knowledge.

The questions themselves should be straightforward and cover basic variables. You should avoid asking about aggregate variables that combine various levels of uncertainty. For example, instead of asking hotel executives to forecast total room-nights that will be sold in an area, you could break this down by market segment, for example, meetings and conventions, individual business travellers, group leisure, etc. This takes advantage of the fact that some of the subvariables may be known with more certainty than others.

The next step is to ask for answers. This should be done to elicit probability distributions from the judges. Figure 9.3 is an example of how to pose the questions and ask for responses.

You, as forecast manager, then process the returned reporting forms. If the number of judges reporting is twenty or more, you can show the distribution of the expected values reported by the judges. The expected value for an individual judge is simply the sum of the products of the values with their probabilities. For example, assume a judge using the reporting form in Figure 9.3 reported the following probabilities:

1. Room nights sold in 2000 (millions)	2. Probability of this outcome	3. Product of value and probability (1 × 2)
16	0%	0
17	0%	0
18	5%	0.9
19	35%	6.65
20	40%	8.0
21	20%	4.2
Total	100%	19.8

The numbers in the third column are simply the product of the value in the first column and the probability in the second column. When the third column values are summed, we obtain the expected value for this particular

---

We Need Your Best Judgement

Following are historical statistics on hotel/motel room demand in the Washington, D.C., metropolitan area.

	Room nights sold (millions)
1992	16.0
1993	16.3
1994	16.6
1995	16.8
1996	16.9
1997	17.7
1998	17.9
1999	18.9

Based on your best judgement, please assign probabilities to each of the possible values of total room demand in the Washington, D.C., metropolitan area in the year 2005. The probabilities for each measure must sum to 100%. No individual probability can be less than 0% or greater than 100%.

Room nights sold in 2005 (millions)	Probability of this outcome
16	_____%
17	_____%
18	_____%
19	_____%
20	_____%
21	_____%
Total	_____%
	(Should sum to 100%)

When you have completed your form, please return it to the forecast manager. Thank you for your co-operation.

Figure 9.3 Form for gathering subjective probability assessments of hotel/motel room demand in 2005

1. Select the judges: people familiar with the variables you are forecasting, their recent history, and what affects them.

2. Pose the questions to the judges either individually or in a group where discussion is discouraged; provide background data on recent trends.

3. Ask for answers: the judges record their probability distributions on paper or computer and transmit these to the forecast manager.

4. Obtain forecasts: the forecast manager combines the forecasts into one probability distribution for each variable and presents the mean and standard deviation for each.

Figure 9.4   The subjective probability assessment process

judge. We can array all of the expected values reported in a distribution and determine the expected value (mean) of the distribution and its dispersion (standard deviation). These then serve as the group's best forecast value and its range.

If the number of judges is fewer than twenty, then the distribution may not be a smooth one. You can still calculate the mean, but the standard deviation may not make much sense.

Figure 9.4 summarizes the process for the subjective probability assessment method.

Delphi method

The Delphi method is designed to produce a group consensus on forecasts while avoiding some of the problems of other group forecasting methods, such as the jury of executive opinion. These problems include:

- specious persuasion
- undue influence of 'recognized experts'
- unwillingness to abandon publicly expressed views
- the 'herd' or 'bandwagon' effect where individuals are reluctant to state views at odds with a developing consensus.

Specifically, the Delphi method has three distinctive characteristics that set it apart from other judgemental techniques:

1   Respondent anonymity – reducing unwanted group discussion effects.
2   Iteration and controlled feedback – the researcher conducting the Delphi method transmits a summary of the emerging group consensus back to the

judges, who are encouraged to reassess their prior responses and provide new ones based on this feedback over several iterations or 'rounds'.

3 Statistical group response – the group opinion is defined by certain statistics from each round.

Since successful application of the Delphi method requires adherence to a relatively complex process, each of the four steps in qualitative forecasting applied to this method will be discussed in detail.

1 Select the judges

You should recognize from the beginning that the quality of Delphi forecasting depends heavily on the expertise of the judges and their willingness to remain involved over a substantial period of time. Panels of Delphi judges have numbered from a dozen to as many as 900. Some researchers believe that fifteen to twenty members are the minimum panel size required (Yong, Keng and Leng, 1989: 38).

Some researchers have found that the reliability of Delphi method results is directly related to the size of the group, but this has not been confirmed for tourism forecasting. Recruiting these judges may take a substantial amount of time, to ensure they have the qualifications and the judgement required for serious forecasting, and that enough of them make a firm commitment to participate to the end of the process. Studies have indicated that the Delphi method is often more accurate than the jury of executive opinion, so the extra time involved may be more than compensated for.

You should make special efforts to recruit a panel of judges representing a wide range of tourism interests and experience. For example, it would be wise to include qualified managers, business researchers, academics, government officials, consultants and even business forecasters. If you are focusing on destination demand, then the judges should represent lodging, food service, transportation (both inbound/outbound and local), attractions and other specific elements of the tourism industry at the destination.

A significant threat to the validity of the Delphi method is attrition. It is not uncommon for one-half of the panel to drop out over the course of the project. This raises serious issues as to the validity of the results, because the dropouts may unbalance the panel in a significant way. Moreover, attrition makes interpretation of progress towards consensus more difficult: is the developing convergence due to true consensus or just the withdrawal of maverick judges? Investing time in informing judges of the time requirements of the study and securing their commitment to remain through to the end will pay handsome dividends in terms of study validity.

You should plan carefully for your Delphi study by laying out a schedule of contacts, response stimulation, processing and reporting of the results. You should tighten it as much as possible, allowing for a maximum of four rounds. The more you can shorten the Delphi process by quick processing and contacting judges with results, the less attrition you are likely to have. Note that communicating over the Internet may dramatically reduce response times. A four-round Delphi study, from beginning to end, should take no longer than six months by post, and considerably less time by e-mail.

2 Pose the questions to the judges

Three elements need to be considered in forming Delphi questions:

1 Probability that some event will occur.
2 Date that it will occur.
3 Magnitude of the event.

Delphi questions comprise some combination of these three elements. In our consideration of the future of hotel/motel room demand in the Washington, D.C., metropolitan area, we might ask for forecasts in one of the following three questions or 'event statements':

1 What is the probability that room-nights sold will reach 22 million annually by 2005?
2 In what year will room-nights sold reach 22 million?
3 What will the volume of room-nights sold in 2005 be?

You should clearly understand the nature of the forecasting problem you are trying to solve with the Delphi technique in order to choose one of these three event statements. For example, if a hotel developer wants to know if total market size will be large enough to make a profit in a hotel that would open in 2005, you as the forecast manager will choose the third question. In contrast, if a city convention and visitors bureau is concerned whether there will be enough room capacity to serve demand when it exceeds 22 million room-nights, you would pose event question 2. Finally, if management is interested in the certainty among qualified experts that room demand will reach a specific level in the year 2005, you should pose question 1.

Sometimes the Delphi method is used to assess the timing of a range of factors that could affect tourism demand in the future. Here, you can ask each of the judges for a list of such factors, and the results can be used to develop event statements in the Delphi questionnaire.

**DELPHI SURVEY OF HOTEL/MOTEL ROOM DEMAND
IN THE WASHINGTON, D.C., METROPOLITAN AREA**

Round 1

Name of respondent: _____

Thank you for agreeing to participate in this Delphi survey of future hotel/motel room demand in the Washington, D.C., area.

Following is the recent history of hotel/motel room demand in the Washington, D.C., metropolitan area:

Year	Room-nights sold (millions)
1994	16.59
1995	16.80
1996	16.88
1997	17.65
1998	17.92
1999	18.86

Based on your knowledge of the hotel/motel business and tourism demand in this area, please record below your forecast of the volume of room-nights that will be sold in the year 2005. Please record at least one decimal point in your forecast.

Hotel/motel room-nights that will be sold in the year 2005:

_____ . _____ million

Your response will be kept confidential and will not be reported outside of the research staff.

Please complete this form and return it as soon as possible in the envelope provided to

Dr D. C. Frechtling,
International Institute of Tourism Studies,
The George Washington University,
Washington, D.C.,
20052 U.S.A.

Thank you for your help.

Figure 9.5 Sample form for gathering Delphi survey data

DELPHI SURVEY OF HOTEL/MOTEL ROOM DEMAND
IN THE WASHINGTON, D.C. METROPOLITAN AREA

Round 2

Name of respondent: ___John Smith_____

Some time ago, you reported your forecast of the number of hotel/motel room-nights that will be sold in the Washington, D.C., area in the year 2005, as follows. Below this is the summary of the responses by the complete Delphi panel:

Your forecast 20.95 million room-nights

Group median (the mid-point in the range of all values reported) = 19.45 million room-nights

Interquartile range (comprises the middle two quarters of the values reported) = 18.10–20.00 million room-nights

Based on this information, please record your forecast hotel/motel room demand in the Washington, D.C., area in the year 2005, below.

_____._____ million room-nights

If your forecast falls outside of the interquartile range reported above, please indicate your reasons for this high or low forecast value, below:

_____

_____

_____

Your response will be kept confidential and will not be reported to any one outside of the immediate research staff.

Please complete this form and return it as soon as possible in the envelope provided to

Dr D. C. Frechtling,
International Institute of Tourism Studies,
The George Washington University,
Washington, D.C.,
20052 U.S.A.

Thank you for your help.

It is important to phrase the questions clearly and unambiguously. It is wise to break complicated topics down into simple questions. It is even wiser to pretest the Delphi questionnaire by sending it to a sample of a dozen or so individuals and asking for their identification of ambiguous or confusing questions. You can then use this information to revise your language to promote understanding during the actual Delphi survey.

You may want to provide background information so that the judges have a common basis to start from. This background could, for example, include the recent history of the variables you wish to forecast. Make sure you enclose a postage-paid return address envelope, and include the return address on the questionnaire in case it and its envelope become separated.

3 Ask for answers

An important part of the Delphi process is the recording of judges' forecasts and the processing of these responses for re-submission to the panel. This process comprises a number of 'rounds', normally two to four in number, where responses are received, summarized, and sent back to the judges. During rounds subsequent to the first, judges are asked to reconsider their forecasts based on the emerging group consensus.

Figure 9.5 presents two sample questionnaires for a very simple Delphi survey of demand for hotel/motel rooms in the Washington, D.C., metropolitan area. (Normally a Delphi questionnaire will ask for responses to a number of event statements, not just one.) The first questionnaire differs from the others in that it presents the recent history of the forecast variable and asks only for the judge's initial forecast. The round 2 questionnaire reminds the judge of his or her initial forecast and summarizes the entire panel response through the median and the interquartile range. It is typical of the questionnaires to be used in successive rounds, as well.

Summarizing consensus: median or mean?

The median is one of three statistics often used to summarize a distribution of values by indicating the 'centre' or typical value of the distribution. It is computed by listing the values in the distribution in order of size (usually from lowest value to highest) and determining the middle value that divides this list into two equal parts. If there are an odd number of values in the distribution then the median is the middle of the order listing. If there are an even number of values, then the median is the mean of the two middle values.

Managers of tourism demand Delphi studies have variously used the mean and standard deviation, or the median and interquartile range to summarize the group consensus. The original Delphi studies used the median, and it has three advantages over the mean as the summary of the panel's responses.

First, it is not sensitive to extreme outliers that may be reported by the panel. For example, assume the mean reported by twenty Delphi judges is 22.0 million room-nights sold in 2005, with a range of twenty to twenty-four reported. If the twenty-first judge reports 32 million room-nights, then this value alone increases the mean to nearly 22.5 , or by more than 2.2 per cent. On the other hand, such a value generally will have little impact on the median, moving it only toward the next highest value reported above the original median.

A second advantage of the median is that it deals with ordinal values – those that can be ranked from lowest to highest but do not have the properties of either interval (for example, years) or ratio (for example, distance) data – in a valid way. Theoretically, the mean of an ordinal data set is meaningless because the intervals are arbitrary. While most forecast data you may wish to gather in a Delphi survey may be interval or ratio data, this is not always the case. For example, often the response, 'never', is permitted when asking in what year the judge thinks an event will occur. 'Never' cannot be part of computing the mean year, but it is enlisted to compute the median: it takes the position just above the highest year reported.

Finally, there is a theoretical reason for preferring the median over the mean as the representative value of the distribution of responses. The sum of the absolute deviations around the median is smaller than for any other measure of the distribution's centre. Looking at this another way, the median is always closer to the actual value than 50 per cent of the responses given, and may well be closer than more than 50 per cent. The mean, on the other hand, may be further away from the true value than two-thirds or more of the Delphi responses.

The standard deviation or the variance is the appropriate measure of a distribution's dispersion around the mean. The analogous measure of dispersion for the median is the *interquartile range* – the range for the middle 50 per cent of the values reported. In other words, it is the range of reported values when the highest one-quarter and the lowest one-quarter of these values have been eliminated from the distribution. Its centre is the median and, like the median, it is not very sensitive to extreme values.

Calculating the interquartile range is conceptually simple but computationally complex. Figure 9.6 presents a simple set of steps to compute this range for any set of data.

Reporting the median and interquartile range to Delphi judges in the second and successive round questionnaires gives each a summary of the panel's reports as to the typical value and how tightly the consensus is grouped around

1. Order the values reported from lowest to highest.

2. Count the values and add 1 to the count.

3. Divide this sum by 4 and round to nearest whole number: this is the number of steps or reported values in a quartile.

4. Beginning with the highest value, count the number of steps found in (3) toward the lowest value: this is the lower bound of the third quartile.

5. Beginning with the smallest value, count the number of steps in (3) toward the highest: this is the upper bound of the first quartile.

6. The interquartile range is the range of values between these two bounds.

Figure 9.6 Calculating the interquartile range
Source: After Witte (1989: 68)

it. If a judge reports a value outside of the interquartile range, then ask him or her to provide a written reason for being outside of the consensus. Then report this reason anonymously to the Delphi judges during the next round so that each might consider it in re-evaluating his or her next forecast.

4 Obtain the forecast

An important decision in the Delphi method is how many rounds to conduct before settling on the group's forecasts. On the initial round, there will normally be a wide range of answers. Over successive rounds the distribution of responses will narrow towards convergence, and this convergence is expected to be a more accurate estimate of the variable sought than either an individual's response or the simple median of a number of responses.

The most severe rule is to continue the process until there is no significant change in the median or the interquartile range from the penultimate round to the last one, a clear signal the panel will not move further towards consensus. A somewhat less severe rule is to continue the process until the interquartile range becomes relatively narrow around the median, say no more than 10 per cent higher or lower than the median. This suggests consensus has been achieved.

Finally, the loosest guide to the number of rounds is to cut them off after two or three. There is no theoretical foundation for this rule but it does reflect monetary and time cost considerations. There is a natural decay in response rate as the process is extended. Achieving consensus of five remaining judges after seven rounds is certainly less meaningful than accepting the consensus of twenty judges after three rounds.

When you report your results, be sure to include both the median and the interquartile range. The latter indicates the strength of the consensus, which may vary widely among the variables you are seeking to forecast.

Delphi advantages and disadvantages

Compared to other qualitative forecasting methods where groups are brought together to develop consensus, the Delphi method has the following advantages:

- It prevents specious persuasion, dominant individuals, and the 'herd' effect from biasing the consensus result.
- Redundant or irrelevant 'noise' is controlled by the forecast manager.
- It presents the spread of opinion as well as consensus points.
- It allows judges to consider the opinions of others without emotion.
- It allows judges to reconsider their own forecasts in light of information on the group consensus and reasons for outliers.
- The method has proved more accurate than jury of executive opinion and traditional group meetings.

Disadvantages include the following:

- Delphi results are extremely sensitive to the degree of the judges' expertise and the clarity of the events and schedules presented.
- It requires a substantial period of time from start to finish, potentially resulting in significant panel attrition.
- The Delphi forecaster can exercise considerable influence over the panel results through the way he or she reports reasons for outliers.
- It treats events as independent of one another.
- It assumes each judge bases his or her forecast of outcomes on perspectives shared with other judges.

Applications of the Delphi method

Kaynak and Macaulay (1984) reported on a Delphi study conducted among public officials, educators, tourism business operators and other business people with an interest in tourism in Nova Scotia, Canada. Questions regarding changes in society's values that may affect tourism development to 2000, structural changes in the tourism industry and their impact, and events that would impact tourism training were posed to 150 judges, and after two rounds forty-four completed questionnaires were returned.

The authors reported means and standard deviations, but it is unclear how they concluded that maximum convergence of opinion was achieved after two rounds. Consensus included relatively little change in society's values by 2000, and a significant increase in bus tours to the province and in government involvement in tourism. The event statements with the greatest likelihood of occurrence and critical impact on Nova Scotia's tourism include more specialized educational programmes for hotel and restaurant managers, increased demand for part-time training programmes, and one-half of the world's cash transactions occurring through computerized systems.

Uysal and Crompton (1985: 8–9) discuss some early applications of the Delphi method to forecast the occurrence of events that would affect tourism demand in the distant future.

Liu (1988) conducted a Delphi survey in 1984–5 among forty-two tourism managers in Hawaii regarding the volume of visitor arrivals in the state in 2000 and the split between international and domestic visitors, Oahu island's share and the maximum accommodation capacity on the island in 2000. Seventeen judges returned completed second-round questionnaires, but it is unclear why the process was cut off at this point. The consensus was that visitor arrivals will total 9 million by 2000, with an increase in the international visitors' share of the state total but a decline in total visitation to Oahu.

Yong, Keng and Leng (1989) recruited sixty-seven members for a Delphi panel on future factors affecting tourism in Singapore, and twenty-three judges agreed to participate. The study was concluded after three rounds, with seventeen judges participating in the last round. Twenty-six event statements were assessed as to (a) the likelihood of occurrence, (b) the year of probable occurrence, and (c) the importance of the event to tourism in Singapore. The major factors affecting tourism demand to the country included the People's Republic of China becoming a major tourism destination, technological advances lowering travel costs to Singapore, and tourism spending becoming a non-discretionary part of household budgets in developed countries.

Moeller and Shafer (1994) describe a Delphi study conducted in 1973–4 among 900 experts as to the social, managerial and technological events likely to shape the future of park and recreation management to 2000 and beyond. Four rounds were conducted, and the number of judges dropped to nearly 400. The forecasters summarized the judges' consensus as an 'optimistic future.'

Müller (1998) reports on a Delphi survey of fifty experts in each of Austria, Germany and Switzerland conducted in April–December 1996 on future development patterns in long-haul tourism. The survey was concluded at the end of three rounds (no criteria were given for stopping at this point) with a 97 per cent response rate. Salient findings for the 1995–2005 period include:

Austria is expected to post the fastest rate of long-haul tourism growth among the three origin countries, this travel from all three countries will outpace domestic tourism, occurrence of violence and disease in destination areas would be the major constraints on this growth, and radio/television and the Internet will become the most important sources of information for long-distance travellers.

The consumer intentions survey

The three qualitative methods used so far rely on the forecasts of experts as judges and the processing of these to achieve a consensus. An alternative in the tourism demand forecasting situation is to ask the source of the demand himself: that is, survey consumers as to whether they anticipate taking a trip over a short- to medium-term, say six months to a year. Asking the actual purchaser may provide advantages over the expert judges.

'Intentions' are statements that consumers make about their planned behaviour or about events they can control. Consumer intentions models assume there is a quantifiable relationship between intentions and actual behaviour in the future. Intentions data are most useful if they meet the following conditions.

The event is important. The more important the event, the more likely it is that intentions will provide good forecasts. Consumers are more likely to have reliable plans to take a two-week vacation trip than a weekend trip. They are more likely to follow through on a planned visit to another country than to a nearby city. An anticipated once-a-year vacation trip is more likely to occur than one among six or seven planned in a year's time.

Closely related to this is how far in the future the event is likely to occur. A visit to another continent a year from now may be known with more certainty than a weekend trip to visit friends in the next city in a month or two.

Responses can be obtained. Potential respondents must be identified and queried, and they must provide their intentions. The objective is to gather enough information from a portion of the entire population to generalize to that population. This is a classic sample survey project, and much has been written on this (for example, Alreck and Settle, 1995; WTO, 1995d). There are three major types of errors that can render the intentions invalid as indicators of future behaviour:

- *Sampling errors* create problems in generalizing from the sample to the population; these are estimated through applying statistical sampling theory and can be resolved through theory, as well.

- *Non-response errors* create problems in generalizing from the respondents to the sample; these are resolved by achieving high response rates.
- *Response errors* create problems in generalizing from the response to the respondent; these are resolved by encouraging respondents to answer carefully constructed, practicable questions honestly and completely.

The respondent has a plan. In accessing tourism demand intentions, this includes asking whether the respondent has made lodging or transportation reservations. An even stronger plan is purchasing non-refundable airline tickets or travel packages that carry cancellation penalties. Intentions accompanied by such actions are more likely to be acted upon than those unaccompanied by any action.

The respondent can fulfil the plan. This is a major obstacle to accurate intentions on business-related trips. Management may mandate or terminate trips outside of the respondent's control. This is also problematic with family vacation travel as well. Little is known about the decision-making dynamics of these trips, and obtaining intentions from one adult may not accurately reflect the family's final behaviour.

The respondent reports correctly. In some cases, vacation trips are conspicuous consumption and the respondent may be trying to impress the interviewer or others with plans that may never be fulfilled. A guard against this is to qualify respondents as to the number of vacation trips they have taken over a previous period. Those who have not taken any such trips are less likely to follow through on plans to take a major one.

New information is unlikely to change the plan. This is another reason why it is so difficult to obtain reliable intentions of business trips. The announcement of an important meeting or problems with a customer or client

---

1. Select the judges: define your population of consumers, design a plan for sampling a portion of them who are representative of the whole, select the sample.

2. Pose the questions to the judges: in carefully worded questionnaires administered by postal mail, e-mail, telephone or in person.

3. Ask for answers: stimulate response through follow up contacts and/or incentives; receive the responses and process them.

4. Obtain forecasts: generalize from the sample responses as to the percentages of the population that will demand tourism services or absolute numbers of these; condition these with past experience on the relationship between intentions and actual behaviour.

Figure 9.7 The consumer intentions survey process

that arise after the intentions have been stated will make them inaccurate. Ultimately, some information will affect many business and leisure travel plans: for example, outbreak of war, transportation labour disruptions, petroleum shortages, airline fare wars.

Figure 9.7 outlines the consumer intentions survey process.

Applications of the consumer intentions survey to tourism

For several decades, the Conference Board in the city of New York has included a question about intentions to take a vacation trip in the next six months in its monthly Survey of Consumer Confidence and Buying Plans. This survey is conducted by mail among 5000 U.S. households drawn from a panel maintained by National Family Opinion, Inc. (NFO) of Columbus, Ohio, U.S.A. Each month, NFO draws a new sample of 5000 U.S. households from its database of householders who have agreed to participate in such surveys. Typically, about 3500 return completed questionnaires covering consumer appraisal of current business conditions, expected conditions, and plans to buy certain durable goods in the next six months.

Every other month beginning in 1978, the NFO panels have received questions on vacations intended in the next six months. Responses are tabulated in the following categories as a percentage of the adult U.S. population intending to take one or more vacation trips:

- destination
  - USA
  - foreign country
- means of travel
  - automobile
  - airplane
  - other.

The Conference Board intentions survey achieves a response rate of about 70 per cent, and the respondent results are generalized to cover non-respondents as well. Research on non-response to tourism surveys has indicated that non-respondents tend heavily to be non-travellers. This suggests the percentages of the population intending to take a vacation derived from this survey may be biased upward to a significant extent.

Another problem with the Conference Board Survey occurs in trying to apply step 4 of the process in Figure 9.7. Since the vacation intentions sample is drawn from the NFO database of householders who have agreed to participate in such surveys, it is not a probability sample of the U.S. adult population.

Both of these drawbacks affect estimates of the absolute numbers of potential vacationers. However, they may not affect *changes* in these numbers. That is, this survey may be a good guide to trends or turning points in future vacation travel activity. This is discussed below.

The U.S. Travel Data Center of Washington, D.C., and its successor, the Travel Industry Association of America Research Department conducted monthly surveys of U.S. tourism activity from 1979 to 1995. Early each month, a new probability sample of 1500 U.S. households was selected and interviewed by telephone about their travel activities over the previous month.

Beginning in early 1992, the Travel Industry Association of America employed this survey to develop the Travelometer$_{sm}$, a set of seasonal forecasts of travel activity away from home. In four months of the year, respondents who had taken at least one trip to a place 100 miles or more away from home were queried about their intentions to travel during the approaching season, according to the schedule in Table 9.1. In 1999, the Association ceased relying on consumer intentions for the Travelometer$_{sm}$, and now relies on an economic forecasting service.

The pleasure travel results were reported for major demographic categories, purpose of trip, duration, expected participation in selected activities (for example, visit a city or take a cruise), type of destination and planned spending. Business travel intentions were tabulated by demographic characteristics.

The Travelometer$_{sm}$ had the advantage over the Conference Board's survey of being based on the intentions expressed by a probability sample of the U.S. population. Moreover, it covered travel during a three-month period rather than the six months by the Conference Board. A final advantage was that the Travelometer$_{sm}$ could report the numbers of 'person-trips' potential vacationers plan to take. This is more useful to industry planners and marketers than the proportion of the population planning to take one or more vacation

Table 9.1   Relationship of Travelometer$_{sm}$ vacation intention interviews to season of intended travel

Month of interview	Season of intended travel	Months in season
January	Spring	March, April, May
April	Summer	June, July, August
July	Fall	September, October, November
October	Winter	December, January, February

trips – the Conference Board approach. Moreover, these intentions forecasts could be directly compared to the number of vacation person-trips respondents to National Travel Survey actually report, to assess the accuracy of the intention estimates.

A disadvantage was that the Travelometer$_{sm}$ was conducted only four times a year to the Conference Board's six. Moreover, past Travelometer$_{sm}$ reports did not report vacation person-trips intended consistently. In the twenty-five Travelometer$_{sm}$ reports beginning with the summer 1992, vacation person-trips were projected only six times.

Evaluation of tourism consumer intentions surveys

If the intentions forecasts were reported, we could evaluate the accuracy of the Travelometer$_{sm}$ by computing the MAPE from the National Travel Survey (NTS) estimates of actual vacation person-trips. For the six periods for which such estimates are available, the MAPE is 2.4 per cent. The seasonal naive model produces a MAPE of 2.2 per cent for the same group of periods. Consequently, it is not clear that the Travelometer$_{sm}$ provides any useful information about future vacation travel in terms of error magnitude accuracy. Given the lack of an unbroken time series of person-trip forecasts, it is not possible to evaluate the Travelometer$_{sm}$ on the directional change accuracy and trend change accuracy criteria discussed in Chapter 2.

On the other hand, with the help of the NTS monthly vacation person-trip series, the Conference Board vacation intentions series can be evaluated on all three forecasting accuracy criteria. The steps required are:

1 Obtain a seasonally adjusted monthly series of NTS vacation person-trips.
2 Combine months into six-month blocks consistent with the Conference Board vacation intentions series; for example, the Conference Board estimate in February 1990 of the percentage of the population planning a vacation trip in the next six months should be associated with the six consecutive monthly NTS vacation person-trip estimates beginning in March 1990.
3 Transform the Conference Board percentage intention estimates into numbers of the population intending to take such a trip; this takes account of population growth over the time series period.
4 Regress the six-month NTS blocks on the Conference Board series as a regression forecast model.
5 Evaluate the regression model forecasts against the NTS six-month blocks on the three accuracy criteria.

This intentions regression model was significant at the 0.05 significance level according to the F-test, although the $\overline{R}^2$ is only 0.163 as is to be expected with univariate regression models of tourism demand. The coefficient of the vacation intentions variable is 1.613 and is significant at the 0.05 level. This suggests that the average number of vacation trips taken by each person with such intentions over the subsequent six months is 1.6.

The actual NTS estimates of U.S. vacation person-trips and the intentions model forecasts are shown in Figure 9.8. Table 9.2 summarizes the evaluation of this model on the three forecast measures of accuracy discussed in Chapter 2.

This vacation intentions model, based on the Conference Board's bimonthly survey of the vacation intentions of a sample of the U.S. population, does not perform well on any of the three accuracy criteria. It comes closest to the naive model in forecasting directional change. Overall, there is no reason to place much confidence in this particular intentions measure in forecasting future vacation travel demand on the basis of the NTS series. Perhaps other time series, validly representing actual pleasure travel activity, could be developed where the Conference Board measure would prove an accurate predictor.

In summary, surveying consumers about their future travel plans may appear to be a reasonable source of valid information about future tourism

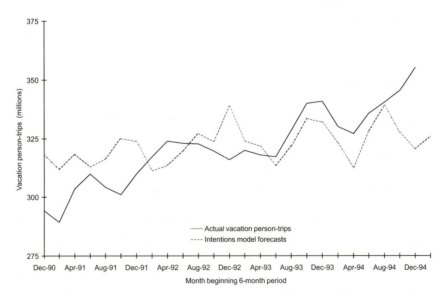

Figure 9.8 Actual and intentions model forecast U.S. vacation person-trips, six-month periods, 1990–94
Source: U.S. Travel Data Center, the Conference Board and the author

Table 9.2 Comparison of forecasting accuracy measures for the vacation intentions and the simple naive model

Measure of accuracy	Measure	Intentions model	Simple naive model
Error magnitude	MAPE	3.7%	1.7%
Directional change	Percentage forecast correctly	12/25 = 48%	50%*
Trend change	Percentage forecast correctly	3/8 = 38%	50%*

Note: *Since the simple naive model always forecasts no change, it will generate neither a correct nor an incorrect forecast of direction most of the time, so an alternative model must forecast directional change or trend change correctly more than 50 per cent of the time or we are better off accepting the naive model forecast of no change (see Witt and Witt, 1992a: 125, 129)

demand. However, the two efforts applied in the U.S.A. have not fulfilled this promise. This conclusion is based on admittedly sketchy data because that is all that has been available. Perhaps a consumer intentions survey that focuses on activities of value to tourism planners and marketers and that can be accompanied by a sound time series of actual behaviour will prove a fruitful source of tourism demand forecasts in the future.

Conclusion

Judgemental, that is, qualitative, forecasting methods are appropriate, and often the only feasible alternative, when any one or more of the following conditions obtains:

- a valid time series of the variable being forecast is not available or is unacceptable
- a long-term (three years or more) forecast is desired, or
- major disturbances in the future macroenvironment are likely.

In contrast to quantitative forecasting methods, qualitative methods use individual judges to organize information and present the futures. These judges may be experts on the tourism demand variable at hand, or consumers likely to generate the demand.

Armstrong (1985: 147–9) provides a number of recommendations to improve the accuracy of judgemental forecasting methods. The following seem most applicable to forecasting tourism demand:

1 On selecting judges:
   (a) for expert opinion studies, do not use judges who have a personal stake in the situation being forecast
   (b) use probability samples for consumer intentions surveys to select samples most representative of their populations.
2 On posing questions:
   (a) word each question carefully so that all judges understand it in the same way and know how to answer it
   (b) word the question in different ways in the same questionnaire when uncertainty is high, e.g., very long-range forecasting
   (c) provide the minimum background information in an easy-to-understand format.
3 On obtaining the forecast:
   (a) consider potential judge–judge and researcher–judge interactions that could bias results, and implement ways of preventing this
   (b) if group meetings must be held to obtain a forecast, structured meetings are more effective than unstructured ones, although participants prefer the latter.
4 On assessing uncertainty:
   (a) ask judges to rate their own confidence in their predictions, although they tend to overestimate this
   (b) groups in consensus tend to make riskier predictions than individuals.
5 Use combined forecasts of futures from different methods (e.g., subjective probability and Delphi) where uncertainty is high, using different methods.

For further information

Alreck, P. L. and Settle, R. B. (1995). *The Survey Research Handbook*. 2nd edition. Richard D. Irwin.

Armstrong, J. S. (1985). *Long-range Forecasting: From Crystal Ball to Computer*. 2nd edition. Wiley.

Dalkey, N. C. (1969). *The Delphi Method: An Experimental Study of Group Opinion*, ch. 6. Rand Corporation.

Granger, C. W. J. (1989). *Forecasting in Business and Economics*. 2nd edition, pp. 215–21 and 153–7. Academic Press.

Jarrett, J. (1991). *Business Forecasting Methods*. 2nd edition, ch. 10. Blackwell.

Makridakis, S., Wheelwright, S. C. and Hyndman, R. J. (1998), *Forecasting: Methods and Applications*. 3rd edition, ch. 10. Wiley.

Makridakis, S., Wheelwright, S. C. and McGee, V. (1983). *Forecasting: Methods and Applications*. 2nd edition, ch. 13. Wiley.

Mentzner, J. T. and Bienstock, C. C. (1998). *Sales Forecasting Management*, ch. 5. Sage.

Moeller, G. H. and Shafer, E. L. (1994). The Delphi technique: a tool for long-range travel and tourism planning. In *Travel, Tourism, and Hospitality Research: A Handbook for Managers and Researchers* (J. R. Brent Ritchie and C. R. Goeldner, eds) 2nd edition, pp. 473–80, Wiley.

Moutihno, L. and Witt, S. F. (1995). Forecasting the tourism environment using a consensus approach. *Journal of Travel Research*, **33** (4), Spring, 46–50.

Saunders, J. A., Sharp, J. A. and Witt, S. F. (1987). *Practical Business Forecasting*, ch. 10. Gower.

Shim, J. K., Siegel, J. G. and Liew, C. J. (1994). *Strategic Business Forecasting*, pp. 384–7. Probus.

Smith, S. L. J. (1995). *Tourism Analysis: A Handbook*. 2nd edition, pp. 143–7. Longman Scientific and Technical.

10

Conclusion

Forecasting is essentially organizing information about the past in order to predict one or more futures. In this book, we are specifically interested in saying something intelligent about the future of tourism demand in order to reduce the risks of operating a tourism organization in that future.

In the previous chapters, we have discussed the reasons for undertaking tourism forecasting, how to approach such a forecasting project, how to evaluate forecasting models, and the application of thirteen different quantitative and qualitative methods of forecasting tourism demand. In this final chapter, we review the accumulated wisdom of those who have studied business forecasting, especially tourism demand forecasting. This advice may well save you time and money by indicating the most fruitful paths to follow, as well as blind alleys and false leads you need to know about in advance of your forecasting efforts.

However, first we present an essential topic for determining how well your preferred forecasting model is operating in actually predicting your measure of tourism demand as the future unfolds.

Monitoring your forecasts

Ideally, your tourism forecasting model, chosen after much blood, sweat, toil and tears in examining alternatives, testing validity and checking accuracy, should produce forecasts over time that fluctuate narrowly around the actual time series unfolding. If this is so, then the cumulative sum of your forecast errors will tend toward zero as time goes by.

Occasionally, however, due to randomness in the forecasting error or the actual data, several positive (or several negative) errors may accumulate in a row, pushing the sum away from zero. It is helpful to have a rule for determining when this sum has strayed too far from zero to reflect only random forecast errors, indicating that the model needs to be revised or a new model chosen.

Forecasters have developed a 'tracking signal' for this very purpose:

$$\text{TS} = \frac{\sum (A_t - F_t)}{\sum |A_t - F_t|/n} \tag{10.1}$$

where   TS = tracking signal
        A   = actual value
        F   = forecast value
        t = some time period
        n = number of time periods.

Ideally, the forecast values should fluctuate around the actual values. If so, the numerator of Equation 10.1 will approximate zero. But if the forecasts tend to exceed or fall short of the actual series as time goes by, then the numerator will depart from zero. If the ratio of these cumulative errors to the cumulative mean absolute errors (the denominator of Equation 10.1) falls outside of the range of –4 to +4, this is a signal that your model is not tracking actual behaviour correctly. Forecasters prefer to use all data available, including those from backcasting, to compute this cumulative mean, not just the values from the beginning of the forecast period.

Consider Figure 10.1, where a forecaster has developed a model to forecast monthly hotel/motel room demand in the Washington, D.C., area for 1999. The forecast model's values do not track the actual series perfectly through 1998, but fluctuate around them. This is consistent with a random pattern of errors, suggesting the forecast model is adequate to its task.

However, as 1999 unfolds, the errors tend towards the negative as the forecast values uniformly exceed the actual series. The tracking signals are

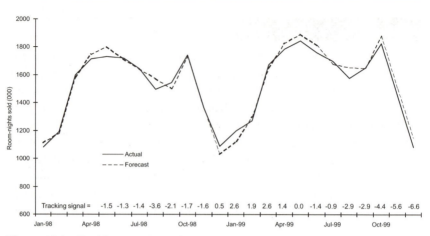

Figure 10.1 Tracking actual and forecast hotel/motel room demand in
Washington, D.C., monthly, 1998–99
Source: Smith Travel Research and author

shown at the bottom of the chart (Figure 10.1), associated with their months.
Reflecting this path, they begin to decline in June, 1999. By October, they
have exceeded the lower bound of our tracking range of –4. At this point, we
need to either re-estimate the parameters of this model or go through the
model selection process again as described in Chapter 3.

Through experience and management's preference, you can adjust the
tracking signal threshold. For example, if your data are very well behaved and
management places a premium on accuracy, you might set the threshold at
between –3 and +3. On the other hand, if you have difficulty fitting a good
forecasting model to your time series, you may want to set the threshold at –5
to +5.

Guides for developing tourism forecasting strategies

Serious tourism demand forecasting spans over three decades. Over this
period, the published experiences of many forecasters give rise to a number of
generalizations about forecasting this demand. The following are provided as
strategic guides for the tourism forecaster, to help you avoid dead ends, traps
and pitfalls that waste time and money.

As with any generalization, you will encounter exceptions to one or more
of the following, but they are a fruitful place to start. Note that most of them
deal with quantitative forecasting. By their idiosyncratic nature, qualitative
forecasting methods do not give rise to many useful generalizations.

Every tourism demand time series has a personality. Some grow strongly year after year while others are flat or even in decline. Some show seasonality that varies from year to year while others display a regular pattern that changes little. Some appear to follow linear paths while others follow curves or even waves over time. Some fluctuate wildly while others show mild increases and decreases. It is the forecaster's challenge to tease out these patterns from a time series for replication in a forecasting model.

No one method works best for all. Related to the previous finding, there is no one forecasting method that works best for all measures of tourism demand. Even in the limited arena of international tourism flows, no one model stands out as the most reliable. In addition, as one of the leading econometricians of our day has concluded: 'It is rare for one model to be superior for all possible purposes: forecasting, policy making, conditional forecasts, testing hypotheses, or investigating the effects of a previous policy change' (Granger, 1999: 18).

No one method is best in reducing all three types of forecasting error. For a given tourism demand series, it is quite unlikely you will find a single model that will be the most accurate predictor of magnitude, direction and trend. Rather, it appears that regression models are somewhat more accurate on forecasting direction and trend while extrapolative models work better on reducing forecast error. But this is not a firm finding across a multitude of time series.

Parsimony rules in tourism demand forecasting. A number of tourism forecasters have noted that complex forecasting models are seldom more accurate in predicting the future than simple ones. This echoes findings across a wide variety of business forecasting situations and methods (Makridakis, Wheelwright and Hyndman, 1998: 526–7). This is especially true of the short to medium term (up to three years). The seasonal patterns and momentum found in most tourism demand series can be expected to continue, unless large shocks (energy crises, wars, economic recessions, etc.) occur. The latter are unlikely in the short to medium term.

Visitor volume is easier to forecast than expenditures. Methods of measuring international and domestic tourism are more accurate in counting people than their expenditures. The latter are usually developed through visitor surveys, records of financial institutions, tourism industry records, or some combination of these. This idiosyncratic approach prevents generation of valid and consistent data series for visitor expenditures, and forecasting models applied to them fall prey to these measurement irregularities.

International tourism demand series tend to be more valid than domestic ones. Validity is the art of measuring precisely what you intend to measure. International visitor counts tend to be more valid than domestic visitor estimates, because the former cross international borders. Even though border formalities are declining throughout the world in the name of facilitating visitor flows, the physical international boundaries remain and at a minimum serve as points to count visitors. There are normally no such boundaries within most of the world's nations where domestic travellers can be observed and surveyed.

Domestic tourism demand is easier to forecast than international tourism demand. While international tourism demand series more accurately reflect visitor flows among countries, they are more difficult to forecast accurately. This is because in addition to all of the factors that influence domestic travel away from home, international travel is also affected by exchange rates, changing government policies towards international tourism, bilateral treaties covering air transportation and other activities affecting tourism, and political upheavals such as war, insurrections and terrorism.

Long-haul tourism flows differ from short-haul flows in patterns and explanatory variables. Over the past decade, world long-haul travel, that is, visitor flows from countries to destinations outside the origin's region, grew about twice as fast as short-haul (intra-regional) travel did (Frechtling, 2000). There are a number of explanations for this, including rising affluence stimulating distant travel and the mature nature of short-haul markets. The two types of travel differ in their reaction to shocks, such as war, terrorism and petroleum shortages. Overall, it appears long-haul visitor flows are more responsive to real income growth while short-haul travel is affected more by exchange rate changes and the age structure of the generating populations.

Consumer price indexes appear to be good proxies for the cost of travelling within a country. A good deal of experimentation with consumer price indexes versus indexes specifically designed to track the prices that visitors pay has indicated that the former are just as good as the latter in forecasting visitor flows. Since the former are available for nearly all countries, the rule of parsimony requires they be used in demand models. However, the costs of transport among countries should be considered separately from in-country prices.

Exchange rates do not represent travel costs well. They have been found to indicate poorly trends in international transport costs or in-country visitor-related prices. However, they are quite visible to the traveller and should be considered carefully for inclusion in causal models.

Relationships can change dramatically in causal models in the long run. The coefficients that indicate the relationship of each explanatory variable to a measure of tourism demand should not be considered fixed in the long run. Major shocks, such as petroleum shortages, wars, terrorism and natural disasters can change their course over the ensuing period. But minor shocks operate on them as well. These include changes in political structures, increased capacity in infrastructure and superstructure, dramatic marketing programmes and reduced restraints on international trade, to name a few. In tourism, the long run appears to be about three years or more, arguing for the application of qualitative forecasting models to signal the shapes of these futures.

Use qualitative models to forecast events that can be verified. Like all other approaches, qualitative forecasting methods should be continually evaluated as to their accuracy in suggesting the shapes of the future. If the events they predict are too vague to be observed, such as 'visitor flows from Canada will increase substantially', such assessment is prevented. A good rule in phrasing an event statement is to clearly define the future situation that would correspond to the event's non-occurrence.

Seasonality is an ally in tourism model-building. Tourism demand in many areas is extremely sensitive to the passing of months, seasons and quarters, and this sensitivity appears to be quite regular. By first describing seasonal patterns accurately, you remove a good bit of the volatility of sub-annual series. This enables you to concentrate on simulating the non-seasonal series, a less daunting challenge.

Look for convergent validity. You can be much more confident in your forecasts if you have two or more models converging on a prediction than if you have only one. Compare the results of several models, looking for corroboration among them and with informed judgement. Combining quantitative and qualitative forecasting methods is an especially effective way of achieving convergent validity. Related to this concept is the value of combining forecasts from different models into a single forecast, as advocated by several leading economic forecasters (for example, Granger, 1999: 67; Makridakis, Wheelwright and Hyndman, 1998: 537–42). Unfortunately, this has received as yet little serious attention in the tourism forecasting literature.

Doing sound forecasting

Each of the thirteen tourism demand forecasting methods discussed in this book are accompanied by a set of rules for applying them. These serve several essential purposes:

- They distinguish one method from another.
- They embody important theories, reasoning and common sense.
- They have proved superior to alternative rules in producing sound forecasts in practice.

- They allow the valid comparisons of results across various studies that help build a body of knowledge about a phenomenon such as tourism demand.

When a researcher ignores or intentionally violates the rules of a forecasting method, he or she cannot:

- claim to have applied the method
- claim to have incorporated the theories inherent in that method in his or her forecasting model
- avoid the implicit declaration that his or her judgement supersedes the accumulated experience of other forecasters
- confirm or deny the conclusions of other forecasters who have rightly applied the method.

In short, the rules of a method are its discipline applied to data about the past of a phenomenon. In the absence of such discipline, sloppy forecasts and ignorance reign.

Using forecasts wisely

Reviewing the process applied in a giving forecasting method, that is, the sequential steps followed, is the best technique for evaluating forecasts prepared by others. Test a forecast study, in its assumptions, method and results, by examining its underlying rationality embodied in its process. In order to do this fruitfully you need to:

- determine the nature of the time series or other past information used
- understand the assumptions on which the model is based
- review the process applied
- test the results for statistical significance and/or reasonableness.

This frequently means that you must request additional information to what is usually published on a forecasting study. For some reason, forecasters seldom detail all of the process they employed when writing up the results. But without this, you cannot validly assess the validity of a forecasting model or the accuracy of its future forecasts.

A final word

It is wise to never underestimate the role that judgement plays in successful tourism demand forecasting. Initially, you use judgement to select the demand series to forecast and the range of methods to apply in doing so. If using a causal model, you choose carefully which explanatory variables to include and the valid measures of these. Moreover, you must decide on the form or structure of your causal model, using sound judgement. Then, you must assess the quality of alternative models to choose the most effective one for your purposes. Finally, monitoring your model over time requires judgement as to when to estimate new parameters or test a new set of models.

When applying a qualitative forecasting technique, judgement plays a more critical role. You must carefully choose the judges and select from among alternative ways of phrasing the questions or event statements. Finally, you employ judgement in deciding when a consensus is reached and its shape.

The point is, tourism demand forecasting is as much an art as it is a science. As you become familiar with the series you are forecasting or are reviewing from someone else's forecasts, you gain insights into what makes it tick. This knowledge is invaluable to you and the managers who use your forecasts. Never rely strictly on a mechanical process to produce tourism forecasts, such as computer programs that uncritically test dozens of models before selecting one based on the mechanical application of some criteria. For, like the activity itself, tourism demand forecasting is a diverse, dynamic and changeable process that rewards the quick and observant but leaves the careless and inattentive behind.

For further information

Choy, D. J. L. (1985). Forecasting tourism revisited. *Tourism Management*, **5** (3), September, 171–6.

Crouch, G. I. (1994a). The study of international tourism demand: a survey of practice. *Journal of Travel Research*, **22** (4), Spring, 41–57.

Doorn, J. W. M. van (1984). Tourism forecasting and the policymaker. *Tourism Management*, **5** (1), March, 24–39.

Faulkner, B. and Valerio, P. (1995). An integrative approach to tourism demand forecasting. *Tourism Management*, **16** (1), February, 29–37.

Gardner, E. S. Jr (1992). How to monitor your forecasts. *Lotus*, April, 54–7.

Makridakis, S., Wheelwright, S. C. and Hyndman, R. J. (1998), *Forecasting: Methods and Applications*. 3rd edition, ch. 11. Wiley.

Shim, J. K., Siegel, J. G. and Liew, C. J. (1994). *Strategic Business Forecasting*, pp. 152–3. Probus.

Witt, S. F. and Witt, C. A. (1992). *Modeling and Forecasting Demand in Tourism*. Academic Press.

Appendix 1

Hotel/motel room demand in Washington, D.C., metropolitan area, 1987–99

Month-year	Room-nights sold	Month-year	Room-nights sold
Jan-87	833 540	Jan-89	1 024 179
Feb-87	942 257	Feb-89	1 012 762
Mar-87	1 257 846	Mar-89	1 373 618
Apr-87	1 374 051	Apr-89	1 573 360
May-87	1 409 306	May-89	1 577 236
Jun-87	1 379 109	Jun-89	1 502 090
Jul-87	1 336 128	July-89	1 437 579
Aug-87	1 273 230	Aug-89	1 389 409
Sep-87	1 277 086	Sep-89	1 369 246
Oct-87	1 458 479	Oct-89	1 546 566
Nov-87	1 140 943	Nov-89	1 222 075
Dec-87	869 707	Dec-89	918 369
Jan-88	896 394	Jan-90	947 077
Feb-88	946 856	Feb-90	1 028 502
Mar-88	1 308 786	Mar-90	1 403 753
Apr-88	1 475 893	Apr-90	1 510 096
May-88	1 516 362	May-90	1 572 016
Jun-88	1 463 186	Jun-90	1 502 584
Jul-88	1 357 937	Jul-90	1 425 576
Aug-88	1 366 384	Aug-90	1 382 619
Sep-88	1 315 898	Sep-90	1 342 028
Oct-88	1 508 838	Oct-90	1 468 964
Nov-88	1 196 734	Nov-90	1 174 218
Dec-88	919 491	Dec-90	907 915

Month-year	Room-nights sold	Month-year	Room-nights sold
Jan-91	930 735	Jul-94	1 527 117
Feb-91	1 023 216	Aug-94	1 451 875
Mar-91	1 344 399	Sep-94	1 427 977
Apr-91	1 509 480	Oct-94	1 616 543
May-91	1 540 774	Nov-94	1 249 960
Jun-91	1 522 091	Dec-94	926 882
Jul-91	1 425 895	Jan-95	1 042 982
Aug-91	1 366 495	Feb-95	1 072 021
Sep-91	1 354 675	Mar-95	1 497 490
Oct-91	1 522 474	Apr-95	1 607 372
Nov-91	1 222 896	May-95	1 717 348
Dec-91	881 834	Jun-95	1 614 752
Jan-92	985 756	Jul-95	1 515 646
Feb-92	1 092 020	Aug-95	1 423 935
Mar-92	1 357 445	Sep-95	1 474 590
Apr-92	1 509 958	Oct-95	1 646 477
May-92	1 607 385	Nov-95	1 235 845
Jun-92	1 465 604	Dec-95	953 185
Jul-92	1 486 785	Jan-96	943 730
Aug-92	1 490 040	Feb-96	1 094 699
Sep-92	1 418 154	Mar-96	1 505 839
Oct-92	1 515 650	Apr-96	1 618 048
Nov-92	1 175 048	May-96	1 712 998
Dec-92	938 187	Jun-96	1 612 733
Jan-93	1 085 429	Jul-96	1 545 371
Feb-93	1 085 551	Aug-96	1 476 328
Mar-93	1 453 431	Sep-96	1 474 887
Apr-93	1 594 843	Oct-96	1 639 643
May-93	1 646 695	Nov-96	1 293 068
Jun-93	1 571 177	Dec-96	963 481
Jul-93	1 546 755	Jan-97	1 107 590
Aug-93	1 485 541	Feb-97	1 153 672
Sep-93	1 448 775	Mar-97	1 511 055
Oct-93	1 627 643	Apr-97	1 693 930
Nov-93	1 303 063	May-97	1 767 343
Dec-93	988 510	Jun-97	1 660 747
Jan-94	1 016 512	Jul-97	1 588 866
Feb-94	1 085 531	Aug-97	1 468 612
Mar-94	1 442 961	Sep-97	1 545 274
Apr-94	1 597 851	Oct-97	1 758 807
May-94	1 624 204	Nov-97	1 380 837
Jun-94	1 626 355	Dec-97	1 015 355

Month-year	Room-nights sold	Month-year	Room-nights sold
Jan-98	1 081 908	Jan-99	1 200 251
Feb-98	1 191 814	Feb-99	1 273 448
Mar-98	1 600 256	Mar-99	1 672 202
Apr-98	1 713 693	Apr-99	1 788 572
May-98	1 732 843	May-99	1 845 950
Jun-98	1 721 516	Jun-99	1 760 220
Jul-98	1 645 277	Jul-99	1 700 385
Aug-98	1 495 092	Aug-99	1 578 068
Sep-98	1 542 887	Sep-99	1 652 127
Oct-98	1 743 790	Oct-99	1 825 682
Nov-98	1 362 818	Nov-99	1 453 314
Dec-98	1 089 460	Dec-99	1 113 279

Appendix 2

Dealing with super-annual events

Seasonality refers to patterns of demand within a year, that recur over a number of years, a common feature of tourism demand series. Sometimes, however, an event occurs periodically over a period of years that effects tourism demand related to a destination. For example, the U.S. presidential inauguration occurs in Washington, D.C., in January of the year following every year evenly divisible by four. This boosts the demand for hotel and motel rooms in and around the city to capacity levels for a week to ten days.

You may have to deal with a similar periodic super-annual event in forecasting demand to a destination. It poses two problems for the forecaster:

1 It inflates somewhat the value of the seasonal factor for the month in which it occurs and deflates somewhat the values for the other months.
2 Your forecasting model will underestimate this month's value in any future year in which the event takes place.

Figure A.2.1 helps us deal with the bias in number 1 for the hotel/motel room demand series for Washington, D.C. The solid line makes it clear that the inaugural festivities in 1989 and 1993 boosted January room-nights considerably above the more typical January. The 1997 inauguration year is more difficult to interpret. It followed a year-earlier January depressed by the Presidential–Congressional budget deadlock. The latter shut down most national government offices in Washington, D.C., including museums popular with visitors. Consequently, January 1997 hotel/motel demand benefited from a recovery from the depressed levels of a year earlier as well as the inauguration festivities.

How do we keep this recurring bulge from affecting the seasonal factors for the more typical Januarys?

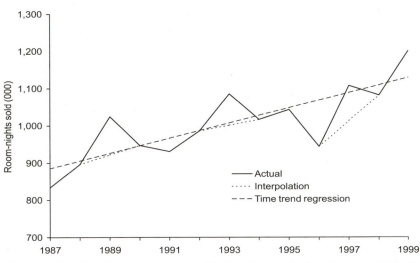

Figure A.2.1 Hotel/motel room demand in Washington, D.C., in January, 1987–99
Source: Smith Travel Research and author

One option is to determine the long-term trend of January room demand and use the resulting trend values for 1989 and 1993 in computing the seasonal factors. A popular representation of this trend is the linear time trend regression model, discussed in the context of regression analysis in Chapter 7. This causal model employs the years as the explanatory variable and room demand as the dependent or forecast variable to develop a straight line that has the virtue of minimizing a measure of the distances from it to the actual values.

The linear time trend for the thirteen years for which we have January hotel/motel room demand figures is shown as the line with the long dashes in Figure A.2.1. It clearly shows that the Januarys of 1989 and 1993 lie significantly above the trend for all Januarys. We could compute the additional boost that presidential inaugurations give to January room demand as the distance from the trend line to the actual value for the two years.

This boost will be understated because of the logic of the time trend model. It minimizes the squared differences between it and the actual time series. As a result, it responds to the high values in 1989 and 1994 by moving upward closer to these values. In so doing, it underestimates the bonus associated with the inaugural Januarys and still biases the seasonal factor for the month upward.

Moreover, this approach fails to deal appropriately with the recovery aspects of January 1997. The difference between the trend line and that month's demand is miniscule, suggesting the inauguration did little to boost occupancies that month.

A better solution for separating out the impact of the inaugural festivities on certain Januarys is to estimate what their values would be in their absence by interpolation. The interpolated value for January 1989 hotel/motel room demand is the average of the actual values for the years immediately prior and subsequent to it, 1988 and 1990. The interpolated values for Januarys 1993 and 1997 are similarly computed. Both of these are represented by the short-dashed lines in Figure A.2.1.

These estimates have the virtue of being unaffected by the size of the inaugural boost and being anchored by two actual values. Both of these interpolations follow an upward trend as the time trend regression model does, but are positioned somewhat lower for 1989 and 1993. This value for 1997 represents the recovery from 1996 considerably more realistically than the time trend estimate does.

The interpolated values shown in Table A.2.1 are substituted for their actual values in computing the seasonal adjustment factors for the Washington, D.C., hotel/motel room demand time series. These cause the seasonal factors for January to be reduced somewhat, and the factors for the other months each to increase a little. Figure A.2.2. compares the two sets of seasonal factors.

The differences between the two series are negligible except for January. However, the seasonal factors resulting from the interpolated values should improve the decomposition forecasting model for the non-inaugural Januarys. The forecasts for inaugural Januarys (2001, 2005, etc.) will need to be adjusted for the boost to room demand that the festivities give (problem 2 noted above). This can be done by applying either a percentage increase from Table A.2.1 or an absolute increase. We might average the values in Table A.2.1. or pick a value within their ranges.

Table A.2.1   Comparison of actual and interpolated values for January hotel/motel room demand in Washington, D.C., affected by presidential inaugurations (thousands of room-nights sold)

	January 1989	January 1993	January 1997
Actual value	1024	1085	1108
Interpolated value	922	1001	1013
Actual value compared to interpolated value			
Absolute difference	102	84	95
Percentage difference	11%	8.4%	9.4%

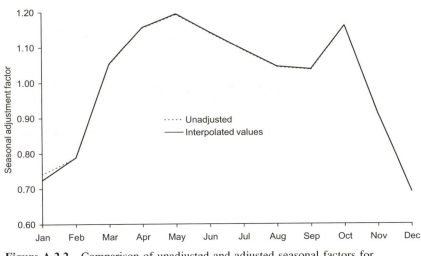

Figure A.2.2 Comparison of unadjusted and adjusted seasonal factors for Washington, D.C., hotel/motel room demand

In summary, this discussion suggests how to deal with special events that affect tourism demand and recur over periods of years in forecasting that demand. The above method deals with biased seasonal adjustment factors and inaccurate monthly or quarterly forecasts resulting from such events. It can be applied whether the event occurs in a regular pattern, or varies by number of years when it occurs. It is designed to improve forecasts of tourism demand for the periods affected.

Appendix 3

Splicing a forecast to a time series

Consider Figure A.3.1, based on the best forecasting model (7.10) found in Chapter 7. Using forecasts of real disposable personal income from a reputable forecasting firm (Panel Publishers, 2000), forecast values are produced from model (7.10) for 2000 through 2002.

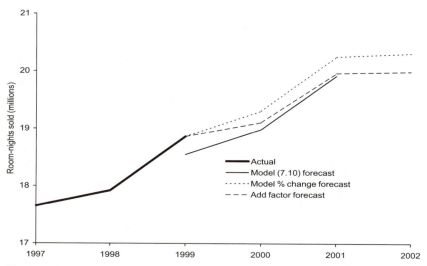

Figure A.3.1 Alternative forecasts of hotel/motel room demand for Washington, D.C., annual, 1997–2002
Source: Smith Travel Research and author

Table A.3.1   Hotel/motel room demand in the Washington, D.C., area, actual and forecast, annually, 1999–2002

1. Year	2. Actual value (millions)	3. Model (7.10) forecast value (millions)	4. Forecast change from previous year (%)
1999	18.86	18.55	2.9
2000	NA	18.99	2.4
2001	NA	19.92	4.9
2002	NA	19.98	0.3

Note: NA = not available

If the forecast for 2000 is simply spliced on to the actual time series, the change from 1999 to 2000 appears as only 130 000 room-nights or only 0.7 per cent. But using the model (7.10) forecast series, the model reckons this at 437 000 room-nights, up 2.4 per cent. This is because the model produces a value for 1999 that is 1.6 per cent (314 000) lower than the actual value.

There are two methods commonly used to splice the first forecast value on to the last actual value in such situations. The 'percentage change' method takes the annual percentage changes from the forecast model and applies these to the actual time series. In our example, the 2.4 per cent increase for the model (7.10) forecast series from 1999 to 2000 shown in the fourth column of Table A.3.1 is added to the actual value for 1999 to obtain 19.31 million room-nights as the forecast for 2000. For the next year, the percentage change in the time trend forecast model is 4.9 per cent (again from column 4), and this is added to our 19.31 million forecast for 2000 to obtain a 2001 forecast of 20.26 million room-nights.

While this is a simple approach with some intuitive appeal, it has a major drawback. As evident in Figure A.3.1, this forecast never reaches the values forecast by our time trend model. Rather, it is always about 1.6 per cent above the forecast line. For another forecasting model, this difference could be considerably greater. By adopting this method, we abandon the values our preferred model predicts for the future.

There is a second technique that both links the last actual value to our model's forecast values and reaches our model's forecast series in the future. Called the 'addfactor method', it is based on the Durbin-Watson statistic, which we observed in Chapter 7 indicates the degree of autocorrelation among the residuals in our regression equation.

To begin the addfactor method of adjusting our forecast values, we compute a factor represented by the Greek letter, rho, or ρ:

$$\rho = 1 - \frac{DW}{2} \tag{A.3.1}$$

where ρ = rho factor
$\qquad$ DW = Durbin–Watson statistic.

The next step is to compute the addfactor that will be applied to our first forecast value after the last actual data point:

$$AF_{f+1} = \rho * (A_f - F_f) \tag{A.3.2}$$

where AF = addfactor
$\qquad \rho$ = rho factor
$\qquad$ A = actual value
$\qquad$ F = forecast value
$\qquad f$ = time period of the last actual value.

This addfactor is added to the first forecast value after the last actual data point $(f+1)$ to obtain the revised forecast:

$$RF_{f+1} = F_{f+1} + AF_{f+1} \tag{A.3.3}$$

where RF = revised forecast value
$\qquad$ F = forecast value
$\qquad$ AF = addfactor
$\qquad f$ = time period of the last actual value.

The revised forecast for the second period after the last actual data point $(f+2)$ is produced by adding the product of rho times the previous period's addfactor to the forecast value for period $f+2$:

$$RF_{f+2} = F_{f+2} + (\rho * AF_{f+1}) \tag{A.3.4}$$

where RF = revised forecast value
$\qquad$ F = forecast value
$\qquad \rho$ = rho factor
$\qquad$ AF = addfactor
$\qquad f$ = time period of the last actual value.

If the value for RF_{f+2} is not sufficiently different from zero, you have reached the forecast line and need apply no more adjustments. If RF_{f+2} is sufficiently different from zero, then apply equation A.3.4 again for period $f+3$. Continue this until RF_{f+2} approximates zero for the number of significant digits you are working with.

Table A.3.2 illustrates the computational process embodied in Equations A.3.1 to A.3.4 using model (7.10) shown in Figure A.3.1, the best model we found in Chapter 7.

In this case, we have reached the forecast line during the third forecast year and future forecasts can be taken directly from our model. In other cases, you might reach the forecast line in one or two future periods.

Table A.3.2 Process for splicing hotel/motel room demand forecasts for the Washington, D.C., area to the actual time series

Step	Computation
1. Compute the rho factor through equation (A.3.1)	$\rho = 1 - (1.22/2) = 0.390$
2. Compute the addfactor by multiplying the rho factor by the error for the last actual value in the time series (from Table A.3.1) through Equation A.3.2	$Af_{f+1} = 0.390 * (18.86 - 18.55)$ $= 0.121$
3. Add the addfactor to the first forecast value after the last actual value (from Table A.3.1) through Equation A.3.3	$RF_{f+1} = 18.99 + 0.121 = 19.11$
4. Compute the addfactor for the next period after the last actual value ($f+2$) through Equation A.3.4	$Af_{f+1} = 0.390 * 0.121$ $= 0.047$
5. If this addfactor is sufficiently different from zero, then add it to the forecast value for period $f+2$	$RF_{f+2} = 19.92 + 0.047 = 19.97$
6. Compute the addfactor for the next period ($f+3$) through Equation A.3.4	$Af_{f+2} = 0.390 * 0.047 = 0.018$
7. If this addfactor is sufficiently different from zero, then add it to the forecast value for period $f+3$	$RF_{f+3} = 19.98 + 0.018 = 20.00$. This is virtually equal to the model (7.10) forecast value of 19.98 so we can stop the process at this point and accept all future years ($f+4$ and later)

In conclusion, as Figure A.3.1 indicates, the addfactor procedure develops transition values that smooth the path between the last actual value of the time series and the values forecast by the model. It avoids both simply jumping up to the forecast line for the first future year and trending up at the same rate as the forecast model but never reaching its values.

For further information

Moore, T. W. (1989). *Handbook of Business Forecasting*, pp. 209–18. Harper & Row.

Glossary and abbreviations

Note: terms defined in this glossary are indicated by bold type. '(WTO)' refers to definitions established by the United Nations and the World Tourism Organization.

Accuracy – the degree of conformity of a forecast to the actual event being forecast, i.e., the correctness of a forecast; for **quantitative forecasting methods**, this is measured by the **MAPE**, among other measures.

ARIMA – autoregressive/integrated/moving average model, the **time series forecasting method** that adds differencing a time series to the **ARMA** method.

ARMA – 'autoregressive moving average' method combines the **auto-regressive model** and the **moving average model;** used in the **Box–Jenkins approach**.

ASM – available seat-miles.

ATC – Australian Tourist Commission.

Autocorrelation – refers to correlation that may occur between adjacent values of **residual** or **error** terms after the application of a **forecasting method**.

Autoregressive model – a **regression** model where the forecast variable is related to past values of itself at varying time lags.

Backcasting – the process of applying a **forecasting model** to the period covered by the **time series** on which it is based; used to establish the **accuracy** of a **forecasting model**.

Bias – refers to the amount by which an estimation method fails to produce the actual value of the statistic being estimated.

Box–Jenkins approach – a popular process for applying **ARIMA** models to time series forecasting.

Causal forecasting method – is a class of **quantitative forecasting method** that attempts to mathematically simulate cause and effect relationships among **time series**.

Chow predictive failure test – a test of structural stability between two sub-samples of a time series.

Coefficient – a number multiplying a variable to produce an equation's solution; in **regression analysis**, the coefficients are determined by **least squares estimation**.

Coefficient of determination – in **regression analysis** the square of the correlation between the values in the **time series** being forecast and the **forecast series**; it indicates the proportion of the **variance** in the latter explained by the former; indicated by R^2 ('R squared'); it should be adjusted for the number of **explanatory variables** in a **regression model**, in which case it is indicated by $\overline{R}^2$ ('R-bar squared').

Confidence level – see **level of confidence**.

Correlation coefficient – a standardized measure of the relationship between two **variables**, representing the amount by which they vary together in deviating from their respective **means**.

Country of residence – the country where the visitor has lived for most of the past twelve months, or for a shorter period if he or she intends to return within twelve months to live there (WTO).

CPI – Consumer Price Index.

Data point – an individual value in a **time series**.

Data series – same as a **time series**.

Decomposition method – a forecasting method designed to break down the patterns in a time series into season, cycle, trend and random components.

Delphi method – that **qualitative forecasting method** designed to develop group consensus by following specific rules that ensure respondent anonymity, iteration and controlled feedback and statistical group response.

Dependent variable – see **forecast variable**.

DES – double exponential smoothing.

Deseasonalize – the process of removing the recurrent seasonal variations in a monthly, quarterly or other sub-annual **time series**.

Destination – a place where a **visitor** stops, either over night or for a shorter period not necessarily including a night (WTO).

Differencing – the act of creating a new **time series** by subtracting the previous value of the original time series from the current one (called 'short differencing') or subtracting the **sub-annual time series** value one year earlier from the current value ('long differencing').

Domestic visitor – any person residing in a country who travels to a place within the country outside his or her usual environment for a period not exceeding twelve months and whose main purpose of visit is other than the exercise of an activity remunerated from within the place visited (WTO).

Double exponential smoothing method – an exponential smoothing method that adjusts a **single exponential smoothing** model for trend in a **time series**.

Downward trend series – a **time series** that declines rather steadily in a linear fashion; its **mean** decreases over time.

Dummy variable – an artificial variable constructed such that it takes the value of one whenever the qualitative phenomenon it represents occurs, and zero otherwise.

Durbin–Watson statistic – allows us to test the hypothesis that there is no **autocorrelation** among the **residuals** obtained by forecasting.

DW – Durbin–Watson.

Endogenous variable – a variable whose value is determined within a **structural forecasting model**.

Error – the value obtained by subtracting a **forecast value** from the actual value for the same point in time; same as **residual**.

Establishment – a single physical location at which business is conducted; distinct from a **firm**, which is a business organization or entity consisting of one or more establishments under common ownership or control.

Ex ante forecasting – using a **forecasting model** to produce estimates of a **historical time series** beyond the known values of that series; see also **ex post forecasting**.

Ex post forecasting – holding out the final one or more **observations** from our **historical time series** when estimating a **forecasting model** and then evaluating the model on how well it forecasts these final observations; see also **ex ante forecasting**.

Exogenous variable – a variable whose value is determined outside a **structural forecasting model**.

Explanatory variable – a variable that affects the **forecast variable** in a **regression** model but is not affected by it; same as **independent variable**.

Exponential smoothing method – one of several **extrapolative forecasting methods** that uses one or more smoothing constants and past **errors** to simulate a **time series;** includes **single exponential smoothing** and **double exponential smoothing**.

Extrapolate – to estimate a value of a **variable** outside a known range from values within a known range by assuming that the estimated value follows logically from the known values.

Extrapolative forecasting methods – also called 'time series methods' employ patterns in a **time series** to project or **extrapolate** future values, ignoring causal relationships.

Firm – a business organization or entity consisting of one or more **establishments** under common ownership or control.

Forecast process – the formal structure of sequential steps that produce a forecast.

Forecast series – a **time series** of future values produced by some method.

Forecast variable – the variable to be forecast based upon its **time series**; the dependent variable in a **regression** equation that is determined by some other factor or factors.

Forecast, tourism demand – a prediction of **tourism demand** for some time period subsequent to the most recent period for which such data are available.

Forecasting method – a systematic way of organizing information from the past to infer the occurrence of an event in the future; a forecasting method normally permits more than one **forecasting model** to be developed.

Forecasting model – one specific application of a **forecasting method.**

Forecasting – the process of organizing information about a phenomenon's past in order to predict a future.

Functional form – the form of the mathematical relationship between **the forecast variable** and one or **more explanatory variables**, e.g., linear, exponential, quadratic.

GDP – gross domestic product.

GNP – gross national product.

Gross domestic product – a measure of the total amount of goods and services produced within a country's borders over a specified period of time, usually one year or quarter.

Gross national product – a measure of the total primary incomes of all sectors of a country, regardless of where produced, over a specified period of time, usually one year or quarter.

Heteroscedasticity – the condition where the variance of a time series increases or decreases over the series; opposite of **homoscedasticity**.

Historical time series – a **time series** of past values.

Homoscedasticity – the condition where the **variance** of a **time series** remains constant over the series; opposite of **heteroscedasticity**.

Inbound international tourism – the activities of non-residents of a given country travelling to and within the country as **visitors** (WTO).

Independent variable – see **explanatory variable**.

Intercept – the constant term in a **regression** equation, often viewed as estimating the value of the **forecast variable** when all **explanatory variables** equal zero.

Interquartile range – the range of the middle 50 per cent of the values in a distribution; its centre is the **median**.

Judge – an expert chosen to provide forecasts according to the rules of a specific **qualitative forecasting method**.

Least squares estimation – a statistical estimation method that estimates the **coefficients** or **parameters** of a **regression** equation by minimizing the squared **errors** between the **forecast series** and the **time series**.

Level of confidence – the probability that a confidence level around an estimated **regression** model statistic encompasses the analogous **population parameter**.

Level of significance – the risk of rejecting the hypothesis that a **regression model** parameter, such as the coefficient of an **explanatory variable**, is significantly different from zero when it is not.

Linear time trend regression – a **regression model** where time is the only **explanatory variable**.

Ljung–Box test – a test for significant autocorrelations in building an **ARIMA** model.

Long-haul tourism – travel to destinations outside the WTO region in which an origin country is located.

MA(2) – **moving average model** of two lags

MAPE – see **mean absolute percentage error**.

Market – those people who may have an interest in purchasing a good or service and have the financial means to do so.

Market segment – a subgroup of an overall **market** that comprises consumers who are similar in their response to a **tourism** product and its marketing.

Mean – the value found by dividing the sum of all **observations** by the number of observations.

Mean absolute percentage error – a measure of forecasting **error** equal to $[(1/N) * \sum(|F_t - A_t|/A_t) * 100]$, where 'N' is the number of time periods covered, 'F' is the forecast for specific time period, t, and 'A' is the actual value for the specific time period t.

Median – the point in a distribution of values, ranked from lowest to highest, that divides the distribution into two equal parts.

Microcomputer – a compact and relatively inexpensive computer consisting of a microprocessor and other components of a computer, miniaturized where possible; sometimes called a 'personal computer'.

Misspecification – the condition of a **regression model** where the **dependent variable** is not an unchanging linear function of the model's **explanatory variables**; that is, important explanatory variables are missing.

Model – a simplified representation of reality that attempts to capture the major relationships at work among certain variables.

Moving average – the **time series** produced by computing the **means** of some number of past consecutive values of a time series at each point in time; not related to **moving average model**.

Moving average model – an **extrapolative forecasting model** employing current and past **errors** to explain current values of a **time series**; not related to **moving average**.

Multicollinearity – in a **regression model**, the condition where two or more **explanatory variables** are highly correlated with each other.

Multiple regression model – see **regression model**.

Naive forecasting model – the simplest **forecasting model**, predicting that the next period's value will be the same as the current period's (the 'simple naive model' or Naive 1), or the same percentage change in the current period (Naive 2) or if a seasonal series, the same as the value one year earlier (the 'seasonal naive model').

NFO – National Family Opinion, Inc.

Non-linear trend series – a **time series** that does not follow a straight line as it rises or falls over time, but often follows a curve or wave.

NTO – national tourism office.

NTS – National Travel Survey.

Observation – same as a **data point**, reminding us that each data point must be observed and measured, introducing the possibility of measurement **error**.

OLS – ordinary least squares regression.

Origin country – the country where the **visitor** has lived for most of the previous twelve months or has lived for a shorter period and intends to return within twelve months (WTO).

Outbound international tourism – the activities of **residents** of a given country travelling to and within another country (WTO).

Outlier – a single **observation** in a **time series** that is unusually large or small relative to the rest of the values.

Paradigm – a **model** of the world or view of how the world works.

Parameter – an **intercept** constant or slope **coefficient** in a quantitative **forecasting model**

Parsimony – the principle that, all else being approximately equal, the simpler of two **forecasting models** is the better one.

Partial autocorrelation – a measure of **correlation** indicating the strength of the relationship between current values of a **variable** and an earlier value at a specific time lag while holding the effects of all other time lags constant.

Partial correlation – a measure of correlation between a **forecast variable** and an **explanatory variable** while holding the effects of all other explanatory variables constant.

Personal income – income received by persons from employment, investments, and transfer payments in the form of wages, salaries, other forms of labour earnings, dividends, interest and rent.

Person-trip – a standard measure of **tourism** activity, this is recorded each time one person goes on a qualified **trip**; for instance, four persons travelling together correspond to four person-trips.

Phenomenon – an occurrence, a circumstance, or a fact that is perceptible by the senses.

Population – all values, objects or people of interest to the survey researcher and from among whom the **sample** will be selected.

Precision – the exactness with which a number is specified, indicated by the number of significant digits with which it is expressed.

Probability sample – a **sample** where every element of the **population** it represents has a known, non-zero chance of being included.

Qualitative forecasting methods – also called 'judgemental methods' these employ experts or judges to organize past information about the **forecast variable** by following some rule or set of rules.

Quantitative forecasting method – a **forecasting method** that organizes past information about a **phenomenon** by specific mathematical rules.

R^2 – see **coefficient of determination**.

$\overline{R}^2$ – see **coefficient of determination**.

Random walk model – one that assumes every observation in a time series is independent of every other observation, so that the best forecast for the next period is no change from the last.

RDPI – real disposable personal income.

Receiving country – a country that receives **visitors** who are **residents** of another country (WTO).

Regression analysis – the method of determining the statistical relationship between a **forecast variable** and one or more **explanatory variables** utilizing their **time series** and least squares estimation or other statistical method.

Regression model – an equation where the **coefficients** relating one or more **explanatory variables** to the **forecast variable** are estimated by least squares estimation or some other statistical method; if there is only one explanatory variable then it is a simple regression model; if there are two or more explanatory variables, then it is a multiple regression model.

Reliability – the extent to which repeated use of a **forecasting model** will yield the same results.

Research – the process by which we gather, organize and analyse information in a systematic manner to solve problems or confirm solutions.

Resident of a country – a person who has lived in the country for most of the past twelve months, or for a shorter period if he or she intends to return within twelve months to live there (WTO).

Residual – in forecasting, commonly used as a synonym for **error**.

RMSPE – root mean square percentage error.

SA – seasonally adjusted.

Same-day visitor – a **visitor** who does not spend the night in a collective or private accommodation in the place visited; this includes cruise passengers who debark in a country but spend their nights on board ship (WTO).

Sample – the number and/or identification of respondents in the **population** who will be or have been included in a **sample survey**.

Sample survey – a research technique where a **population** is identified, a **sample** is selected and systematically questioned, and the results analysed and expanded to represent the population.

SAS – Statistical Analysis System.

Scatter diagram – a graphical display showing two **time series** as a single point at each time period.

Seasonal factor – a value associated with a given month, quarter or other sub-annual period which represents the average ratio of that value to the value for the average period for the year; this is used to compute **seasonally adjusted time series.**

Seasonal naive model – see **naive forecasting model**.

Seasonality – movements in a **time series** within a year which recur roughly the same every year; these are usually the result of weather, social customs, holidays and business policies.

Seasonally adjusted time series – a **time series** of monthly, quarterly or other sub-annual data from which recurring seasonal fluctuations have been removed; these series are usually produced through computing **seasonal factors**.

Serial correlation – same as **autocorrelation**.

SES – single exponential smoothing.

Short-haul tourism – travel to destinations within the WTO region in which the **origin country** is located.

Single exponential smoothing method – an **extrapolative forecasting method** where a single smoothing constant and **errors** are used to adjust the forecast series to the **time series**; works best with a **stationary series**.

SMA – simple moving average.

Spreadsheet – a type of software for **microcomputers** that offers the user a matrix of rows and columns into which data can be entered and processed.

SPSS – Statistical Package for the Social Sciences.

Spurious regression – some explanatory variables may appear to be significant in an ordinary **least squares** regression model when they are not due to **autocorrelation** of errors.

Stationary series – a **time series** that exhibits a constant **mean** and constant **variance** over time.

Stepped series – a **time series** that exhibits a series of increases (or decreases) followed by a horizontal or level trend indicating no change.

Structural econometric forecasting model – a set of interdependent, or simultaneous, equations intended to represent how **endogenous** and **exogenous variables** are interrelated.

Sub-annual time series – a **time series** for regular periods of time less than one year, such as months, seasons or quarters.

Survey – a sampling, or partial collection, of facts, figures, or opinions taken from a **population** and used to approximate or indicate what a complete collection of information, or census, might reveal.

Theil's U-statistic – an objective measure of the accuracy of a forecasting model relative to the Naive 1 model for the same data series.

Time plot – a graph that displays a **time series** related to its periods at equally spaced intervals.

Time series – an ordered sequence of values of a **variable** observed at equally spaced time intervals.

Time series forecasting methods – see **extrapolative forecasting methods**.

Time trend method – a **forecasting method** that uses **regression analysis** to estimate the relationship of a deseasonalized **time series** to time, expressed in months, quarters or years.

Tourism – the activities of persons travelling to and staying in places outside their usual environment for not more than one consecutive year for leisure, business and other purposes (WTO).

Tourism demand – a measure of **visitors'** use of quantity of a good or service; such measures commonly found in **tourism** forecasting include **visitors** to a destination, transportation passengers and **tourism expenditures**.

Tourism expenditure – the total consumption expenditure made by a **visitor** or on behalf of a visitor for and during his/her **trip** and stay at a **destination** (WTO).

Tourism Industries – the set of **firms, establishments** and other organizations with a principal activity of providing products directly to **visitors**.

Tourist – a **visitor** who stays at least one night in a collective or private accommodation in a place visited (WTO).

TPI – Travel Price Index.

Tracking signal – an indicator of whether the **errors** occurring as the future unfolds are due to chance or indicate that the **forecasting model** no longer simulates the **time series** and should be revised or replaced.

Transformation – changing the measurement scale of one or more **variables**; used to achieve a **stationary series** and to improve the accuracy of a **regression model**.

Travel – the act of taking any **trip**.

Travel party – members of a single household travelling together on a **trip**.

Traveller – any person on a **trip** between two or more localities (WTO).

Trip – a basic measure of **tourism** from the standpoint of the generating place or country (the origin) and covers the whole period that a person travels away from home (WTO).

UN – United Nations.

Upward trend series – a **time series** that moves upward rather steadily in a linear fashion; its **mean** increases over time.

Vacation trip – a pleasure **trip**, usually of several days or more and often requiring a leave of absence from work.

Validity – the extent to which a variable or a regression model actually measures what it is intended to measure.

Variable – any phenomena that can be measured; in this book, it usually refers to a **phenomenon's time series**.

Variance – a summary statistic that represents how closely the values of a **time series** cluster around its **mean**; it is the mean of the squared deviations from the mean.

VFR – visit friends and relatives.

Visitor – any person travelling to a place other than that of his usual environment for less than twelve consecutive months and whose main purpose of travel is other than the exercise of an activity remunerated from within the place visited (WTO).

Visitor party – same as **travel party**.

World Tourism Organization – an affiliate of the United Nations, is an intergovernmental body devoted to the promotion and development of domestic and international **tourism** throughout the world.

WTO – World Tourism Organization.

Select bibliography

Akis, S. (1998). A compact econometric model of tourism demand for Turkey. *Tourism Management*, **19** (1), February, 99–102.

Almon, C. (1989). *The Craft of Economic Modeling*. 2nd edition. Ginn Press.

Alreck, P. L. and Settle, R. B. (1995). *The Survey Research Handbook*. 2nd edition. Richard D. Irwin.

Archer, B. (1994). Demand forecasting and estimation. In *Travel, Tourism, and Hospitality Research: A Handbook for Managers and Researchers* (J. R. Brent Ritchie and C. R. Goeldner, eds) 2nd edition, pp. 105–14, Wiley.

Armstrong, J. S. (1985). *Long-range Forecasting: From Crystal Ball to Computer*. 2nd edition. Wiley.

Arrow, K. J. (1992). I know a hawk from a handsaw. In *Eminent Economists: Their Life and Philosophies* (M. Szenberg, ed.) pp. 42–50, Cambridge University Press.

Bernstein, P. L. (1996). *Against the Gods: The Remarkable Story of Risk*. Wiley.

Brady, J. and Widdows, R. (1988), The impact of world events on travel to Europe during the summer of 1986. *Journal of Travel Research*, **26** (3), Winter, 8–10.

Brown, L. (ed.) (1993). *The New Shorter Oxford English Dictionary on Historical Principles*. Oxford University Press.

Calantone, R. J., di Benedetto, C. A. and Bojanic, D. (1987). A comprehensive review of the tourism forecasting literature. *Journal of Travel Research*, **26** (2), Fall, 28–39.

Carraro, C. and Manente, M. (1994). *The TRIP Forecasting Models of World Tourism Flows from and to Italy*. Centro Internazionale di Studi sull'Economia Turistica Venice.

Chan, Y.-M. (1993). Forecasting tourism: a sine wave time series regression approach. *Journal of Travel Research*, **32** (2) Fall, 58–60.

Chan, Y.-M., Hui, T.-K. and Yuen, E. (1999). Modeling the impact of sudden environmental changes on visitor arrival forecasts: the case of the Gulf War. *Journal of Travel Research*, **37** (4), May, 391–4.

Choy, D. J. L. (1984). Forecasting hotel industry performance. *Tourism Management*, **6** (1), March, 4–7.

Choy, D. J. L. (1985). Forecasting tourism revisited. *Tourism Management*, **5** (3), September, 171–6.

Chu, F.-L. (1998a). Forecasting tourism: a combined approach. *Tourism Management*, **19** (6), 515–20.

Chu, F.-L. (1998b). Forecasting tourism arrivals: nonlinear sine wave or ARIMA? *Journal of Travel Research*, **36** (3), Winter), 79–84.

Chu, F.-L. (1998c). Forecasting tourism demand in Asian-Pacific countries. *Annals of Tourism Research*, **25** (3), 597–615.

Clifton, P., Nguyen, H. and Nutt, S. (1992). *Market Research: Using Forecasting in Business*, pp. 223–49. Butterworth-Heinemann.

Coates, J. F. and Jarratt, J. (1989). *What Futurists Believe*. Lomond.

Coopers & Lybrand (1997). Coopers & Lybrand's U.S. lodging forecasts: the estimation and review processes. *Hospitality Directions*, February, 30–6.

Cornish, E. (1977). *The Study of the Future*. World Future Society.

Crouch, G. (1995). A meta-analysis of tourism demand. *Annals of Tourism Research*, **22** (1), 103–18.

Crouch, G. I. (1992). Effect of income and price on international tourism. *Annals of Tourism Research*, **19**, 643–64.

Crouch, G. I. (1994a). The study of international tourism demand: a survey of practice. *Journal of Travel Research*, **22** (4), Spring, 41–57.

Crouch, G. I. (1994b). The study of international tourism demand: a review of findings. *Journal of Travel Research*, **23** (1), Summer, 12–23.

Crouch, G. I., Schultz, L. and Valerio, P. (1992). Marketing international tourism to Australia: a regression analysis. *Tourism Management*, **13** (2), June, 196–208.

Cunningham, S. (1991). *Data Analysis in Hotel and Catering Management*, pp. 184–201. Butterworth-Heinemann.

Dalkey, N. C. (1969). *The Delphi Method: An Experimental Study of Group Opinion*. Rand Corporation.

Dalrymple, K. and Greenidge, K. (1999). Forecasting arrivals to Barbados. *Annals of Tourism Research*, **26** (1), 189–90.

Darnell, A., Johnson, P. and Thomas, B. (1990). Beamish Museum – modelling visitor flows. *Tourism Management*, **11** (3), September, 251–7.

Dharmaratne, G. S. (1995). Forecasting tourist arrivals. *Annals of Tourism Research*, **22** (4), 804–18.

di Benedetto, C. A. and Bojanic, D. C. (1993). Tourism area life cycle extensions. *Annals of Tourism Research*, **20**, 557–70.

Doorn, J. W. M. van (1982). Can futures research contribute to tourism policies. *Tourism Management*, **3** (3), September, 149–66.

Doorn, J. W. M. van (1984). Tourism forecasting and the policymaker. *Tourism Management*, **5** (1), March, 24–39.

Elkins, R. D. and Roberts, R. S. (1987). Evaluating the human resource (employment) requirements and impacts of tourism developments. In *Travel, Tourism, and Hospitality Research: A Handbook for Managers and Researchers* (J. R. Brent Ritchie and C. R. Goeldner, eds) pp. 403–11, Wiley.

Faulkner, B. and Valerio, P. (1995). An integrative approach to tourism demand forecasting. *Tourism Management*, **16** (1), February, 29–37.

Florida Department of Commerce (1995). *Florida Visitor Study/1994*. Florida Department of Commerce.

Frechtling, D. C. (1992). World marketing and economic research priorities for tourism. *Tourism Partnerships and Strategies: Merging Vision with New Realities, 23rd Annual Conference Proceedings*, pp. 20–7, Travel and Tourism Research Association.

Frechtling, D. C. (2000). International travel generating models to 2010. *Lights camera, action: spotlight on tourism in the new millennium. 31st Annual Conference Proceedings*, Travel and Tourism Research Association, pp. 322–31.

García-Ferrer, A. and Queralt, R. (1997). A note on forecasting international tourism demand in Spain. *International Journal of Forecasting*, **13** (4). December, 539–49.

Gardner, E. S. Jr (1992). How to monitor your forecasts. *Lotus*, April, 54–7.

González, P. and Moral, P. (1995). An analysis of the international tourism demand in Spain. *International Journal of Forecasting*, **22** (2), June, 233–51.

Granger, C. W. J. (1989). *Forecasting in Business and Economics*. 2nd edition. Academic Press.

Granger, C. W. J. (1999). *Empirical Modeling in Economics: Specification and Evaluation*. Cambridge University Press.

Gujarati, D. (1992). *Essentials of Econometrics*. McGraw-Hill.

Holden, K., Peel, D. A. and Thompson, J. L. (1990). *Economic Forecasting: An Introduction*. Cambridge University Press.

Holman, R. L. (1993). Egypt hurt by drop in tourists. *The Wall Street Journal*, 16 February.

Jarrett, J. (1991). *Business Forecasting Methods*. 2nd edition. Blackwell.

Jenkins, D. and Frechtling, D. C. (1991). World tourism model simulations for West Germany, 1990–93. In *World Travel and Tourism Review: Indicators, Trends and Forecasts, Volume 1* (D. E. Hawkins and J. R. Brent Ritchie, eds) pp. 83–90, CAB. International.

Johnston, J. (1972). *Econometric Methods*. 2nd edition. McGraw-Hill.

Jørgensen, F. and Solvoll, G. (1996). Demand models for inclusive tour charter: the Norwegian case. *Tourism Management*, **17** (1). February, 17–24.

Kaynak, E., Bloom, J. and Leibold, M. (1994). Using the Delphi technique to predict future tourism potential. *Marketing Intelligence and Planning*, **12** (7), 18–29.

Kaynak, E. and Macaulay (1984). The Delphi technique in the measurement of tourism market potential: the case of Nova Scotia. *Tourism Management*, **5** (2), June, 87–101.

Kennedy, P. (1992). *Guide to Econometrics*, 3rd edition. MIT Press.

Kennedy, P. (1998). *A Guide to Econometrics*. 4th edition. MIT Press.

Kmenta, J. (1971). *Elements of Econometrics*. Macmillan.

Landsburg, S. E. (1993). *The Armchair Economist: Economics and Everyday Life*. Free Press.

Levenbach, H. and Cleary, J. P. (1981). *The Beginning Forecaster: The Forecasting Process through Data Analysis*. Lifetime Learning.

Lewis, C. D. (1982). *Industrial and Business Forecasting Methods*, p. 40. Butterworth; quoted in Witt and Witt (1992a, p. 86).

Lim, C. (1997). An econometric classification and review of international tourism demand models. *Tourism Economics*, **3** (1), March, 69–81.

Lim, C. (1999). A meta-analytic review of international tourism demand. *Journal of Travel Research*, **37** (3), February, 373–84.

Liu, J. (1988). Hawaii Tourism for the year 2000: a Delphi forecast. *Tourism Management*, **9** (3), September, 279–90.

Makridakis, S. (1990). *Forecasting, Planning and Strategy for the 21st Century*. Free Press.

Makridakis, S., Wheelwright, S. C. and Hyndman, R. J. (1998), *Forecasting: Methods and Applications*. 3rd edition. Wiley.

Makridakis, S., Wheelwright, S. C. and McGee, V. (1983). *Forecasting: Methods and Applications*. 2nd edition. Wiley.

Martin, C. A. and Witt, S. F. (1989). Accuracy of econometric forecasts of tourism. *Annals of Tourism Research*, **16**, 407–28.

Maurer, A. (2000). Email message to D. C. Frechtling regarding Bill Gates's address to the 1998 Governors Meeting for Travel and Tourism of the World Economic Forum, transmitted 11 August.

Mentzner, J. T. and Bienstock, C. C. (1998). *Sales Forecasting Management.* Sage.

Middleton, V. T. C. (1994). *Marketing in Travel and Tourism.* 2nd edition. Heinemann Professional.

Miller, J. J., McCahon, C. S. and Miller, J. L. (1991). Foodservice forecasting using simple mathematical models. *Hospitality Research Journal,* **15** (1), 43–58.

Moeller, G. H. and Shafer, E. L. (1994). The Delphi technique: a tool for long-range travel and tourism planning. In *Travel, Tourism, and Hospitality Research: A Handbook for Managers and Researchers* (J. R. Brent Ritchie and C. R. Goeldner, eds) 2nd edition, pp. 473–80, Wiley.

Moore, T. W. (1989). *Handbook of Business Forecasting.* Harper & Row.

Morley, C. L. (1994). The use of CPI for tourism prices in demand modelling. *Tourism Management,* **15** (5), 342–6.

Moutihno, L. and Witt, S. F. (1995). Forecasting the tourism environment using a consensus approach. *Journal of Travel Research,* **33** (4), Spring, 46–50.

Müller, H. (1998). Long-haul tourism 2005 – Delphi study. *Journal of Vacation Marketing,* **4** (2), April, 192–201.

Naisbitt, J. (1994). *Global Paradox.* Morrow.

Nolan, B. (1994) Data Analysis: an Introduction. Polity Press.

Panel Publishers (2000). *Blue Chip Economic Indicators,* **25** (9), 10 September.

Paulos, J. A. (1991). *Beyond Numeracy: Ruminations of a Numbers Man.* Alfred A. Knopf.

Pindyck, R. S. and Rubinfeld, D. L. (1981). *Econometric Models and Economic Forecasts.* 2nd edition. McGraw-Hill.

Qiu, H. and Zhang, J. (1995), Determinants of tourist arrivals and expenditures in Canada. *Journal of Travel Research,* **34** (2), Fall, 43–9.

Qu, H. and Lam, S. (1997). A travel demand model for Mainland Chinese tourists to Hong Kong. *Tourism Management,* **18** (8), December, 593–7.

Qu, H. and Zhang, H. Q. (1996). Projecting international tourism arrivals in East Asia and the Pacific to the year 2005. *Journal of Travel Research,* **25** (1), Summer, 27–34.

Rao, P. and Miller, R. L. (1971). *Applied Econometrics.* Wadsworth.

Saunders, J. A., Sharp, J. A. and Witt, S. F. (1987). *Practical Business Forecasting.* Gower.

Schulmeister, S. (1979). *Tourism and the Business Cycle.* Austrian Institute for Economic Research.

Sheldon, P. (1993). Forecasting tourism: expenditures versus arrivals. *Journal of Travel Research,* **22** (1), Summer, 13–20.

Shim, J. K., Siegel, J. G. and Liew, C. J. (1994). *Strategic Business Forecasting*. Probus.

Smeral, E. (1988). Tourism demand, economic theory and econometrics: an integrated approach. *Journal of Travel Research*, **26** (4), Spring, 38–43.

Smeral, E. (1994). Economic models. In *Tourism Marketing and Management Handbook* (S. F. Witt and L. Moutinho, eds) 2nd edition, pp. 497–503. Prentice-Hall.

Smeral, E. and Weber, A. (2000). Forecasting international tourism trends to 2010. *Annals of Tourism Research*, **27** (4), 982–1006.

Smeral, E. and Witt, S. F. (1992). The impacts of Eastern Europe and 1992 on international tourism demand. *Tourism Management*, **13** (4), December, 368–76.

Smeral, E., Witt, S. F. and Witt, C. A. (1992). Econometric forecasts: tourism trends to 2000. *Annals of Tourism Research*, **19**, 450–66.

Smith, S. L. J. (1995). *Tourism Analysis: A Handbook*. 2nd edition. Longman Scientific and Technical.

Song, H. and Witt, S. F. (2000). *Tourism Demand Modelling and Forecasting: Modern Econometric Approaches*. Pergamon.

Summary, R. (1987), Estimation of tourism demand by multivariable regression analysis. *Tourism Management*, **8** (4), December, 317–22.

Turner, L. W., Kulendran, N. and Fernando, H. (1997a). Univariate modelling using periodic and non-periodic analysis: inbound tourism to Japan, Australia and New Zealand compared. *Tourism Economics*, **3** (1), March, 39–56.

Turner, L. W., Kulendran, N, and Fernando, H. (1997b). The use of composite national indicators for tourism forecasting. *Tourism Economics*, **3** (4), December, 309–17.

Turner, L. W., Kulendran, N. and Pergat, V. (1995). Forecasting New Zealand tourism demand with disaggregated data. *Tourism Economics*, **1** (1), March, 51–69.

Turner, L. W., Reisinger, Y. and Witt, S. F. (1998). Tourism demand analysis using structural equation modelling. *Tourism Economics*, **4** (4), December, 301–23.

United Nations and World Tourism Organization (UN and WTO) (1994). *Recommendations on Tourism Statistics*. United Nations Department for Economic and Social Information and Policy Analysis.

Uysal, M. and Crompton, J. L. (1985). An overview of approaches used to forecast tourism demand. *Journal of Travel Research*, **23** (4), Spring, 8–13.

Van Doren, C. (1991). *A History of Knowledge Past, Present and Future*. Ballantine Books.

Vandaele, W. (1983). *Applied Time Series and Box-Jenkins Models*. Academic Press.

Witt, C., Witt, S. F. and Wilson, N. (1994). Forecasting international tourist flows. *Annals of Tourism Research*, **21** (3), 612–28.

Witt, C. A. and Witt, S. F. (1990). Appraising an econometric forecasting model. *Journal of Travel Research*, **28** (3), Winter, 30–4.

Witt, C. A. and Witt, S. F. (1992b), Tourism forecasting: accuracy comparisons across aggregated/disaggregated data. Unpublished paper.

Witt, C. A., and Witt, S. F. (1994). Demand elasticities. In *Tourism Marketing and Management Handbook* (S. F. Witt and L. Moutinho, eds) 2nd edition, pp. 521–9, Prentice-Hall.

Witt, S. F. (1994). Econometric demand forecasting. In *Tourism Marketing and Management Handbook* (S. F. Witt and L. Moutinho, eds), 2nd edition, pp. 516–20, Prentice-Hall.

Witt, S. F. and Martin, C. A. (1987). International tourism demand models – inclusion of marketing models. *Tourism Management*, **8** (1), March, 33–40.

Witt, S. F. and Witt, C. A. (1991). Tourism forecasting: error magnitude, direction of change error, and trend change error. *Journal of Travel Research*, **30** (2), Fall, 26–33.

Witt, S. F. and Witt, C. A. (1992a). *Modeling and Forecasting Demand in Tourism*. Academic Press.

Witt, S. F. and Witt, C. A. (1995). Forecasting tourism demand: a review of empirical research. *International Journal of Forecasting*, **11** (3), September, 447–75.

Witt, S. F., Newbould, G. D. and Watkins, A. J. (1992). Forecasting domestic tourism demand: application to Las Vegas arrivals data. *Journal of Travel Research*, **31** (1), Summer, 36–41.

Witte, R. S. (1989). *Statistics*. 3rd edition. Holt, Rinehart and Winston.

Wong, K. K. F. (1997a). An investigation of the time series behaviour of international tourist arrivals. *Tourism Economics*, **3** (2), June, 185–99.

Wong, K. K. F. (1997b). The relevance of business cycles in forecasting international tourist arrivals. *Tourism Management*, **18** (8), December, 581–6.

World Tourism Organization (WTO) (1995a). *Concepts, Definitions and Classifications for Tourism Statistics: Technical Manual No. 1*. WTO.

World Tourism Organization (WTO) (1995b). *Collection of Tourism Expenditure Statistics: Technical Manual No. 2*. WTO.

World Tourism Organization (WTO) (1995c). *Collection of Domestic Tourism Statistics: Technical Manual No. 3*. WTO.

World Tourism Organization (WTO) (1995d). *Collection and Compilation of Tourism Statistics: Technical Manual No. 4*. WTO.

World Tourism Organization (WTO) (1999). *Tourism Satellite Account (TSA): The Conceptual Framework*. WTO.

World Travel and Tourism Council (1995). *United States Travel and Tourism: A New Economic Perspective*. World Travel and Tourism Council.

Yong, Y. W., Keng, K. A. and Leng, T. L. (1989). A Delphi forecast for the Singapore tourism industry: future scenario and marketing implications. *International Marketing Review*, **6** (3), 35–46.

Index